# The Advanced Econometrics of Tourism Demand

# Routledge Advances in Tourism

STEPHEN PAGE, *University of Stirling, Scotland*

**1. The Sociology of Tourism**
Theoretical and Empirical Investigations
Edited by Yiorgos Apostolopoulos,
Stella Leivadi and Andrew Yiannakis

**2. Creating Island Resorts**
Brian King

**3. Destinations**
Cultural Landscapes of Tourism
Greg Ringer

**4. Mediterranean Tourism**
Facets of Socioeconomic
Development and Cultural Change
Edited by Yiorgos Apostolopoulos, Lila
Leontidou, Philippos Loukissas

**5. Outdoor Recreation Management**
John Pigram and John Jenkins

**6. Tourism Development**
Contemporary Issues
Edited by Douglas G. Pearce and
Richard W. Butler

**7. Tourism and Sustainable
Community Development**
Edited by Greg Richards and
Derek Hall

**8. Tourism and Political Boundaries**
Dallen J Timothy

**9. Leisure and Tourism Landscapes**
Social and Cultural Geographies
Cara Aitchison, Nicola E MacLeod and
Stephen J Shaw

**10. Tourism in the Age of
Globalisation**
Edited by Salah Wahab and
Chris Cooper

**11. Tourism and Gastronomy**
Edited by Anne-Mette Hjalager and
Greg Richards

**12. New Perspectives in
Caribbean Tourism**
Edited by Marcella Daye, Donna
Chambers and Sherma Roberts

**13. The Advanced Econometrics
of Tourism Demand**
Haiyan Song, Stephen F. Witt
and Gang Li

# The Advanced Econometrics of Tourism Demand

## Haiyan Song, Stephen F. Witt and Gang Li

Routledge
Taylor & Francis Group
New York   London

First published 2009
by Routledge
711 Third Avenue, New York, NY 10017

Simultaneously published in the UK
by Routledge
2 Park Square, Milton Park, Abingdon, Oxon OX14 4RN

*Routledge is an imprint of the Taylor & Francis Group, an informa business*

First issued in paperback 2011

*Library of Congress Cataloging in Publication Data*
Song, Haiyan.
The advanced econometrics of tourism demand / by Haiyan Song, Stephen F. Witt, and Gang Li.
p. cm. -- (Routledge advances in tourism)
Includes bibliographical references and index.
1. Tourism--Econometric models.   2. Tourism--Forecasting.   I. Witt, Stephen F.
II. Li, Gang, 1975–   III. Title.

G155.A1S592 2009
910.01'5195--dc22                                                    2008014951

ISBN: 978-0-415-99120-9 (hbk)
ISBN: 978-0-415-52346-2 (pbk)

# Contents

*List of Figures*    vii
*List of Tables*    ix
*Preface*    xi

1   Introduction to Tourism Demand Analysis    1

2   Recent Developments in Tourism Demand Analysis    13

3   Traditional Methodology of Tourism Demand Modelling    35

4   General-to-Specific Modelling    46

5   Cointegration    70

6   Error Correction Model    88

7   Vector Autoregression (VAR) and Cointegration    105

8   Time Varying Parameter Modelling    138

9   Panel Data Analysis    149

10   Systems of Demand Equations    167

11   Evaluation of Forecasting Performance    181

*Notes*    197
*References*    199
*Author Index*    213
*Subject Index*    217

# Figures

5.1   Consumer price indices of Spain and the UK (log).                    71

5.2   Comparison of stationary and non-stationary time series.              75

7.1   Impulse responses to one SE shock in the UK LTA equation.           123

7.2   Impulse responses to one SE shock in the US LTA equation.           123

7.3   Impulse responses to one SE shock in the UK LGDP equation.          124

7.4   Impulse responses to one SE shock in the US LGDP equation.          124

7.5   Forecast error variance decomposition for variable LTA (UK).        125

7.6   Forecast error variance decomposition for variable LTA (US).        125

8.1   Recursive estimates of coefficients in UK model.                    140

8.2   Recursive estimates of coefficients in USA model.                   141

8.3   Estimated coefficients in UK model based on Kalman filter
      approach.                                                           147

8.4   Estimated coefficients in USA model based on Kalman filter
      approach.                                                           148

11.1  Time horizon of forecasts.                                          183

# Tables

| | | |
|---|---|---:|
| 2.1 | Summary of Econometric Studies of Tourism Demand Modelling | 14 |
| 4.1 | Variations of the Autoregressive Distributed Lag Model | 48 |
| A4.1 | Worked Example: Data Used in Estimation | 68 |
| 5.1 | Critical Values for the DF Tests | 77 |
| 5.2 | Critical Values of the Dickey-Fuller $\Phi_3$ Statistic | 79 |
| 5.3 | Empirical Results for General ADF Regression (5.17) | 82 |
| 5.4 | Empirical Results for ADF Regression (5.24) | 83 |
| 5.5 | ADF Test Results for $LPPDI_t$, $LRCSP_t$ and $LPVSP_t$ | 84 |
| 5.6 | Critical Values for Cointegration ADF Test | 85 |
| 6.1 | Dickey-Fuller (DF) and Phillips-Perron (PP) Test Results | 95 |
| 6.2 | Forecast Errors Generated from the Three UK ECMs | 102 |
| A6.1 | Data Used in Chapter 6 | 103 |
| 7.1 | Choice Criteria for Selecting the Order of the VAR Model (UK) | 115 |
| 7.2 | Choice Criteria for Selecting the Order of the VAR Model (USA) | 116 |
| 7.3 | LR Test of Block Granger Non-causality in the VAR Model (UK) | 117 |
| 7.4 | LR Test of Block Granger Non-causality in the VAR Model (USA) | 118 |
| 7.5 | OLS Estimation of Tourist Arrivals Equation in the Unrestricted VAR Model | 119 |
| 7.6 | OLS Estimation of GDP Equation in the Unrestricted VAR Model | 120 |

7.7   OLS Estimation of Trade Volume Equation in the
      Unrestricted VAR Model                                    121

7.8   OLS Estimation of Tourist Prices Equation in the
      Unrestricted VAR Model                                    122

7.9   *Ex Post* Forecast Errors of Selected Models             126

7.10  Johansen Cointegration Test Based on $\lambda_{max}$ (UK)   132

7.11  Johansen Cointegration Test Based on $\lambda_{trace}$ (UK)  133

7.12  Johansen Cointegration Test Based on $\lambda_{max}$ (USA)  134

7.13  Johansen Cointegration Test Based on $\lambda_{trace}$ (USA) 134

7.14  Estimated Cointegrated Vectors in Johansen
      Estimation (UK)                                           135

7.15  Estimated Cointegrated Vectors in Johansen
      Estimation (USA)                                          136

7.16  Long-Run Cointegration Vectors Based on Different
      Estimation Methods                                        137

7.17  *Ex Post* Forecast Errors of the VECMs                   137

8.1   Kalman Filter Estimates of the TVP Models (Dependent
      Variable: $lnTA_{it}$)                                     146

9.1   Low, Medium and High Income Country Groups:
      Descriptive Statistics                                    157

9.2   Simple Double-Log Regression of TSP on GDP              159

9.3   Fixed and Random Effects Models: Estimation Results     162

10.1  Estimates of Unrestricted Static LAIDS                  175

10.2  Estimates of Unrestricted EC-LAIDS                      176

10.3  Restriction Tests for Homogeneity and Symmetry         177

10.4  Long-Run and Short-Run Expenditure and Own-Price
      Elasticities                                             177

10.5  Long-Run and Short-Run Compensated Cross-Price
      Elasticities                                             178

11.1  Summary of Model Selection Criteria                     182

11.2  Rankings of Forecasting Accuracy Comparison            186

# Preface

An earlier version of this book entitled *Tourism Demand Modelling and Forecasting: Modern Econometric Approaches* was published by Pergamon in 2000. This has been well received by researchers, students and practitioners, as it has become one of the most cited works in the field of tourism demand modelling and forecasting according to the Google Scholar citation system (http://scholar.google.com). Over 120 journal articles on tourism demand modelling and forecasting were published during the period 2000 to 2007, suggesting that this is one of the most important areas for tourism research, given its relevance to tourism planning, marketing and destination management. Many of these published studies have benefited from the methodologies introduced in the book. With the increasing interest in tourism demand modelling and forecasting research, a revised and updated version of this book has become necessary.

In the new edition of the book, we include an additional chapter (Chapter 2), which provides a comprehensive review of tourism demand studies. Another new chapter (Chapter 9), which introduces system of equations modelling, has been added to reflect the growing interest in the literature in this approach to modelling and forecasting tourism demand. The chapter on the evaluation of forecasting performance (Chapter 11) has also been rewritten to incorporate the system of equations methodology. Finally, the reference list has been updated with the latest publications.

The purpose of this book is to introduce students, researchers and practitioners to advanced econometric methodology within the context of tourism demand analysis, and to illustrate this methodology with actual tourism applications. The book is designed for final-year undergraduates, postgraduates and research students in tourism studies, as well as researchers and practitioners who wish to apply advanced econometric modelling and forecasting methodologies to tourism demand analysis. It is assumed that the reader has taken an introductory course in statistics and multiple regression analysis and has some knowledge of tourism. The concepts and computations of advanced econometric modelling methodologies are introduced at a level that is accessible to non-specialists. The methodologies introduced include general-to-specific modelling, cointegration, vector autoregression, time varying parameter modelling, panel data analysis and system demand models. In order to help the reader understand the various methodologies, extensive tourism demand examples are provided.

The book starts with an introduction to the fundamentals of tourism demand analysis (Chapter 1). A comprehensive review of recent publications in tourism demand modelling and forecasting is provided in Chapter 2. The problems of traditional tourism demand modelling and forecasting, that is, data mining and spurious regression due to common trends in the time series, are addressed in Chapter 3. General-to-specific modelling, including the use of autoregressive distributed lag processes, cointegration analysis and error correction models, has been regarded as a remedy for the problems of data mining and spurious regression. Therefore, the general-to-specific approach to tourism demand modelling and forecasting is explained in Chapters 4 through 7. The size of the tourism industry has increased rapidly over the last three decades, and it is also known that the demand for international tourism (both inbound and outbound) is sensitive to regime shifts (changes in government policy, political and economic conditions); therefore, demand elasticities are unlikely to have remained unchanged over time. The time varying parameter model, together with the use of the Kalman filter as an estimation method, is a useful tool for examining the effects of regime shifts on tourism demand elasticities, and this is explained in Chapter 8. Often there is a lack of sufficient time series data in terms of the number of observations on the tourism demand variables and this can result in estimation and forecasting biases. The panel data approach is introduced in Chapter 9 as a possible solution to this problem. Chapter 10 introduces the demand system model with a view to overcoming the inherent problems in single equation models. The last chapter (Chapter 11) evaluates the empirical forecasting performance of the various models and puts forward general conclusions.

The authors have considerable research experience related to modelling and forecasting the demand for international tourism, with over 100 publications in this area. They have also been teaching tourism demand modelling and forecasting for many years.

Our sincere appreciation goes to Professor Stephen Page, the Editor of the *Routledge Advances in Tourism* series, for his advice and encouragement. We would also like to thank Mr Benjamin Holtzman, our Commissioning Editor from Taylor and Francis, for his support. Clerical assistance from Ms Eling Yim is also kindly acknowledged.

July 2008                                                    Haiyan Song
                                                             Stephen F. Witt
                                                             Gang Li

# 1 Introduction to Tourism Demand Analysis

## 1.1 INTRODUCTION

Tourism demand is the foundation on which all tourism-related business decisions ultimately rest. Companies such as airlines, tour operators, hotels, cruise ship lines, and many recreation facility providers and shop owners are interested in the demand for their products by tourists. The success of many businesses depends largely or totally on the state of tourism demand, and ultimate management failure is quite often due to the failure to meet market demand. Because of the key role of demand as a determinant of business profitability, estimates of expected future demand constitute a very important element in all planning activities. It is clear that *accurate* forecasts of tourism demand are essential for *efficient* planning by tourism-related businesses, particularly given the perishability of the tourism product. For example, it is impossible for an airline to recoup the potential revenue lost by a flight taking off with empty seats. The loss resulting from these unsold seats contrasts with the case of, say, a car manufacturer, where if a car does not sell on a particular day it can still be sold subsequently.

The tourism forecasting methods examined in this book are advanced econometric approaches. Here, the forecast variable is specifically related to a set of determining forces; future values of the forecast variable are obtained by using forecasts of the determining variables in conjunction with the estimated quantitative relationship between the forecast variable and its determinants.

In section 1.2 the tourism demand function is examined, and measurement issues relating to demand variables are discussed. The functional form of the demand equation and its relationship to demand elasticities are presented in section 1.3, and the chapter is summarised in section 1.4.

## 1.2 DETERMINANTS OF TOURISM DEMAND

Tourism visits can take place for various reasons: holidays, business trips, visits to friends and relatives (VFR), conferences, pilgrimages and so on.

Most empirical studies of tourism demand examine either total tourist trips (including all the above-mentioned purposes) or just holiday trips (Witt and Witt, 1995). Since the majority of tourist visits take place for holiday purposes, the determinants of demand are generally taken to be the same as those for holiday trips in those published studies which examine total trips. We shall therefore also focus on the determinants of the demand for holiday tourism.

The term 'tourism demand' may be defined for a particular destination as the quantity of the tourism product (that is, a combination of tourism goods and services) that consumers are willing to purchase during a specified period under a given set of conditions. The time period may be a month, a quarter or a year. The conditions that relate to the quantity of tourism demanded include tourism prices for the destination (tourists' living costs in the destination and travel costs to the destination), the availability of and tourism prices for competing (substitute) destinations, potential consumers' incomes, advertising expenditure, tastes of consumers in the origin (generating) countries, and other social, cultural, geographic and political factors.

The demand function for the tourism product in destination $i$ by residents of origin $j$ is given by

$$Q_{ij} = f(P_i, P_s, Y_j, T_j, A_{ij}, \varepsilon_{ij}) \tag{1.1}$$

where $Q_{ij}$ is the quantity of the tourism product demanded in destination $i$ by tourists from country $j$; $P_i$ is the price of tourism for destination $i$; $P_s$ is the price of tourism for substitute destinations; $Y_j$ is the level of income in origin country $j$; $T_j$ is consumer tastes in origin country $j$; $A_{ij}$ is advertising expenditure on tourism by destination $i$ in origin country $j$; $\varepsilon_{ij}$ is the disturbance term that captures all other factors which may influence the quantity of the tourism product demanded in destination $i$ by residents of origin country $j$.

In empirical investigations it can be difficult to find exact measures of the determinants of tourism demand due to lack of data availability. The variables used in empirical studies of tourism demand functions are now reviewed, and the problems associated with these measures are also addressed.

## 1.2.1   Dependent Variable

International tourism demand is generally measured in terms of the number of tourist visits from an origin country to a destination country, or in terms of tourist expenditure by visitors from the origin country in the destination country. The number of tourist nights spent by residents of the origin in the destination is an alternative tourism demand measure.

International tourism demand data are collected in various ways. Tourist visits are usually recorded by frontier counts (inbound), registration at accommodation establishments (inbound) or sample surveys (inbound and outbound). A problem with frontier counts is that in certain cases a substantial transit traffic element may be present. Accommodation establishment records exclude day-trippers and tourists staying with friends or relatives or in other forms of unregistered accommodation. Sample surveys may be applied at points of entry/exit to returning residents or departing non-residents, or household surveys may be carried out (outbound), but in both cases often the sample size is relatively small. International tourist expenditure data are usually collected by the bank reporting method or sample surveys. The former method is based on the registration by authorised banks and agencies of the buying and selling of foreign currencies by travellers. There are many problems associated with this method of data collection, such as identifying a transaction as a tourism transaction, the non-reporting of relevant transactions and the unreliability of its use for measuring receipts from specific origin countries (the geographic breakdown relates to the denomination of the currency and not the generating country). Sample surveys provide more reliable data on tourist expenditures, but as with visit data the sample size is often relatively small.

## 1.2.2   Explanatory Variables

Among the various influencing factors on tourism demand, the following are most often considered in tourism demand modelling studies as explanatory variables.

### 1.2.2.1   *Population*

The level of foreign tourism from a given origin is expected to depend upon the origin population. Although population features as a separate explanatory variable in some tourism demand studies, more often the effect of population is accommodated by modifying the dependent variable to become international tourism demand per capita. However, in many cases the impact of population changes is ignored. The main justification for not having population as a separate variable is that its presence may cause multicollinearity problems, as population tends to be highly correlated with income (see section 1.2.2.2.) On the other hand, the procedure adopted whereby demand is specified in per capita terms in effect constrains the population elasticity to equal unity (if a power model is under consideration). Although it is theoretically incorrect to exclude population, it is likely that population changes in the generating countries will be small over the short-medium term, and hence the model will only be affected marginally.

### 1.2.2.2   *Income*

In tourism demand functions, origin country income or private consumption is generally included as a key explanatory variable, and usually enters the demand function in per capita form (corresponding to the specification of demand in per capita terms). If (mainly) holiday demand or visits to friends and relatives are under consideration then the appropriate form of the variable is personal disposable income or private consumption. However, if attention focuses on business visits (or they form an important part of the total), then a more general income variable (such as national income or GDP) should be used, or a measure of business activity such as aggregate imports/exports between the origin and destination countries.

### 1.2.2.3   Own Price

The appropriate measure of tourism prices is difficult to obtain. In the case of tourism there are two elements of price: the cost of travel to the destination and the cost of living for tourists in the destination.

Although the theoretical justification for including transport cost as a demand determinant does not appear to be disputed, many empirical studies exclude this variable from the demand function on the grounds of potential multicollinearity problems and lack of data availability. However, it is possible to obtain an approximate measure of transport cost using representative airfares between origin and destination for air travel, and representative petrol costs and/or ferry fares for surface travel.

Usually the consumer price index (CPI) in a destination country is taken to be a proxy for the cost of tourism in that country. The problem of using the CPI as the cost of tourism in the destination is that the cost of living of the local residents does not always reflect the cost of living of foreign visitors to that destination, especially in poor countries. However, this procedure is adopted on the grounds of lack of more suitable data, that is, an index 'defined over the basket of goods purchased by tourists, rather than over the usual typical consumer basket' (Kliman, 1981, p. 490). Potential tourists base their decisions on tourism costs in the destination measured in terms of their local currency, and therefore the destination price variable should be adjusted by the exchange rate between the origin and destination currencies.

Exchange rates are also sometimes used separately to represent tourists' costs of living. Although they usually appear in addition to a consumer price index proxy, they may also be used as the sole representation of tourists' living costs. The justification for including a separate exchange rate variable in international tourism demand functions is that consumers are more aware of exchange rates than destination costs of living for tourists, hence they are driven to use exchange rate as a proxy variable. However, the use of exchange rate alone in the demand functions can be very misleading because even though the exchange rate in a destination may become more favourable, this could be counterbalanced by a relatively high inflation rate. Empirical results presented by Martin and Witt (1987) suggest that the exchange-rate-adjusted consumer price index is a reasonable proxy for the cost of tourism, but that exchange rate on its own is not an acceptable proxy.

### 1.2.2.4 Substitute Prices

Mostly, those substitution possibilities allowed for in international tourism demand studies are restricted to tourists' destination living costs. There are two possible ways in which these substitute prices may enter the demand function. First, the tourists' cost-of-living variable may be specified in the form of the destination value relative to the origin value, thus permitting substitution between tourist visits to the foreign destination under consideration and domestic tourism. The justification for this form of relative price index is that domestic tourism is the most important substitute for foreign tourism. Second, substitute prices may enter the demand function in a form that allows for the impact of competing foreign destinations by specifying the tourists' cost-of-living variable as destination value relative to a weighted average value calculated for a set of alternative destinations, or by specifying a separate weighted average substitute destination cost variable.

Just as tourists' living costs in substitute destinations are likely to influence the demand for tourism to a given destination, so travel costs to substitute destinations may also be expected to have an impact. However, although some theoretical attention has been paid to the notion of substitute travel costs in the literature, they do not often feature in tourism demand functions. Substitute travel costs may enter the demand function by specifying the travel cost variable as travel cost to the destination relative to a weighted average value calculated for a set of alternative destinations, or by specifying a separate weighted average substitute travel cost variable.

### 1.2.2.5 Tastes

Consumer tastes can have an important influence on tourism demand. They are affected by socio-economic factors such as age, sex, education and marital status, and can change as a result of innovation and advertising, and more fundamentally as a consequence of changing values and priorities, and rising living standards. However, due to data limitations most empirical studies which allow for consumer tastes use a time trend to represent a steady change in the popularity of a destination country over the period considered as a result of changing tastes. The intention of using a time trend is also to capture the time-dependent effects of all other explanatory variables not explicitly included in the demand equation, such as changes in air service frequencies and demographic changes in the origins. However, the problem of including a time trend in tourism demand functions is its ambiguity. We normally do not know exactly what the trend variable actually captures. In many cases, the inclusion of a time trend also causes problems with the income variable, since these two variables are likely to be highly correlated. Song *et al.* (1999) make an attempt to examine the influence of tastes on tourism demand by using a destination preference index. However, much work is still needed to incorporate appropriately consumer tastes in tourism demand functions.

### 1.2.2.6   Marketing

National tourist organisations engage in sales-promotion activities specifically to attempt to persuade potential tourists to visit the country, and these activities may take various forms, including media advertising and public relations. Hence, promotional expenditure is expected to play a role in determining the level of international tourism demand. Much tourism-related marketing activity is not, however, specific to a particular destination (for example, general travel agent and tour operator advertising) and therefore is likely to have little impact on the demand for tourism to that destination. The promotional activities of national tourist organisations are destination specific and are therefore more likely to influence tourism flows to the destination concerned.

Marketing has not featured often in tourism demand models, but a critical review of studies which do include some form of marketing variable appears in Witt and Martin (1987a) and a subsequent review appears in Crouch *et al.* (1992).

### 1.2.2.7   Expectations and Habit Persistence

Tourist expectations and habit persistence (stable behaviour patterns) are usually incorporated in tourism demand models through the use of a lagged dependent variable, that is, an autoregressive term (Witt, 1980a). Once people have been on holiday to a particular country and liked it, they tend to return to that destination. There is much less uncertainty associated with holidaying again in that country compared with travelling to a previously unvisited foreign country. Furthermore, knowledge about the destination spreads as people talk about their holidays and show photographs, thereby reducing uncertainty for potential visitors to that country. In fact this 'word of mouth' recommendation may well play a more important role in destination selection than does commercial advertising. A type of adaptive expectation or learning process is in operation and as people are, in general, risk averse (especially in the case of large outlays of money such as for holidays), the number of people choosing a given destination in any year depends on the numbers who chose it in previous years.

A further justification for the inclusion of a lagged dependent variable in tourism demand functions, which is not related to expectations or habit persistence, is that there may be constraints on supply. These constraints may take the form of shortages of hotel accommodation, passenger transportation capacity and trained staff, and these often cannot be increased rapidly.

Time is also required to build up contacts among tour operators, hotels, airlines and travel agencies. Similarly, once the tourist industry in a country has become highly developed it is unlikely to dwindle rapidly. If a partial adjustment mechanism is postulated to allow for rigidities in supply, this results in the presence of a lagged dependent variable in the tourism demand function. This is now demonstrated.

$$Q_t - Q_{t-1} = \mu(Q_t^* - Q_{t-1}), \qquad 0 < \mu < 1 \qquad (1.2)$$

where $Q_t$ is the quantity of the tourism product provided in destination *i* for residents of country *j* in period *t*; $Q_t^*$ is the quantity of the tourism product demanded in destination *i* by residents of country *j* in period *t*; $\mu$ is the speed of adjustment of the level of tourism provided to the level demanded. (Subscripts *i* and *j* have been omitted for simplicity.)

The left-hand side of Equation (1.2) denotes the change in the level of the tourism product provided between periods *t*–1 and *t*. The bracketed term on the right-hand side of Equation (1.2) is the difference between the level of demand for the tourism product in period *t* and the level provided in period *t*–1, that is, the change demanded in the level of tourism. Thus Equation (1.2) states that the change in the level of tourism provided is a proportion, $\mu$, of change demanded. If $\mu = 0$, then $Q_t = Q_{t-1}$, and there is no movement of the quantity of tourism provided towards the quantity demanded. If $\mu = 1$, then $Q_t = Q_t^*$, that is, there is complete adjustment of the quantity of tourism provided to the quantity demanded. As we are specifying a *partial* adjustment process, $\mu$ lies strictly between zero and unity—there is some adjustment but it is incomplete.

Equation (1.2) may be rewritten as

$$Q_t = (1 - \mu)Q_{t-1} + \mu Q_t^* \qquad (1.3)$$

Now $Q_t^*$ is the quantity of tourism demanded and is a function of the set of explanatory variables such as income, own price and substitute prices. Therefore, the only difference between the explanatory variables present in models (1.1) and (1.3) is that the latter includes the dependent variable with a one-period lag—hence the justification for including a lagged dependent variable in tourism demand functions to accommodate supply constraints.

### 1.2.2.8   *Qualitative Effects*

Dummy variables can be included in international tourism demand models to capture the impacts of 'one-off' events. For example, when governments impose foreign currency restrictions on their residents (such as the £50 annual limit introduced in the UK during 1966 to late 1969), this is expected to reduce outbound tourism. Similarly, the 1973 and 1979 oil crises are expected to have temporarily reduced international tourism demand; although the impacts of the oil crises on holiday prices and consumer incomes are incorporated in these explanatory variables, a further reduction in international tourism demand is likely on account of the psychological impact of the resultant uncertainties in the world economic situation. Witt and Martin (1987b) discuss a range of 'one-off' events which have been accommodated by dummy variables. A more recent example is the reduction in outbound and inbound tourism for those countries affected by the Severe Acute Respiratory Syndrome (SARS) outbreak in 2003.

## 1.3    FUNCTIONAL FORM AND DEMAND ELASTICITIES

Equation (1.1) is a theoretical model of tourism demand which is simply a mathematical statement that indicates that there is a relationship between the variables under consideration. However, in exactly what form these variables are related is unknown. In practice, we need to specify the form of the tourism demand function, that is, the manner in which tourism demand is related to its determinants. The two commonly used demand equations assume either a linear relationship or a power relationship between $Q_{ij}$ and its determinants.

The simplest relationship is the linear relationship and this is expressed as

$$Q_{ij} = \alpha_0 + \alpha_1 P_i + \alpha_2 P_s + \alpha_3 Y_j + \alpha_4 T_j + \alpha_5 A_{ij} + \varepsilon_{ij} \tag{1.4}$$

where the variables $Q_{ij}$, $P_i$, $P_s$, $Y_j$, $T_j$ and $A_{ij}$ are defined as in Equation (1.1); $\alpha_0, \alpha_1, \ldots, \alpha_5$ are the coefficients that need to be estimated empirically; and $\varepsilon_{ij}$ is the disturbance term.

Linear tourism demand equations are popular for the following two reasons. First, empirical studies have shown that many tourism demand relationships can be approximately represented by a linear relationship over the sample period under consideration (Edwards, 1985; Smeral *et al.*, 1992). Second, the coefficients in the linear model can be estimated relatively easily.

Based on Equation (1.4), we can examine how sensitive tourism demand is to changes in the independent variables. The measure of responsiveness of demand to changes in the independent variables is the demand elasticity, which is measured by

$$\tilde{\omega}_X = \frac{\Delta Q_{ij} / Q_{ij}}{\Delta X / X} = \frac{\Delta Q_{ij}}{\Delta X} \times \frac{X}{Q_{ij}} \tag{1.5}$$

where $X$ denotes an independent variable and $\Delta$ denotes 'change in'.

Equation (1.5) shows the percentage change in quantity demanded, $Q_{ij}$, attributable to a given percentage change in an independent variable, $X$. This equation measures arc elasticity, namely the elasticity over some finite range of the function. At the limit, where $\Delta X$ and $\Delta Q_{ij}$ are very small, the point elasticity may be obtained:

$$\tilde{\omega}_X = \frac{\partial Q_{ij}}{\partial X} \times \frac{X}{Q_{ij}} \tag{1.6}$$

The partial derivative sign denotes that we are examining the impact on quantity demanded resulting from a change in $X$, holding all other factors constant. Applying formula (1.6) to Equation (1.4) allows various demand elasticities to be calculated. For example, the own price elasticity is calculated as

$$\tilde{\omega}_X = \frac{\partial Q_{ij}}{\partial P_i} \times \frac{P_i}{Q_{ij}}$$
$$= \frac{\partial(\alpha_0 + \alpha_1 P_i + \alpha_2 P_s + \alpha_3 Y_j + \alpha_4 T_j + \alpha_5 A_{ij} + \varepsilon_{ij})}{\partial P_i} \times \frac{P_i}{Q_{ij}} = \alpha_1 \times \frac{P_i}{Q_{ij}} \tag{1.7}$$

From Equation (1.7) we can see that the point elasticity is obtained from a linear demand function by multiplying the regression coefficient of the variable $X$ by the value of $X/Q_{ij}$ at that point. Given that the value of $X/Q_{ij}$ varies over the time period, the point elasticities based on the linear demand model therefore also vary over time. The substitute price elasticity, income elasticity and so on are calculated in the same manner.

The most commonly used functional form in tourism demand analysis is the power model (Witt and Witt, 1995). This can be expressed as

$$Q_{ij} = A P_i^{\alpha_1} P_s^{\alpha_2} Y_j^{\alpha_3} T_j^{\alpha_4} A_{ij}^{\alpha_5} u_{ij} \tag{1.8}$$

where $A, \alpha_0, \alpha_1, \ldots, \alpha_5$ are coefficients; the variables are as defined previously; and $u_{ij}$ is the disturbance term.

The popularity of the power function is due to its features discussed below, but also due to its relatively good empirical performance. For example, Witt and Witt (1992) and Lee *et al.* (1996) found that the power model outperformed the linear model in terms of expected coefficient signs and statistical significance of the coefficients.

The power function has three important features. First, Equation (1.8) implies that the marginal effects of each independent variable on tourism demand are not constant, but depend on the value of the variable, as well as on the values of all other variables in the demand function. This can be seen by taking the partial derivative of Equation (1.8) with respect to, say, income:

$$\frac{\partial Q_{ij}}{\partial Y_j} = A\alpha_3 P_i^{\alpha_1} P_s^{\alpha_2} Y_j^{\alpha_3 - 1} T_j^{\alpha_4} A_{ij}^{\alpha_5} u_{ij} \tag{1.9}$$

Equation (1.9) shows that the marginal effect of a change in income on tourism demand depends not only on the level of income but also on all the other explanatory variables. This changing marginal relationship is perhaps more realistic than the constant relationship assumed in the linear model. For example, when consumers' disposable income is low, a given increase in income tends to have a large impact on foreign holiday expenditure; but when disposable income is high, the increase in foreign holiday expenditure resulting from the given increase in income is likely to be smaller. This may be due to external constraints imposed on consumers' leisure time, or because consumer demand shifts to a higher order, such as to buying new houses.

The second feature of the power tourism demand function is that Equation (1.8) may be transformed into a linear relationship using logarithms, again making estimation relatively easy. The transformed Equation (1.8) is

$$\ln Q_{ij} = \alpha_0 + \alpha_1 \ln P_i + \alpha_2 \ln P_s + \alpha_3 \ln Y_j + \alpha_4 \ln T_j + \alpha_5 \ln A_{ij} + \varepsilon_{ij} \tag{1.10}$$

where $\alpha_0 = \ln A$ and $\varepsilon_{ij} = \ln u_{ij}$.

The third feature of the power demand function is that the estimated coefficients in Equation (1.10) are estimates of demand elasticities (which are constant over time). For example, own price elasticity is measured by

$$\tilde{\omega}_{P_i} = \frac{\partial Q_{ij}}{\partial P_i} \times \frac{P_i}{Q_{ij}} \tag{1.11}$$

From Equation (1.8):

$$\tilde{\omega}_{P_i} = A\alpha_1 P_i^{\alpha_1 - 1} P_s^{\alpha_2} Y_j^{\alpha_3} T_j^{\alpha_4} A_{ij}^{\alpha_5} u_{ij} \frac{P_i}{Q_{ij}}$$

$$= A\alpha_1 P_i^{\alpha_1 - 1} P_s^{\alpha_2} Y_j^{\alpha_3} T_j^{\alpha_4} A_{ij}^{\alpha_5} u_{ij} \times \frac{P_i}{A P_i^{\alpha_1} P_s^{\alpha_2} Y_j^{\alpha_3} T_j^{\alpha_4} A_{ij}^{\alpha_5} u_{ij}} \tag{1.12}$$

$$= \alpha_1 \frac{A P_i^{\alpha_1} P_s^{\alpha_2} Y_j^{\alpha_3} T_j^{\alpha_4} A_{ij}^{\alpha_5} u_{ij}}{P_i} \times \frac{P_i}{A P_i^{\alpha_1} P_s^{\alpha_2} Y_j^{\alpha_3} T_j^{\alpha_4} A_{ij}^{\alpha_5} u_{ij}}$$

$$= \alpha_1$$

Hence, the own price elasticity is the same as the coefficient of the own price variable, and does not depend on the price/quantity ratio. This constant demand elasticity feature holds for all the variables in Equation (1.8) (and therefore also Equation (1.10)). The constant demand elasticity property is useful in that it is easy to understand from a managerial point of view; it allows policymakers to assess the percentage impact on tourism demand resulting from a 1% change in one of the independent variables, while holding all other explanatory variables constant.

The magnitude of the estimated price elasticity of demand can provide useful information for policymakers. Total tourism revenue may increase, decrease or remain the same as a result of a change in tourism prices, and this depends on the value of the price elasticity. There are three ranges of values that are relevant.

$|\tilde{\omega}_{P_i}| > 1$: If the absolute value of the price elasticity exceeds unity, the demand for tourism is price elastic. An increase in tourism price will result in a more than proportionate decrease in quantity demanded, and as a result total tourism revenue will fall.

$|\tilde{\omega}_{P_i}| = 1$: If the absolute value of the price elasticity equals unity, the demand curve is a rectangular hyperbola. Total tourism revenue will remain constant with a change in tourism price.

$|\tilde{\omega}_{P_i}| < 1$: If the absolute value of the price elasticity is less than unity, the demand for tourism is price inelastic. An increase in tourism price will result in a less than proportionate decrease in quantity demanded, and as a result total tourism revenue will rise.

According to economic theory, the total revenue (*TR*) will continue to increase as long as marginal revenue (*MR*) is positive. If we know the price elasticity of demand at a point, the value of MR can be calculated. This is illustrated as follows:

$$TR = P_i Q_{ij} \tag{1.13}$$

$$MR = \frac{dTR}{dQ_{ij}} = P_i + Q_{ij}\frac{dP_i}{dQ_{ij}} = P_i(1 + \frac{Q_{ij}}{P_i}\frac{dP_i}{dQ_{ij}}) = P_i(1 + \frac{1}{\tilde{\omega}_{P_i}}) \tag{1.14}$$

Equation (1.14) states that the *MR* relates to the price of tourism and price elasticity. If we know the value of the price elasticity, we can calculate the sign of the *MR*, and hence we can see whether or not the *TR* is increasing. For example, if the price elasticity of demand for tourism is estimated to be –1.5, the *MR* revenue will be $0.333P_i$. Since the price of tourism is always positive, the *MR* is positive. The managerial implication of this would be that a decrease in the tourism price holding other variables constant will bring about an increase in total tourism revenue. However, if the calculated price elasticity is –0.5, the *MR* will be $-P_i$, which is negative. This suggests that a decrease in the tourism price holding other variables constant will bring about a less than proportionate increase in tourism demand, and so total tourism revenue will decline.

Knowledge of income elasticities is also important for tourism planners. A low income elasticity of demand implies that the demand for tourism in a particular destination is relatively insensitive to the economic situation in the origin country. However, if the calculated income elasticity exceeds unity, then a rise in income in the origin country will be accompanied by a more than proportionate rise in tourism demand in the destination. Destinations should therefore pay particular attention to forecasting the expected levels of future economic activity in those tourism generating countries with high income elasticities.

Price elasticities for substitute destinations also contain useful information for tourism policymakers. If the substitute price elasticity in the tourism demand function for a particular destination is high, this means that tourism in this destination is very sensitive to price changes in other destinations. Planners and decision-makers in the destination under consideration should therefore keep a close watch on prices in competing destinations in order to ensure that the relative price level does not increase significantly.

## 1.4     SUMMARY

This chapter has introduced some basic concepts related to tourism demand modelling and forecasting. The demand for the tourism product faced by a destination depends on the price of tourism for that destination, the price of tourism for alternative destinations, potential consumers' incomes, consumer tastes, and the promotional efforts of the destination, as well as other social, cultural, geographic and political factors. Demand elasticities such as own price elasticity, income elasticity and substitute price elasticity measure the percentage change in the quantity of tourism demanded in a destination country as a result of a one percent change in one of the determinant variables, while holding the rest of the determinants constant in the tourism demand function. A decline in the price of tourism in a destination results in an increase in total tourism revenue in that destination if demand is price elastic, a decrease in total tourism revenue if demand is price inelastic, and unchanged total tourism revenue if the price elasticity equals unity.

Understanding demand elasticities is very important for tourism policymakers and planners in the destinations. For tourism demand forecasters, correctly identifying the determinants of tourism demand and appropriately specifying the tourism demand models are crucial for the generation of accurate forecasts of future tourism demand.

# 2 Recent Developments in Tourism Demand Analysis

## 2.1    INTRODUCTION

The increasing interest in tourism demand studies is motivated by the rapid growth of the tourism industry across the globe since the ending of World War II. Modelling tourism demand in order to analyze the effects of various determinants and accurate forecasting of the future demand for tourism are the two major focuses of tourism demand studies. The earliest work in this field can be traced back to the 1960s, notably pioneered by Guthrie (1961), followed by Gerakis (1965) and Gray (1966). Since then considerable progress has taken place in this field of study, in terms of the diversity of research interests, the depth of theoretical foundations, and advances in research methodologies. This improvement has accelerated since the early 1990s, when the advanced methodologies for business and economic studies, especially the advances in econometrics, started to be introduced into the tourism literature.

This chapter aims to provide an overview of recent developments and contemporary trends in tourism demand studies using econometric methods. It provides empirical evidence to support the theoretical explanation of the key elements of tourism demand analysis discussed in Chapter 1. More than 200 empirical studies on tourism demand modelling and forecasting have been published since 1990 and the general trends in tourism demand analysis over this period are reviewed. The focus is placed on seven areas: data frequency, origins/destinations under study, measures of tourism demand, explanatory variables, functional form, models and demand elasticities. A detailed summary of the post-1990 econometric studies on tourism demand modelling is shown in Table 2.1.

*Table 2.1* Summary of Econometric Studies of Tourism Demand Modelling

| Study | Frequency and Sample (1) | Region of Focus (2) | Dependent Variable (3) | Independent Variable (4) | Econometric and Other Models (5) | Functional Form (6) |
| --- | --- | --- | --- | --- | --- | --- |
| Aguiló et al. (2005) | A: 60-00 | Balearic Islands (Spain) (I) | TA | Y/P RC ER D cumulated TA | **Information transmission model** | Non-linear |
| Akal (2004) | A: 63-01 | Turkey (I) | TE | TA | **AR(I)MAX SR** | Linear Double-log |
| Akis (1998) | A: 80-93 | Turkey (I) | TA | Y RC | **SR** | Double-log |
| Algieri (2006) | M: 93.12-02.10 | Russia (I) | TE | Y RC TC | **CI** | Double-log |
| Ashworth and Johnson (1990) | A: 72-86 | UK (O) | TE-H | Y P RPI D | **SR** | Double-log |
| Bakkal (1991) | A: 66-85 | Germany (O) | BS (of TN) | TE/aggregated PI RC SC | **Translog utility function** | Semi-log-non-linear |
| Bicak et al. (2005) | A: 83-00 | North Cyprus (I) | TA HA | Y RC D DT | **SR** Trends | Double-log Semi-log |
| Blake et al. (2006) | Q: 79.1-03.3 | Scotland (I) | TA TE | Y/P RC SC | **STSM** CGE | Double-log |
| Cho (2001) | Q: 75.1-97.4 | Hong Kong (I) | TA | CPI IM EX OEIs | **ARIMAX** ARIMA ES | Linear |

| | | | | | | |
|---|---|---|---|---|---|---|
| Croes and Vanegas (2005) | A: 75-00 | Aruba (I) | TA | Y CER D | ADLM | Linear Double-log |
| Crouch et al. (1992) | A: 70-88 | Australia (I) | TA/P | Y/P RP TC ME D DT | ADLM | Double-log |
| Daniel and Ramos (2002) | A: 75-97 | Portugal (I) | TA | Y/P RC TC TS D DT | CI ECM | Double-log |
| De Mello et al. (2002) | A: 69-97 | UK to France, Portugal, Spain | BS | TE/P/SPI RC SC D | LAIDS | Semi-log-linear |
| De Mello and Fortuna (2005) | A: 69-97 | UK (O) | BS | TE/P/SPI RC SC D | Static/Dynamic LAIDS ADLM | Semi-log-linear |
| De Mello and Nell (2005) | A: 69-97 | UK (O) | BS | TE/P/SPI RC SC D | CI-structural VAR LAIDS | Semi-log-linear |
| Di Matteo (1999) | Q: 79.1-95.4 | Canada to US | TE | Y/P ER D | SR NLWSS | Double-log |
| Di Matteo and Di Matteo (1993) | Q: 79.1-89.4 | Canada to US | TE | Y/P ER RC-gas D | ADLM | Double-log |
| Divisekera (2003) | Not reported | UK, US, Japan and New Zealand (O) | BS | TE/P/SPI average of RC+TC SC D | LAIDS | Semi-log-linear |
| Dritsakis (2004) | A: 63-00 | Germany and UK to Greece | TA | Y/P CTC RC | VAR(CI)/ECM | Double-log |
| Dritsakis and Athanasiadis (2000) | A: 60-93 | Greece (I) | TA/P | Y/P $C_d$ SC ER ME DT D OEI | ADLM | Double-log |

*(Continued)*

Table 2.1 (Continued)

| Study | Frequency and Sample (1) | Region of Focus (2) | Dependent Variable (3) | Independent Variable (4) | Econometric and Other Models (5) | Functional Form (6) |
|---|---|---|---|---|---|---|
| Dritsakis and Papanastasiou (1998) | A: 60-93 | Greece (I) | TA TE NAC | $C_d$ DT TE NAC TA OEI | Simultaneous equation model | Double-log |
| Durbarry and Sinclair (2003) | A: 68-99 | France to Italy, Spain and UK | BS | TE/P/SPI RC SC D | EC-LAIDS | Semi-log-linear |
| Eugenio-Martin et al. (2005) | Q: 79.1-01.1 | Scotland (I) | TA TE | Y RC ER | STSM | Double-log |
| Fujii et al. (1985) | A: 58-80 | Hawaii (I) | BS on tourist goods | TE/P/SPI $C_d$ DT SC | LAIDS | Semi-log-linear |
| Gallet and Braun (2001) | A: 60-85 | US (O) | TA | Y $C_d$/ER SC | GSR | Double-log |
| García-Ferrer and Queralt (1997) | M: 79.01-93.12 | Spain (I) | TE TA | Y RC SC D | STSM ARIMA BSM | Double-log |
| Garín-Muñoz and Amaral (2000) | A: 85-95 | Spain (I) | TN/P | Y/P ER C D | Static/dynamic PDR | Linear |
| González and Moral (1995) | M: 79.01-93.12 | Spain (I) | TE TA | Y RC SC D | STSM ECM TFM ARIMA | Double-log |
| González and Moral (1996) | M: 79.01-94.06 | Spain (I) | TE TA | Y RC SC D | STSM TFM ARIMA BSM | Double-log |

| Study | Data | Location | Type | Variables | Method | Form |
|---|---|---|---|---|---|---|
| Greenidge (2001) | Q: 68.1-97.4 | Barbados (I) | TA | Y RC SC ST SS Cir | STSM BSM | Double-log |
| Han *et al.* (2006) | A: 64-96 | US to Europe | TE/P | TE/P/SPI RC SC D DT | LAIDS | Semi-log-linear |
| Holmes and Shamsuddin (1997) | M: 81.01-93.08 | US to British Columbia | TA | Y ER $C_d$ $C_o$ D | Intervention & TFM ARIMA | Double-log |
| Icoz *et al.* (1998) | A: 82-93 | Turkey (I) | TA | Cd ER No. of beds No. of agents | SR | Double-log |
| Ismail *et al.* (2000) | M: 87.01-97.12 | Japan to Guam | TA | Y ER TC D | ADLM | Linear |
| Jensen (1998) | A: 61(70)-95 | Denmark (I) | TE | Y RC SC D weather | ADLM | Double-log |
| Jørgensen and Solvoll (1996) | 69-93 seasonal | Norway (O) | ITC | Y/P Price of ITC weather OEI | ADLM | Double-log |
| Kim and Song (1998) | A: 62-94 | Korea (I) | TA | Y TC TV RC D | CI/ECM VAR AR ES Naïve 1 MA ARMA | Double-log |
| Kim and Uysal (1998) | M: 91.01-95.12 | Hotels in Seoul, Korea | TN | $C_d$ TV No. of events | ARMAX | Double-log |
| Kulendran (1996) | Q: 75.3-95.2 | Australia (I) | TA | Y RC TC D | CI/ECM | Double-log |
| Kulendran and King (1997) | Q: 75.1-94.4 | Australia (I) | TA | Y RC TC D | CI/ECM STSM SR ARIMA AR AR(12) ARMA | Double-log |

*(Continued)*

Table 2.1  (Continued)

| Study | Frequency and Sample (1) | Region of Focus (2) | Dependent Variable (3) | Independent Variable (4) | Econometric and Other Models (5) | Functional Form (6) |
|---|---|---|---|---|---|---|
| Kulendran and Wilson (2000) | Q: 81.1-97.4 | Australia (I) | TA-B | Y $Y_d$ TA-H TV/$Y_d$ RC IM D | CI/ECM Naïve 1 ARIMA | Double-log |
| Kulendran and Witt (2001) | Q: 78.1-95.3 | UK (O) | TA/P | Y/P RC CS TC SF D | CI/ECM SR BSM ARIMA SARIMA Naïve 1 | Double-log |
| Kulendran and Witt (2003a) | Q: 82.1-98.4 | Australia (I) | TA-B | Y $Y_d$ TA-H TV/ $Y_d$ C | ECM STSM ARIMA[1,4] ARIMA[1] AR[4] Naïve 1 BSM | Double-log |
| Kulendran and Witt (2003b) | Q: 78.1-95.4 | UK (O) | TA-H | Y RC ER C D | TFM ECM ARIMA | Double-log |
| Lanza et al. (2003) | A: 75-92 | 13 European countries (O) | BS | $C_d$ SC OEI D | LAIDS | Semi-log-linear |
| Lathiras and Siriopoulos (1998) | A: 60-95 | Greece (I) | TA/P | Y/P RC SC ER D | CI/ECM | Double-log |
| Law (2000) | A: 66-96 | Taiwan to Hong Kong | TA | Y RC ER P ME HR | SR Naïve 1 ES MA FNN ANN | Non-linear |
| Law (2001) | A: 67-98 | Japan to Hong Kong | TA | Y HR ER P ME | SR Naïve 1,2 MA ES ANN | Double-log |
| Law and Au (1999) | A: 77-97 | Japan to Hong Kong | TA | RC P ER ME HR | SR Naïve 1 ES MA FNN | Linear |

| Study | Period | Destination | | Variables Model | Functional form |
|---|---|---|---|---|---|
| Ledesma-Rodríguez et al. (2001) | A: 79-97 | Tenerife (I) | TA | Y/P ER TC ME OEI **Static/Dynamic PDR** | Double-log |
| Lee et al. (1996) | A: 70-89 | Korea (I) | TE/P | Y/P RC ER D **SR** | Double-log |
| Li et al. (2004) | A: 72-00 | UK (O) | BS | TE/P/SPI RC SC D **Static LAIDS EC-LAIDS** | Semi-log-linear |
| Li et al. (2006a) | A: 63/68-00 | Thailand (I) | TA | Y RC SC D **ADLM VAR CI/ECMs TVP ARIMA** | Double-log |
| Li et al. (2006b) | A: 72-00 | UK (O) | BS | TE/P/SPI RC SC D **Static-/EC-/TVP-/TVP-EC-LAIDS** | Semi-log-linear |
| Li et al. (2006c) | A: 72-00 | UK (O) | TE/P | TE/P/SPI RC SC D **TVP-ECM ECMs TVP ADLM VAR** | Semi-log-linear |
| Lim (2004) | Q: 80.1-99.4 | Korea to Australia | TA | Y C ER RC D **ADLM** | Double-log |
| Lim and McAleer (2001a) | Q: 75.1-96.4 | Australia (I) | TA | Y/P TC ER C RC **VAR CI/VECM** | Double-log |
| Lyssiotou (2000) | Q: 79-91 | UK (O) | BS-H | TE-H/recreation-PI RC SC D DT **AIDS** | Semi-log-non-linear |
| Mangion et al. (2005) | A: 73-00 | UK to Malta, Spain and Cyprus | BS | TE/P/SPI RC SC **EC-LAIDS Hedonic Pricing Model** | Semi-log-linear |
| Morley (1996) | A: 72-92 | Australia (I) | TA-H | Y/P TC **SR** | Linear |

(Continued)

*Table 2.1 (Continued)*

| Study | Frequency and Sample (1) | Region of Focus (2) | Dependent Variable (3) | Independent Variable (4) | Econometric and Other Models (5) | Functional Form (6) |
|---|---|---|---|---|---|---|
| Morley (1997) | A: 72-92 | Australia (I) | TA-H TA-VFR | Y/P RC D TC | **ADLM** | Double-log |
| Morley (1998) | A: 72-92 | Australia (I) | TA-H TA-VFR | Y/P RC TC D | **ADLM** | Double-log |
| Morris et al. (1995) | Q: 81.1-93.4 | Australia (I) | TA TA-H TA-VFR | RC TC $\Delta$Y DT D | **SR** | Double-log |
| Narayan (2004) | A: 70-00 | Fiji (I) | TA | Y/P TC HR SC D | **CI ECM** | Double-log |
| Naudé and Saayman (2005) | A: 96-02 | 43 African countries | TA | Y/P RC OEIs D | Static/dynamic **PDR CSR** | Linear |
| O'Hagan and Harrison (1984) | A: 64-81 | US (O) | BS | TE/P/SPI RC SC D DT | **LAIDS** | Semi-log-linear |
| Oh (2005) | Q: 75.1-01.1 | Korea (I) | TE | Y SD DT | **VAR** | Linear |
| Papatheodorou (1999) | A: 57-90 | UK, Germany and France (O) | BS | TE/tourists/SPI RC SC D DT | **LAIDS** | Semi-log-linear |
| Patsouratis et al. (2005) | A: 80-97 | Greece (I) | TA | Y $C_d$ ER $C_s$ | **SR** | Double-log |

| Study | Period | Destination | Demand | Explanatory variables | Method | Functional form |
|---|---|---|---|---|---|---|
| Payne and Mervar (2002) | Q: 93.1-99.4 | Croatia (I) | TE | Y RC D | **SR** | Double-log |
| Pyo et al. (1991) | A: 72-87 | US domestic | TE on tourist goods | TE/SPI $C_d$ SC | LES | Semi-log-linear |
| Qiu and Zhang (1995) | A: 75-90 | Canada (I) | TA TE | Y/P ER $C_d$ D DT ICR | **SR** | Linear Double-log |
| Qu and Lam (1997) | A: 84-95 | Mainland China to Hong Kong | TA | Y/P C ER D | **SR** | Linear |
| Riddington (1999) | A: 73-94 | UK Skiing place | TA | OEI DT | TVP LCM | Linear |
| Riddington (2002) | A: 73-00 | UK Ski Resorts | TA | OEI DT | **Supplemented LCM TVP LCM** | Linear |
| Roget and González (2006) | A: 96-01 | Spain (I) | TN-rural | Y $C_d$ PB | **dynamic PDR** | Linear |
| Rosselló (2001) | M: 75.01-99.12 | Balearic Islands (I) | TA | ER RC OEIs | **ADLM** Naïve1 ARIMA | Linear |
| Rosselló et al. (2004) | M/A: 82-01 | Balearic Islands (I) | Gini-coefficient | Y/P ER RC | ECM | Linear |
| Rosselló et al. (2005) | A: 60-01 | Balearic Islands (I) | TA | Y RC ER D | **SR SR+diffusion** | Non-linear |
| Sakai et al. (2000) | A: 68-95 | Japan (O) | TP | Y/P ER labour age participation gender | **PDR** | Linear |

*(Continued)*

*Table 2.1 (Continued)*

| Study | Frequency and Sample (1) | Region of Focus (2) | Dependent Variable (3) | Independent Variable (4) | Econometric and Other Models (5) | Functional Form (6) |
|---|---|---|---|---|---|---|
| Salman (2003) | M: 80.01–98.12 | Sweden (I) | TA | Y RC ER $C_d$ D | CI | Double-log |
| Shan and Wilson (2001) | M: 87.01–98.01 | China (I) | TA Y RC IM+EX ER | TA Y RC IM+EX ER | VAR | Linear |
| Sheldon (1993) | A: 70-86 | US (I) | TE | Y ER RC SC | SR Naïve1,2 Trends | Linear/ Double-log |
| Smeral et al. (1992) | A: 75-00 | 18 OECD countries (I/O) | TM TX | Y $C_o$ D TTX RC D (ST) | Complete system | Linear |
| Smeral (2004) | A: 75-99 | 25 OECD countries (I/O) | TM TX | Y RC D SM RC D | Complete system | Linear |
| Smeral and Weber (2000) | A: 75-96 | 20 OECD countries (I/O) | TM TX | Y RC D (DT) SM RC D (DT) | Complete system | Linear |
| Smeral and Witt (1996) | A: 75-94 | 18 OECD countries (I/O) | TM TX | Y $C_o$ D SM RC D | Complete system | Linear |
| Song et al. (2000) | A: 65-94 | UK (O) | TA/P-H | Y/P RC SC PREF D | CI/ECM VAR MA AR ARMA Naïve 1 | Double-log |
| Song and Witt (2003) | A: 62-98 | Korea (I) | TA | Y TV RC SC D | ADLM ECM | Double-log |

| Study | Period | Destination | Data | Variables | Model | Functional form |
|---|---|---|---|---|---|---|
| Song and Witt (2006) | Q: 93.1-03.2 | Macau (I) | TA | Y RC SC D | **VAR** | Linear |
| Song et al. (2003a) | A: 69-97 | Denmark (I) | TA/P-H | TE/P RC SC TC DT D | **CI/ECM SR VAR ADLM TVP ARIMA Naïve 1** | Double-log |
| Song et al. (2003b) | A: 63/68-00 | Thailand (I) | TA | Y RC SC D | **ADLM VAR TVP CI/ECMs ARIMA Naïve 1** | Double-log |
| Song and Wong (2003) | A: 73-00 | Hong Kong (I) | TA | Y RC SC | **TVP** | Double-log |
| Song et al. (2003c) | A: 73(81)-00 | Hong Kong (I) | TA | Y RC SC D | **ADLM** | Double-log |
| Syriopoulos (1995) | A: 62-87 | Mediterranean countries (I) | TE | Y/P C RC ER D DT(ST) | **CI/ECM** | Double-log |
| Syriopoulos and Sinclair (1993) | A: 60-87 | US, UK, Germany, France and Sweden (O) | BS | TE/P/SPI RC SC D DT | **LAIDS** | Semi-log-linear |
| Tan et al. (2002) | A: 80-97 | Indonesia (I) and Malaysia (I) | TA/P | Y/P C ER RC D | **SR** | Double-log |
| Turner et al. (1998) | Q: 78.1-95.4 | UK (O) | TA-B TA-H TA-VFR | Y RC SC TC SF IM EX OEIs | **SEM** | Linear |
| Turner and Witt (2001a) | Q: 78.1-97.4 | New Zealand (I) | TA-B TA-H TA-VFR | Y P RC TC SF TV/ $Y_d$ IM EX OEIs | **SEM** | Linear |
| Turner and Witt (2001b) | Q: 78.2-98.3 | New Zealand (I) | TA TA-B TA-H TA-VFR | Y RC TC TV/$Y_d$ | **STSM BSM** | Double-log |

(Continued)

*Table 2.1* (Continued)

| Study | Frequency and Sample (1) | Region of Focus (2) | Dependent Variable (3) | Independent Variable (4) | Econometric and Other Models (5) | Functional Form (6) |
|---|---|---|---|---|---|---|
| Uysal and Roubi (1999) | Q: 81.1-96.4 | Canada to US | TE | Y/P RC D | **ADLM** FNN | Double-log |
| Vanegas and Croes (2000) | A: 75-96 | US to Aruba | TA | Y RC ER | **ADLM** | Linear Double-log |
| Var et al. (1990) | A: 79-87 | Turkey (I) | TA | Y/P ER Dis | **SR** | Double-log |
| Veloce (2004) | Q: 72.1-99.4 | Canada (I) | TA/P | Y/P RC D DT | ECM SR VAR ES ARIMA AR | Double-log |
| Vogt and Wittayakorn (1998) | A: 60-93 | Thailand (I) | TE | RC ER Y | **CI/ECM** | Double-log |
| Webber (2001) | Q: 83.1-97.4 | Australia (O) | TA | Y RC $C_d$/ER (C ER) ER-volatility | **CI/VAR** | Double-log |
| White (1985) | A: 54-81 | US (O) | BS | TE/P/SPI RC TC SC D DT | **LAIDS** | Semi-log-linear |
| Witt et al. (2003) | A: 69-97 | Denmark (I) | TA/P-H | TE/P RC SC TC DT D | **CI/ECM SR VAR ADLM TVP** Naïve 1 ARIMA | Double-log |
| Witt and Turner (2002) | A: 82-99 | China (I) | TA | Y RC TC | **STSM** | Double-log |

| | | | | | |
|---|---|---|---|---|---|
| Witt and Witt (1990) | A: 65-80 | US, European countries (I/O) | TA/P | Y/P C_d SC ER TC SF TS TSS D DT | SR | Double-log |
| Witt and Witt (1991) | A: 65-85 | Germany, France UK and US (O) | TA/P TA | Y/P C SC ER, TC SF TS TSS D | SR Naïve1,2 ES AR ARIMA Trends | Double-log |
| Witt and Witt (1992) | A: 65-80 | France, Germany, UK and US (O) | TA/P | Y/P C_d CS ER TC SF D | ADLM Naïve1,2 ES AR ARIMA Trends | Double-log |
| Wong *et al.* (2006) | A: 73-00 | Hong Kong (I) | TA | Y RC SC D | Unrestricted VAR Bayesian VAR | Double-log |

## Legend

**1. Frequency and sample**
A: annual
M: monthly
Q: quarterly

**2. Region of focus**
I: inbound
O: outbound

**3. Dependent variable**
–B: business
–H: holidays
–VFR: visiting friends & relatives
BS: budget share of TE
EX: exports
IM: imports
ITC: No. of inclusive tour charters
NAC: No. of tourist accommodations
TA: tourist arrivals
TAHA: TA in hotels and apartments
TE: tourism receipts/expenditure

TM: tourism imports
TN: number of nights
TP: travel propensity
TX: tourism exports

**4. Independent variable**
C: relative tourism price unadjusted by ER
$C_d$: tourism price in destination
Cir: tourism lifecycle
$C_o$: tourism price in origin country
$C_s$: tourism price in substitute destination
D: dummy variable
Dis: travel distance
DT: deterministic (linear) trend
ER: exchange rate
HR: average hotel rate
ICR: immigration crime rate
ME: marketing expenditure
OEI: other economic indicator
P: population

PB: oil price per barrel
PI: price index
PREF: the preference index
RC: ER-adjusted relative price
RPI: retail price index
SC: substitute price
SF: TC to substitute destinations
SM weighted TM
SPI: Stone's price index
SS: stochastic seasonal component
ST: stochastic trend
TC: travel cost (airfare)
TS: travel cost by surface
TSS: TS to substitute destinations
TTX: total TX
TV: trade volume
Y: income in origin country
$Y_d$: income in destination country

(*Continued*)

Table 2.1 (Continued)

| Study | Frequency and Sample (1) | Region of Focus (2) | Dependent Variable (3) | Independent Variable (4) | Econometric and Other Models (5) | Functional Form (6) |
|---|---|---|---|---|---|---|
| **5. Econometric and other models**<br>ADLM: autoregressive distributed lag model<br>AIDS: almost ideal demand system<br>AR(I)MA(X) autoregressive (integrated) moving average (cause effect) model<br>AR: autoregressive process<br>BNN: back-propogation neural network<br>BSM: non-causal basic structural model<br>CGE: computable general equilibrium<br>CI: cointegration<br>CSR: cross-sectional regression | | | ECM: error correction model<br>ES: exponential smoothing<br>FNN: feed-forward neural network<br>GSR: gradual switching regression<br>LAIDS: linear AIDS<br>LCM: the learning curve model<br>MA: moving average<br>Naïve 1: no-change model<br>Naïve 2: constant growth rate model<br>NLWSS: nonparametric locally weighted scatterplot smoothing | | PDR: panel data regression<br>SEM: structural equation model<br>SR: static regression<br>STSM: structural time series model<br>TFM: transfer function model<br>TVP: time varying parameter model<br>VAR: vector autoregression<br>VECM: vector error correction model<br>Note: the models in bold type indicate econometric approaches | |

## 2.2 DATA FREQUENCY

Three data frequencies are commonly used in tourism demand modelling studies: annual, quarterly and monthly data. Among the studies being reviewed, about two-thirds of them use annual data, a quarter employ quarterly data, and less than 10% are based on monthly data. Although annual data overall dominate the research in this field, quarterly data have been used more often in recent studies, and this is in line with the growing interest in analysing the seasonality of international tourism demand. The increasing number of observations result in more degrees of freedom in model estimation and give more flexibility to include additional influencing factors and/or to extend the lag structure to capture the dynamics of tourism demand more sufficiently. Meanwhile, some advanced econometric models which require the estimation of more parameters, such as the time-varying-parameter (TVP) model, can be introduced into tourism demand studies.

## 2.3 ORIGINS/DESTINATIONS UNDER STUDY

Western Europe and North America have dominated tourism demand studies in the past few decades. This trend is associated with the great contribution of these regions to international tourism development, as both inbound and outbound tourism in these areas account for a large proportion of global tourism flows. These areas have continued to draw a great deal of researchers' attention in the last decade. The UK and USA are the most popular researched countries as both destinations and countries of origin, followed by Germany, France, Spain and Italy. Meanwhile, international tourism in the East Asia and Pacific region has shown the fastest growth in the last decade. Correspondingly, this region has attracted increasing research interest. In East Asia and the Pacific, the well-researched markets are: Hong Kong, predominantly as a destination; Japan, mainly as a source market; and Australia and Korea, as both origin and destination countries. The main travel routes that have been examined are from the UK and the USA to Mediterranean countries, Australia and Hong Kong, and from Japan to Australia and Hong Kong.

## 2.4 MEASURES OF TOURISM DEMAND

Tourist arrivals is the most commonly used measure of international tourism demand, followed by tourist expenditure and tourist nights in registered accommodation. In particular, tourist expenditure, in the form of either absolute values or budget shares, is required by the specification of system demand models, such as the linear expenditure system (LES) and the almost ideal demand system (AIDS).

Most empirical studies are based on aggregate data, that is, total tourist arrivals or total tourist expenditure at the destination level. However, recent trends show that tourism demand analysis at the disaggregated level (for example, in terms of the purpose of travel) is attracting increasing research interest. Different market segments are associated with varying influencing factors and different decision-making processes. Disaggregate demand analysis can provide more detailed insights into each market segment. Therefore, it can better facilitate decision making in terms of developing differentiated and effective marketing strategies for different market segments. Travel purpose is the most often used dimension of data disaggregation. Among various market segments, travel for leisure purposes has attracted the greatest research attention (for example, Ashworth and Johnson, 1990; Kulendran and Witt, 2003b). In addition, some studies focus on business tourism, such as Kulendran and Wilson (2000) and Kulendran and Witt (2003a).

## 2.5   EXPLANATORY VARIABLES

Among all the explanatory variables discussed in Chapter 1, origin country income and relative tourism prices have the most significant effects on international tourism demand, according to a large body of empirical studies. In addition, tourism prices in alternative destinations, travel costs, marketing expenditure and one-off events all have some influence on international tourism demand.

### 2.5.1   Income

Among all the feasible and available measures of the origin country's income, real personal disposable income (PDI) is a relatively satisfactory measure, particularly for holidaymaking or visits to friends and relatives (VFR) types of tourism demand (Kulendran and Witt, 2001; Song *et al.*, 2000; Syriopoulos, 1995). Meanwhile, national disposable income (NDI), gross domestic product (GDP), gross national product (GNP) and gross national income (GNI), all in constant prices, are also used in some studies, particularly those concerned with business tourism (Kulendran and Witt, 2003a). Other plausible proxies include real private consumption expenditure (Song *et al.*, 2003b) and the industry production index (González and Moral, 1995).

Although income is regarded as one of the most important determinants of demand in theory and has been commonly considered in empirical studies, its influence on tourism demand is not always significant, especially in error correction models (ECMs) which are used to examine the short-term dynamics of a demand system. This is demonstrated in studies by Kulendran and King (1997), Kim and Song (1998) and Song *et al.* (2003b). Insignificant income effects are often associated with specific origin countries, particularly those with high income levels, such as Japan, Germany and the USA.

## 2.5.2    Own Price

Alternative measures of tourism prices have been presented in the selected studies. For example, Qiu and Zhang (1995) and Witt and Witt (1991, 1992) use CPIs in the destinations, along with the exchange rates between the destination and the origin, to account for tourism prices separately; Webber (2001) combines these two effects to generate an exchange-rate-adjusted tourism price in the destination; while the majority of tourism studies, especially the most recent studies, commonly define an exchange rate adjusted relative price between the destination and the origin, which is called the *relative tourism price* (see, for example, Li *et al.*, 2006c; Syriopoulos, 1995; Witt *et al.*, 2004). Compared to other price variables, such as substitute tourism prices and travel costs, the own price in a destination appears to be a more important determinant for international tourism demand, as judged by the statistical significance of the coefficients.

## 2.5.3    Tourism Prices in Alternative Destinations

In addition to income and the own price in a destination, tourism prices in alternative destinations are included in some international tourism demand studies. Where a number of alternative destinations are concerned, a weighted average price index of these destinations relative to the tourism price in the origin country is usually used to capture their joint effects (Kulendran and Witt, 2001). The advantage of combining is to save degrees of freedom in the estimated model, while the disadvantage is the inefficiency in distinguishing the different strengths of effects among alternative destinations in the bundle.

## 2.5.4    Travel Costs

In most of the studies that take account of the effects of travel costs, economy airfares between the main cities in the origin country and the destination country are used as proxies (such as Dritsakis, 2004; Lim and McAleer, 2001a and 2002; Kulendran and Witt, 2001). Private gasoline costs are used as proxies for surface travel (Di Matteo and Di Matteo, 1993; Ledesma-Rodriguez *et al.*, 2001; Witt and Witt, 1992). With regard to definitions of travel costs, two alternative forms can be seen, corresponding to tourism prices: the origin-destination-specific form, that is, own price (Kim and Song, 1998; Kulendran and King, 1997; Kulendran and Witt, 2001; Song *et al.*, 2003b), and the weighted average form, that is, taking the substitute effect into account (Kulendran and Witt, 2001). Although travel costs have been considered in a number of empirical studies, they do not always show significant effects on tourism demand (Crouch *et al.*, 1992; Kulendran and King, 1997). A possible reason is the lack of precise measurement of travel costs, especially at the aggregate level. In addition, the use of proxies such as average airfares could be problematic due to the complex structure of airfares.

### 2.5.5   Marketing Expenditure

Only two among all of the reviewed studies included this variable in their demand models: Crouch *et al.* (1992) and Ledesma-Rodriguez *et al.* (2001). On the grounds of lacking precise data in an earlier study, Witt and Martin (1987a, p. 33) pointed out that 'where marketing is used to explain international tourism demand, caution must be exercised in interpreting the empirical results.' This, together with difficulty in accessing marketing expenditure data, explains the unpopularity of this variable in recent tourism demand studies.

### 2.5.6   One-Off Events

Dummy variables are often used to capture the effects of various one-off events, such as the two oil crises in the 1970s, which have shown worldwide effects on tourism demand (Witt *et al.*, 2003; Han *et al.*, 2006). In addition, some regional and country-specific events that are often considered in tourism demand models include the financial crisis in 1997 and SARS in 2003, both in Asia (Lim, 2004; Wong *et al.*, 2007, respectively), the terrorist attack in the USA on September 11, 2001 (Wong *et al.*, 2007), and the foot-and-mouth disease outbreak in the UK in 2001 (Eugenio-Martin *et al.*, 2005). All of these events have shown significant adverse effects on tourism demand in the affected countries and regions. However, some mega events such as the Olympic Games exert positive influences on tourism demand in the host countries (Kim and Song, 1998).

## 2.6   FUNCTIONAL FORM

Double-logarithmic regression has been the predominant functional form in tourism demand modelling studies over the past few decades. Only a small number of studies applied linear models without logarithmic transformation, and even fewer employed non-linear forms. In addition, a semi-log (both linear and non-linear) form is utilised specifically in system-of-equations modelling approaches, principally the AIDS, where independent variables (prices and real expenditure) are transformed into logarithms, but the dependent variables (expenditure shares) are not. In addition to the theoretical merits of the double-log functional form discussed in Chapter 1, Vanegas and Croes (2000) provided empirical evidence of its superiority to its linear counterpart in their study of US demand for tourism in Aruba. They concluded that double-log models generally fitted the data better in terms of the statistical significance of the estimated coefficients, whereas Qiu and Zhang (1995) ran a similar comparison but did not find a significant difference between the two forms. Without a clear justification from the theoretical perspective, it is suggested that the choice of a particular functional form should be subject to statistical testing.

## 2.7    MODELS

Various econometric models have been employed to model and forecast tourism demand. This section provides a brief summary of the applications of these models in the tourism context, while the technical illustrations of these techniques will be presented in the following chapters.

### 2.7.1    Cointegration (CI) Model and Error Correction Model (ECM)

Until the early 1990s, econometric modelling and forecasting of tourism demand had been restricted to static models, which suffered from various problems such as spurious regression (discussed in Chapter 5). Since the mid 1990s, dynamic models, for example a number of specific forms of the autoregressive distributed lag model (ADLM), have appeared in the tourism demand literature (see Chapter 4 for a technical illustration). Particularly because of their merits for long-run and short-run demand elasticity analysis, cointegration and error correction models have attracted great research attention, with many tourism applications being published since 1990. In these studies four estimation methods have been used—the Engle-Granger (1987) two-stage approach (EG), the Wickens-Breusch (1988) one-stage approach (WB), the ADLM approach (Pesaran and Shin 1995), and the most frequently employed, Johansen (1988) maximum likelihood (JML) approach. Due to different modelling strategies, these models yield demand elasticities with large discrepancies for the same data set. Moreover, unlike the other methods, the JML approach may detect more than one CI relationship among the demand and explanatory variables. All of these approaches have their merits, and there has not been clear-cut evidence to show that any one is superior to the others. Sometimes the evaluation is associated with their *ex post* forecasting performance.

### 2.7.2    Time Varying Parameter (TVP) Model

To relax the assumption of constant coefficients (that is, the demand elasticities in a double-log model) associated with traditional econometric techniques, the TVP model was developed and has been applied in tourism demand studies. The TVP model first appeared in the tourism literature in the late 1990s (Riddington, 1999) and there have been only a handful of applications since then. They have all been based on annual tourism data and the main focus of these studies is the evolution of demand elasticities over a relatively long period (discussed in the next section). As it allows for changing tourist behaviours, the TVP model is likely to generate more accurate forecasts of tourism demand, especially as far as short-run forecasts are concerned. This will be discussed in Chapter 8.

### 2.7.3  Vector Autoregressive (VAR) Approach

Where exogeneity is not assured, the vector autoregressive (VAR) model is more appropriate. There have been around ten studies using the VAR approach for tourism demand analysis since the late 1990s. The latest advance in this approach is to incorporate Bayesian restrictions into the original unrestricted VAR model. The empirical study by Wong *et al.* (2006) suggests that Bayesian VAR models can generally improve forecast accuracy in comparison to their unrestricted counterparts.

### 2.7.4  Almost Ideal Demand Systems (AIDS)

The demand system approach has a stronger underpinning of economic theories than the single-equation approach, and is thus more useful for tourism demand analysis, especially as far as the interdependence of tourists' budget allocations is concerned. Among a number of system approaches available, the AIDS introduced by Deaton and Muellbauer (1980b) has been the most often used system-of-equations method. Since the AIDS model was first introduced into tourism demand studies in the 1980s, it has not attracted much attention until recently. There have been only a dozen applications so far. Most of these studies analysed allocations of tourists' expenditure among a group of destination countries, while Fujii *et al.* (1985) investigated tourists' expenditure allocations among different consumer products in a particular destination. The AIDS has been developed from the original static form to the error correction form. Combining the ECM with the linear form of the AIDS (that is, LAIDS), Durbarry and Sinclair (2003), Li *et al.* (2004), and Mangion *et al.* (2005) specified EC-LAIDS models to examine the dynamics of tourists' consumption behaviour. Moreover, Li *et al.* (2006b) further combined the TVP technique with the LAIDS model in both long-run and EC forms to develop the TVP-LAIDS and TVP-EC-LAIDS models. These models are more favourable due to their superior forecasting performance. More detailed discussion of this approach will be provided in Chapter 10.

### 2.7.5  Other Econometric Models

In addition to the above frequently used demand models, the structural time series model (STSM) with causal variables (for example, Kulendran and Witt, 2003a), the transfer function model (for example, Holmes, 1997), the learning curve model, the liner expenditure system (for example, Pyo *et al.*, 1991), the translog utility function (Bakkal, 1991), panel data analysis (for example, Garín-Muñoz and Amaral, 2000) and the structural equation model (for example, Turner and Witt, 2001a) have all appeared in the tourism literature being reviewed. However, their applications are still rare compared to those discussed above. Hence discussion of these techniques will not be covered in this book.

## 2.8   DEMAND ELASTICITIES

Elasticity analysis has received overwhelming attention in econometric studies of tourism demand. This section summarises the findings of recent tourism demand elasticity analyses.

### 2.8.1   General Observations

The majority of tourism demand studies have shown that the income elasticity of tourism demand is greater than one, indicating that international tourism is a luxury product. In addition, it is found that demand for long-haul travel is more income-elastic than the demand for short-haul (that is, intra-regional or domestic) travel. The own-price elasticity of demand is normally negative, although the magnitudes vary considerably. The reasons for the variations, as identified by Crouch (1996), include diverse definitions of tourism prices, different sample periods, functional forms, estimation methods, and the omission of key determinants in the demand models.

Where tourism prices in alternative destinations are included in a tourism demand model such as an AIDS model, cross-price elasticities are examined. The positive and negative signs of cross-price elasticities indicate the substitution and complementary effects, respectively, between the destination concerned and other destinations. Although the substitution effect is often identified between neighbouring destinations, some studies, especially those employing AIDS models, suggest that neighbouring countries may act as complementary destinations. For example, in UK outbound tourism demand studies by Li *et al.* (2004) and Lyssiotou (2000), Greece and Italy are recognised as complementary destinations. It should be noted that the relationship between neighbouring countries, as either substitutes or complements, is dependent on the origin country concerned. For example, Song *et al.* (2003b) found that Malaysia, Indonesia, Philippines and Singapore are regarded as substitute destinations to Thailand by Australian, Japanese and UK tourists, while they appear as complementary destinations to Thailand as far as Korean and US tourists are concerned. In other words, Korean and US tourists are likely to visit multiple destinations in the same region during a single trip.

### 2.8.2   Long-Run and Short-Run Elasticities

In addition to the general observations discussed above, some specific findings can be obtained based on the particular demand model in use. Given that a CI relationship has been identified by statistical tests, long-run and short-run tourism demand elasticities can be calculated from the CI equation and the ECM, respectively. With regard to the income elasticity, the finding of lower levels of significance in ECMs than in CI models indicates that income affects tourism demand more in the long run than in the short run (Syriopoulos, 1995). To some extent, it also indicates that Friedman's (1957) permanent income hypothesis holds. In other words, consumption depends on what people expect to earn over a considerable period of time, and fluctuations in income that are regarded as temporary have little impact on consumption spending. Many empirical studies also show that the values of both the income and own-price elasticities in the long run are greater than their short-run counterparts, suggesting that tourists are more sensitive to income/price changes in the long run than in the short run (see, for example, Kim and Song, 1998; Song *et al.*, 2003b; Song and Witt, 2000). These findings are in line with demand theory. Due to information asymmetry and relatively inflexible budget allocations, it takes time before income changes affect tourism demand (Syriopoulos, 1995).

### 2.8.3    Evolution of Elasticities

Compared to the long-run average demand elasticities, analyzing the evolution of demand elasticities over time has greater importance for short-term forecasting. Crouch (1994, 1996) identified the differences for income and own-price elasticities in different time periods. Using the TVP approach, some studies, such as Li *et al.* (2006b) and Song and Wong (2003), support the above findings in their empirical studies. An example with graphic illustration will be given in Chapter 8. In a fixed-parameter double-log demand model, which is most often used for elasticity analysis, only the average level of a demand elasticity over the sample period is obtained. However, a TVP model can illustrate clearly how the values of a demand elasticity evolve over time. It suggests that the TVP model is preferable to the log-linear fixed-parameter regression when investigating the dynamics of tourism demand.

### 2.9    SUMMARY

This chapter provides a review of the applications of econometric methods in international tourism demand studies since 1990. In addition to the description of the data, variables and models, demand elasticities have been given a particular focus. This review suggests that international tourism in most destinations is generally regarded as a luxury product, and the demand for long-haul travel is more income- and price-elastic than the demand for short-haul travel. A number of advanced econometric methods have been applied to tourism demand studies and their technical features will be introduced in subsequent chapters.

# 3 Traditional Methodology of Tourism Demand Modelling

## 3.1 INTRODUCTION

Most of the published studies on causal tourism demand models before the 1990s were classical regressions with ordinary least squares (OLS) as the main estimation procedure. The functional form of most of these models was single-equation, and either linear or power models. The data used in estimating tourism demand models are mainly time series, and since most of these time series, such as tourist expenditure, tourist arrivals, income (measured by personal disposable income or GDP), tourists' living costs in the destination, transport prices, and substitute prices are trended (non-stationary), the estimated tourism demand models have tended to have high $R^2$ values, due to these common trends in the data. We shall see in Chapters 3 and 4 that statistical tests based on regression models with non-stationary variables are unreliable and misleading, and therefore any inference drawn from these models is suspect. Moreover, tourism demand models with non-stationary variables tend to cause the estimated residuals to be autocorrelated, and this invalidates OLS. The problem of autocorrelation in tourism demand models has normally been dealt with by employing the Cochrane-Orcutt (1949) iterative estimation procedure. However, the use of the Cochrane-Orcutt procedure diverts attention from searching for the correctly specified model (autocorrelation normally indicates model misspecification).

The organisation of this chapter is as follows. Section 3.2 reviews the traditional tourism demand modelling methodology and presents the commonly used criteria for model selection. Section 3.3 discusses the limitations of the traditional approach to tourism demand modelling.

## 3.2 TRADITIONAL METHODOLOGY OF TOURISM DEMAND MODELLING

The traditional tourism demand modelling methodology proceeds with the following steps: *1) formulate hypotheses based on demand theory; 2) decide model's functional form; 3) collect data; 4) estimate the model; 5) test hypotheses; and 6) generate forecasts or evaluate policies.*

### 3.2.1   Hypothesis Formulation

Although O'Hagan and Harrison (1984), Syriopoulos and Sinclair (1993) and Smeral *et al.* (1992) examine tourism demand based on the complete demand system approach as exemplified by Stone (1954), Theil (1965) and Deaton and Muellbauer (1980a), most studies which have appeared in the literature are single-equation models based on the demand theory discussed in Chapter 1. This demand theory suggests that the optimal choice of consumer goods depends on consumers' income and the prices of the goods. In the case of the demand for tourism, the choice of a tourism destination is related to the relative price of tourism products in that destination compared to alternative destinations and income in tourism generating countries. For example, if tourists in a particular origin face a choice of two destinations, the tourists' demand functions can be written as

$$Q_1 = f_1(P_1, P_2, Y) \tag{3.1}$$

$$Q_2 = f_2(P_2, P_1, Y) \tag{3.2}$$

Equations (3.1) and (3.2) are simplified versions of specification (1.1), where the consumer tastes and marketing variables have been excluded. These two equations state that the demand for tourism to destination 1/destination 2 is related to the prices of tourism in the two destinations concerned ($P_1$ and $P_2$) as well as the income level of potential tourists from the origin country ($Y$). The following hypotheses related to the above functions can be formulated based on economic theory.

> Hypothesis I: The Engel curve suggests that if the price of tourism is held constant, an increase in tourists' income will result in an increase in the demand for tourism to both destinations provided that tourism is a normal or necessary good. Therefore, income in the origin country has a positive effect on the demand for tourism to both destinations.
>
> Hypothesis II: If the price of tourism in destination 1 increases while the price of tourism in destination 2 and consumers' income in the origin country remain unchanged, tourists will 'switch' from going to destination 1 to destination 2, and therefore the demand for tourism to destination 1 will decrease. This is known as the substitution effect and the substitution effect always moves in the opposite direction to the price changes.
>
> Hypothesis III: With respect to the demand for tourism to destination 1, the effect of a price change in destination 2 can either be positive or negative. If destination 2 is a substitute for destination 1 the demand for tourism to destination 1 will move in the same

direction as the price change in destination 2. On the other hand, if tourists tend to travel to the two destinations together, that is, the destinations are complementary to each other, tourism demand to one destination will move in the opposite direction to the change in price of tourism in the other.

According to these hypotheses, Equations (3.1) and (3.2) can now be written as

$$Q_1 = f_1(P_1, P_2, Y) \tag{3.3}$$
$$\quad\; -\;\; +/-\;\; +$$

$$Q_2 = f_2(P_2, P_1, Y) \tag{3.4}$$
$$\quad\; -\;\; +/-\;\; +$$

where the minus and plus signs represent the negative and positive effects of the explanatory variables on tourism demand.

Equations (3.3) and (3.4) are theoretical tourism demand models which can be estimated using data on $Q_i$, $P_i$ and $Y$ (where $i = 1, 2$), and hypotheses I, II and III can be statistically tested. (Hypothesis testing is discussed in section 3.2.5.)

## 3.2.2 Model Specification

Although consumer demand theory suggests possible relationships between tourism demand variables, it does not say anything about the precise functional form of the demand model. A researcher has to select an appropriate functional form for estimation, and the functional form is normally decided according to the ease of estimation and interpretation. In Chapter 1 we presented two commonly used functional forms in tourism demand analysis— the linear and power functions. The linear functional form is easy to estimate using OLS, while the power model is linear in logarithms (also known as the double-log or log-log model) and has the additional advantage that the estimated parameters can be interpreted as demand elasticities. Other types of functional form include the log linear model ('log' on the left-hand side of the equation and linear on the right), and the linear log model (linear on the left-hand side of the equation and 'log' on the right).

Functional form selection involves choosing the particular type of model that best fits the data, with the estimated error term satisfying the following conditions: $E(\varepsilon_i) = 0$, $Var(\varepsilon_i) = \sigma^2$, $Cov(\varepsilon_i, \varepsilon_j) = 0$ and $\varepsilon_i$ is normally distributed, that is, $\varepsilon_i \sim N(0, \sigma^2)$.

## 3.2.3 Data Collection

To estimate a tourism demand model, that is, to obtain the numerical values of the $\alpha$ parameters in Equations (1.2) and (1.10), we have to use actual data. The data can be obtained from either primary sources or secondary sources. Three types of data are normally used for model estimation: *1) time series, 2) cross-sectional and 3) pooled (the combination of time series and cross-sectional) data.*

*Time series data* are observed at regular time intervals, such as monthly, quarterly or annually. Most pre-1990s tourism demand models were estimated using time series data without testing the stationarity properties of the data, and therefore have been criticised for generating spurious regression relationships. The spurious regression problem is discussed in detail in subsequent chapters.

*Cross-sectional data* are data on one or more variables collected at the same point in time, such as the data collected from consumer expenditure surveys in the UK and the USA. The use of cross-sectional data has been very popular in modelling demand for non-durable commodities (food, clothing, meat, tobacco and so on), but published studies on tourism demand analysis using cross-sectional data are rare. Exceptions are Quandt and Young (1969) and Mak *et al.* (1977). A major disadvantage of using cross-sectional data is that the estimated residuals of the demand model tend to suffer from the problem of heteroscedasticity. The weighted least squares (WLS) procedure has to be used to correct for heteroscedasticity and this in turn can cause problems if the weights are incorrectly applied.

*Pooled data* combine both time series and cross-sectional components. Pooled data (also called panel or longitudinal data) are data in which the information on cross-sectional units (say, households, firms or tourism receiving/generating countries) is observed over time. One of the advantages of using panel data in tourism demand modelling is that it takes both temporal and cross-unit variations into account. Another advantage of panel data over pure time series or cross-sectional data sets is the large number of observations and the consequent increase in the number of degrees of freedom. This reduces collinearity and improves the efficiency of the estimates.

Carey (1991), Romilly *et al.* (1998a), Tremblay (1989), Witt (1980a, 1980b) and Yavas and Bilgin (1996) pool cross-sectional and time series data in order to estimate tourism demand elasticities with respect to income, exchange rates, relative prices, transport costs and social explanatory variables for various country groupings. Chapter 9 of this book examines in detail the use of pooled data in modelling tourism demand.

The use of panel data is, however, not unproblematic, since the choice of an appropriate model depends *inter alia* on the degree of homogeneity of the intercept and slope coefficients, and the extent to which any individual cross-section effects are correlated with the explanatory variables. If the homogeneity condition for the regression coefficients across individual units is not satisfied, the panel data approach cannot be used.

Tourism demand data are available from various sources. The World Tourism Organization (WTO) publishes figures on tourist arrivals and tourism receipts for most countries, broken down by country of origin, in the

*Yearbook of Tourism Statistics.* The International Monetary Fund (IMF) publishes consumer price index (CPI), exchange rate and gross domestic product (GDP) figures for most countries in the world in *International Financial Statistics* (monthly and annually). Some additional destination country data, such as visitor nights and length of stay, may be obtained from national tourist organisations. Data on personal disposable income, consumers' expenditure and population size are generally published by national statistical offices, for example, the Central Statistical Office (CSO) in the UK, Statistics Canada, the Bureau of Economic Analysis (BEA) in the USA and the National Statistical Bureau of China. For a full list of data sources related to tourism see Bar-On (1989).

Demand analysis at the firm/household level requires company or survey data. Company data cannot be easily accessed due to problems of confidentiality, and the quality of survey data depends on whether the questionnaires are correctly designed and implemented.

Whatever data source is used, one has to bear in mind that the quality of the data may be problematic for one or more of the following reasons. First, most tourism demand analyses are carried out at the national/regional level. The aggregated data may not reflect correctly individual consumer's behaviour. Second, tourism and economic data are non-experimental in nature and therefore observation errors in the data compiling process will be carried over to the modelling process. Third, survey data collected by means of questionnaires may only partially reflect the characteristics of the whole population; in particular, when the response rate is low, the estimated demand model is likely to suffer from the problem of small sample bias. Fourth, when analysing inbound or outbound tourism demand for a country, the data needed may be complied in different countries, and given that data definitions and collection methods differ from country to country, forecasting performance comparisons across models can be difficult.

### 3.2.4 Model Estimation

After obtaining the data on the tourism demand variables, the tourism demand model can be estimated. In traditional tourism demand analysis, the main method of estimation is OLS, and sometimes this method is augmented by the Cochrane-Orcutt procedure if autocorrelated residuals are identified. Lim (1997a) reviewed 100 publications on tourism demand modelling during the period of 1961–1994, and found that more than 70% of these used OLS. The estimation method discussed in this section therefore concentrates on OLS only.

For illustrative purposes, we specify a four variable tourism demand model (3.5). A subscript *t* is attached to every variable to indicate that the model is estimated using time series data.

$$Q_{it} = \alpha_0 + \alpha_1 P_{it} + \alpha_2 P_{st} + \alpha_3 Y_t + \varepsilon_{it} \tag{3.5}$$

The OLS procedure is used to obtain the numerical values of the $\alpha$ parameters in Equation (3.5). In order to obtain valid estimates of the parameters, the following assumptions have to be made:

1. $E(Q_{it}) = \alpha_0 + \alpha_1 P_{it} + \alpha_2 P_{st} + \alpha_3 Y_t$, that is, the expected value of $Q_{it}$ depends on the values of the explanatory variables and the unknown $\alpha$ parameters. This is equivalent to $E(\varepsilon_{it}) = 0$.
2. $Var(Q_{it}) = Var(\varepsilon_{it}) = \sigma^2$. This states that the sample variance of $Q_{it}$ or the variance of the error term remains constant over time. If this assumption does not hold, the model suffers from the problem of heteroscedasticity.
3. $Cov(Q_{it}, Q_{is}) = Cov(\varepsilon_{it}, \varepsilon_{is}) = 0$. This assumes that any two observations on the dependent variable or the residuals are not correlated. Violation of this assumption results in a model with autocorrelated residuals.
4. It is also assumed that the values of the dependent variable are normally distributed about their mean, that is, $Q_{it} \sim N(\alpha_0 + \alpha_1 P_{it} + \alpha_2 P_{st} + \alpha_3 Y_t, \sigma^2)$ which is equivalent to $\varepsilon_{it} \sim N(0, \sigma^2)$.
5. The values of the explanatory variables are known and there is no linear relationship among the explanatory variables. If this condition is not met, the model suffers from the problem of multicollinearity.

OLS minimises the sum of squared residuals (SSR) of Equation (3.5):

$$SSR = \sum_{t=1}^{T}(Q_{it} - \hat{Q}_{it})^2 = \sum_{t=1}^{T}(Q_{it} - \hat{\alpha}_0 - \hat{\alpha}_1 P_{it} - \hat{\alpha}_2 P_{st} - \hat{\alpha}_3 Y_t \tag{3.6}$$

where $\hat{Q}_{it}$ is the estimated value of $Q_{it}$.

To find the OLS estimates of the $\alpha$ parameters that minimise (3.6), the partial derivatives of Equation (3.6) with respect to $\hat{\alpha}_0$, $\hat{\alpha}_1$, $\hat{\alpha}_2$ and $\hat{\alpha}_3$ are taken:

$$\frac{\partial SSR}{\partial \hat{\alpha}_0} = 2(T\hat{\alpha}_0 + \hat{\alpha}_1 \sum P_{it} + \hat{\alpha}_2 \sum P_{st} + \hat{\alpha}_3 \sum Y_t - \sum Q_{it})$$

$$\frac{\partial SSR}{\partial \hat{\alpha}_1} = 2(\hat{\alpha}_0 \sum P_{it} + \hat{\alpha}_1 \sum P_{it}^2 + \hat{\alpha}_2 \sum P_{st} P_{it} + \hat{\alpha}_3 \sum Y_t P_{it} - \sum Q_{it} P_{it})$$

$$\frac{\partial SSR}{\partial \hat{\alpha}_2} = 2(\hat{\alpha}_0 \sum P_{st} + \hat{\alpha}_1 \sum P_{it} P_{st} + \hat{\alpha}_2 \sum P_{st}^2 + \hat{\alpha}_3 \sum Y_t P_{st} - \sum Q_{it} P_{st})$$

$$\frac{\partial SSR}{\partial \hat{\alpha}_3} = 2(\hat{\alpha}_0 \sum Y_t + \hat{\alpha}_1 \sum P_{it} Y_t + \hat{\alpha}_2 \sum P_{st} Y_t + \hat{\alpha}_s \sum Y_t^2 - \sum Q_{it} Y_t)$$

Setting the above equations equal to zero, we have

$$T\hat{\alpha}_0 + \hat{\alpha}_1 \sum P_{it} + \hat{\alpha}_2 \sum P_{st} + \hat{\alpha}_3 \sum Y_t = \sum Q_{it}$$

$$\hat{\alpha}_0 \sum P_{it} + \hat{\alpha}_1 \sum P_{it}^2 + \hat{\alpha}_2 \sum P_{st} P_{it} + \hat{\alpha}_3 \sum Y_t P_{it} = \sum Q_{it} P_{it}$$

$$\hat{\alpha}_0 \sum P_{st} + \hat{\alpha}_1 \sum P_{it} P_{st} + \hat{\alpha}_2 \sum P_{st}^2 + \hat{\alpha}_3 \sum Y_t P_{st} = \sum Q_{it} P_{st}$$

$$\hat{\alpha}_0 \sum Y_t + \hat{\alpha}_1 \sum P_{it} Y_t + \hat{\alpha}_2 \sum P_{st} Y_t + \hat{\alpha}_3 \sum Y_t^2 = \sum Q_{it} Y_t$$

These equations are called *normal equations*. Although it is possible to solve these normal equations algebraically for $\hat{\alpha}_0$, $\hat{\alpha}_1$, $\hat{\alpha}_2$ and $\hat{\alpha}_3$, the notation can be very complex without using matrices. Standard computer programmes do all the calculations once the data on the dependent and independent variables have been entered. If the five assumptions made earlier hold, the parameter estimates generated by OLS ($\hat{\alpha}$) are the best linear unbiased estimates (BLUE) of $\alpha$.

The residuals and estimated values of the dependent variables are obtained as

$$\hat{\varepsilon}_{it} = Q_{it} - \hat{\alpha}_0 - \hat{\alpha}_1 P_{it} - \hat{\alpha}_2 P_{st} - \hat{\alpha}_3 Y_t \tag{3.7}$$

$$\hat{Q}_{it} = \hat{\alpha}_0 + \hat{\alpha}_1 P_{it} + \hat{\alpha}_2 P_{st} + \hat{\alpha}_3 Y_t = Q_{it} - \hat{\varepsilon}_{it} \tag{3.8}$$

and the variance of the residuals $\hat{\sigma}_{it}^2$ is calculated from

$$s_{it}^2 = \hat{\sigma}_{it}^2 = \frac{\sum \hat{\varepsilon}_{it}^2}{T - k} \tag{3.9}$$

where $T$ is the number of observations used in the estimation and $k$ is the number of estimated regression coefficients including the constant term.

OLS minimises the sum of squares of the residuals (SSR) and ensures that the estimated regression equation is the best in terms of the model's 'fit' to the data. However, the 'best fit' does not necessarily mean that the model explains the variations in the dependent variable well, and therefore a statistic that measures the model's explanatory power over the data, that is, the 'goodness of fit', is needed. A frequently used measure of goodness of fit in traditional econometric methodology is the *coefficient of determination*, and it is defined as

$$R^2 = 1 - \frac{\sum \hat{\varepsilon}_{it}^2}{\sum (Q_{it} - \bar{Q}_{it})^2} \tag{3.10}$$

where $\bar{Q}_{it}$ is the mean of $Q_{it}$.

$R^2$ measures the proportion of the total variation in $Q_{it}$ that can be explained by the estimated model. Since $R^2$ is a proportion, the value of $R^2$ must lie between zero and one. A value of one suggests a perfect fit while a value of zero indicates that the model does not explain any variation in the dependent variable at all.

As we can see from formula (3.10), the $R^2$ value is determined by the sum of squared residuals, $\Sigma\hat{\varepsilon}_{it}^2$, and the quantity $\Sigma(Q_{it} - \overline{Q}_{it})^2$. The value of $\Sigma(Q_{it} - \overline{Q}_{it})^2$ is a constant if the sample of $Q_{it}$ is fixed. Therefore, the $R^2$ value is mainly determined by the value of $\Sigma\hat{\varepsilon}_{it}^2$. It is easy to show that adding more explanatory variables to Equation (3.5) will reduce the value of $\Sigma\hat{\varepsilon}_{it}^2$, and hence increase the value of $R^2$, even if the added variables are not actually related to the tourism demand variable, $Q_{it}$. This problem is partially overcome by using 'adjusted' $R^2$, which takes into account the number of explanatory variables present in the model. Adding unimportant or irrelevant variables in the manner of 'data mining' is penalised. The 'adjusted' $R^2$ is calculated as

$$\overline{R}^2 = 1 - \frac{T-1}{T-k}(1-R^2) \tag{3.11}$$

Although the addition of a variable leads to a gain in $R^2$, it also leads to a loss of one degree of freedom. Formula (3.11) is a better measure of the goodness of fit because it allows for the trade-off between an increase in $R^2$ and the loss of degrees of freedom.

The majority of published empirical investigations in the area of tourism demand modelling and forecasting use $R^2$ or $\overline{R}^2$ as the main criterion for model selection. Other criteria used in the model selection process include Akaike's (1974) information criterion (AIC) and Schwarz's (1978) Bayesian criterion (SBC), and these are calculated as:

$$AIC = \ln\frac{\Sigma\hat{\varepsilon}_{it}^2}{T} + \frac{2k}{T} \tag{3.12}$$

$$SBC = \ln\frac{\Sigma\hat{\varepsilon}_{it}^2}{T} + \frac{k\ln T}{T} \tag{3.13}$$

where $\Sigma\hat{\varepsilon}_{it}^2$ is the estimated sum of squared residuals from Equation (3.6), and $k$ and $T$ are the number of estimated parameters and the total number of observations used in the estimation, respectively.

Ideally, we would like a model to have a high $\overline{R}^2$ and low values for the AIC and SBC. But there is always a possibility that one model is superior to another under one criterion and inferior under another. For example, the SBC penalises model complexity more heavily than does the AIC and this may lead to contradictory conclusions.

## 3.2.5 Hypothesis Testing

Apart from estimating unknown parameters in a tourism demand model, testing hypotheses about the parameters in the model is also an important part of the empirical investigation.

### 3.2.5.1 *Testing the Significance of a Single Coefficient*

From section 3.2.1, we know that hypotheses are formulated according to economic theory, and hypothesis-testing statistics are used to provide support for the theoretical hypotheses. For example, as far as Equation (3.5) is concerned, demand theory suggests the following relationships: $\alpha_1 < 0$; $\alpha_2 \neq 0$ and $\alpha_3 > 0$. A commonly used statistic to test these hypotheses is the *t statistic*, which is calculated from

$$t = \frac{\hat{\alpha}_i}{SE(\hat{\alpha}_i)} \tag{3.14}$$

where $\hat{\alpha}_i$ is the estimated regression coefficient and $SE(\hat{\alpha}_i)$ is the standard error of the coefficient. The number of degrees of freedom for the $t$ statistic is $T - k$, where $T$ is the number of observations and $k$ is the number of coefficients in the regression model, including the constant term.

In the cases of $\alpha_1 < 0$ and $\alpha_3 > 0$, a one-tailed $t$ statistic is used, while for $\alpha_2 \neq 0$ a two-tailed statistic is appropriate, if it is not clear whether two destination countries are regarded as substitutes or complements. The decision on whether a one-tailed or two-tailed statistic should be used is based on whether you have a strong belief that the regression coefficient has a positive or a negative value. The sign of the estimated coefficient is easy to observe, but the statistical significance of the coefficient needs to be tested by looking at whether or not the coefficient is significantly different from zero given the observed sign. Suppose we obtain a negative value for the estimated coefficient $\hat{\alpha}_1$, but we want to know whether the coefficient is significantly different from zero. The steps involved in this $t$ test are as follows:

Step 1: Set up the null and alternative hypotheses $H_0 : \alpha_1 = 0$ and $H_1 : \alpha_1 < 0$;
Step 2: Calculate the $t$ statistic based on Equation (3.14);
Step 3: Compare the calculated $t$ statistic, given the degrees of freedom, with the corresponding one-tailed critical value at a specific level of significance, normally 5%;
Step 4: Reject $H_0$ and accept $H_1$ if the calculated $t$ is greater than the critical value, otherwise accept $H_0$ and reject $H_1$.

For a two-tailed $t$ test, the steps are the same except that the critical values for inference are different.

### 3.2.5.2   *Testing the Joint Significance of All Coefficients*

The $t$ test is applied to examine whether the dependent variable $Q_{it}$ is related to a particular explanatory variable. Another statistic that has been frequently reported in traditional tourism demand analyses is the $F$ statistic, which is used to test the relevance of all the explanatory variables in the demand model. The null and alternative hypotheses now become

$H_0 : \alpha_1 = 0,\ \alpha_2 = 0,\ \alpha_3 = 0$

$H_1 :$ at least one of the $\alpha$s is not zero

If the null hypothesis is true, the joint effect of the explanatory variables provides no explanation for $Q_{it}$, and thus the estimated tourism demand model is of no value. If the alternative hypothesis is true, then the model has some explanatory power. However, the alternative hypothesis does not suggest which of the explanatory variables is relevant. Therefore, this test has to be used in conjunction with the $t$ test.

The $F$ test is calculated based on the following formula:

$$F(k-1, T-k) = \frac{(SSR_2 - SSR_1)/(k-1)}{SSR_1/(T-k)} \tag{3.15}$$

where $SSR_1$ is the sum of squared residuals from Equation (3.6), $SSR_2$ is the sum of squared residuals from the regression equation $Q_{it} = \alpha_0 + u_{it}$, and $(k-1, T-k)$ are the degrees of freedom.

The calculated value of this statistic is compared with the critical value from the $F$ distribution table. If the calculated $F$ value is smaller than the critical value, the null hypothesis is accepted and the alternative rejected. If the calculated $F$ is greater than the critical value, we accept the alternative and reject the null.

## 3.2.6   Forecasting and Policy Evaluation

Suppose that an estimated tourism demand model satisfies demand theory and passes all the hypothesis tests. The next step is to use the model for forecasting and policy analysis. Since the forecasting issue will be discussed in Chapter 11, we do not go into any details here with respect to how to generate forecasts using econometric models. However, one thing that is worth mentioning here is that in order to generate forecasts for the dependent variable, $Q_{it}$, we have to forecast the explanatory variables $P_{it}$, $P_{st}$ and $Y_t$ first, and the forecasts for these explanatory variables can be obtained either by time series extrapolation or from other forecasting sources. One of the advantages of econometric demand models is that they can be used for policy evaluations. For example, suppose that we estimate a tourism demand model in which, apart from the three explanatory variables given in (3.5), a marketing variable is also found to be positively related to the dependent variable. This allows us to look at how tourism demand in a destination country responds to the changes in marketing expenditure by this country. If one finds that tourism demand is very responsive to marketing expenditure, the destination country should adopt relevant marketing policies to promote its tourism products in order to attract more tourists.

## 3.3   FAILURE OF THE TRADITIONAL APPROACH TO TOURISM DEMAND MODELLING

In the above section we summarised the traditional econometric approach to tourism demand modelling. From the discussions we can see that this methodology relies heavily on the five assumptions made in section 3.2.3 being satisfied. Witt and Witt (1995, p. 458) argue that 'in the light of the lack of testing to see whether or not the models are well specified and recent developments in econometric methodology which focus the specification of the dynamic structure of time series, the quality of the empirical results obtained is questionable'. The traditional methodology also implicitly assumes that tourism demand data are stationary or at least trended stationary, but it has been shown that most tourism demand data are actually non-stationary, and this can lead to serious problems with statistics such as $t$, $DW$ and $F$, as well as $R^2$, which are reported in most of the empirical studies. The integrating property of the data and the modelling strategy related to non-stationary variables will be further discussed in Chapter 5.

Another serious problem with traditional tourism demand models is that the forecasting performance of these models has been poor in comparison with alternative specifications; in particular, they cannot even compete with the simplest time series models such as the naïve no change model (see, for example, Martin and Witt, 1989; Witt and Witt, 1992). One possible explanation for this could be that the traditional tourism demand method does not take into account both the long-run cointegrating relationship and short-run dynamics in the estimation of the models.

Advanced econometric methodologies such as cointegration, error correction models, vector autoregressive models, time varying parameter models and panel data approaches can be employed to overcome the problems associated with the traditional single-equation demand models. These methodologies will be discussed, and the estimation and forecasting results compared, in subsequent chapters.

# 4 General-to-Specific Modelling

## 4.1 INTRODUCTION

The traditional approach to tourism demand modelling starts by constructing a simple model that is consistent with demand theory. Such a model is then estimated and tested for statistical significance. The estimated model is expected to have a high $R^2$, and the coefficients are expected to be both 'correctly' signed and statistically significant (usually at the 5% level). In addition, the residuals from the estimated model should be properly behaved, that is, they should be normally distributed with zero mean and constant variance.

As an example, consider the following. A simple outbound tourism demand model for country/region $j$ may be specified as

$$q_{it} = \alpha_0 + \alpha_1 y_t + \alpha_2 p_{it} + u_{it} \tag{4.1}$$

where $q_{it}$ is tourism demand, which is normally measured by total/per capita visits/expenditure to destination $i$; $y_t$ is a measure of income in the tourism generating country/region $j$; and $p_{it}$ is a price variable which represents living costs for tourists in destination $i$. The subscript $j$ is omitted for simplicity.

Following the traditional approach, Equation (4.1) is estimated using ordinary least squares (OLS). If the results are 'unsatisfactory', either in terms of a low $R^2$, or 'wrongly' signed/insignificant coefficients, the model is then respecified by introducing new explanatory variables, using a different functional form, or selecting a different estimation method if the residuals exhibit heteroscedasticity, autocorrelation or lack of normality. For example, the exchange rate between the origin and destination countries, tourists' living costs in substitute destinations, or event dummy variables may be added to the model. Alternatively, a lagged dependent variable could be introduced if it is believed that a partial adjustment process of actual to desired tourism demand is in operation. Although such a procedure starts from a relatively simple specification, the final model, that is both theoretically sound and statistically acceptable, may be very complex. This methodology is called the *specific-to-general approach*.

The specific-to-general modelling approach is often criticised for its excessive data mining, since researchers normally only publish their final models, which often appear to be acceptable on both theoretical and statistical grounds, with the intermediate modelling process omitted. With this methodology, the same set of data is simply fitted to a range of potential models and the same statistics are calculated repeatedly until an equation that fits the researcher's a priori beliefs is discovered. It is possible, therefore, that different researchers equipped with the same data set and statistical tools could end up with totally different model specifications. The problems associated with the traditional approach to tourism demand modelling are discussed in Witt and Witt (1995).

## 4.2    GENERAL-TO-SPECIFIC MODELLING

The *general-to-specific* modelling approach was initiated by Sargan (1964), and subsequently developed by Davidson *et al.* (1978), Hendry and von Ungern-Sternberg (1981) and Mizon and Richard (1986). In contrast to the specific-to-general modelling methodology, the general-to-specific approach starts with a general model which contains as many variables as possible suggested by economic theory. According to this framework, if a dependent variable $y_t$ is determined by $k$ explanatory variables, the data generating process (DGP) may be written as an autoregressive distributed lag model (ADLM) of the form:

$$y_t = \alpha + \sum_{j=1}^{k}\sum_{i=0}^{p} \beta_{ji} x_{jt-i} + \sum_{i=1}^{p} \phi_i y_{t-i} + \varepsilon_t \tag{4.2}$$

where $p$ is the lag length, which is determined by the type of data used. As a general guide, $p = 1$ for annual data, $p = 4$ for quarterly data, $p = 6$ for bimonthly data and $p = 12$ for monthly data. However, the lag lengths of the time series may vary, and they are normally decided by experimentation. $\varepsilon_t$ in Equation (4.2) is the error term which is assumed to be normally distributed with zero mean and constant variance, $\sigma^2$, that is, $\varepsilon_t \sim N(0,\sigma^2)$.

For simplicity, let us assume that there are only two variables, $y_t$ and $x_t$, involved in the general model and that the lag length is $p = 1$. Equation (4.2) can now be simplified to give

$$y_t = \alpha + \beta_0 x_t + \beta_1 x_{t-1} + \phi_1 y_{t-1} + \varepsilon_t \tag{4.3}$$

Although the subsequent discussions are based on this simplified ADLM, the principles apply generally to the more complicated specifications.

*Table 4.1* Variations of the Autoregressive Distributed Lag Model

| Model | Restrictions | Equation |
|---|---|---|
| 1. ADLM | None | $y_t = \beta_0 x_t + \beta_1 x_{t-1} + \phi_1 y_{t-1} + \varepsilon_t$ |
| 2. Static | $\beta_1 = \phi_1 = 0$ | $y_t = \beta_0 x_t + \varepsilon_t$ |
| 3. Autoregressive (AR) | $\beta_0 = \beta_1 = 0$ | $y_t = \phi_1 y_{t-1} + \varepsilon_t$ |
| 4. Growth Rate | $\phi_1 = 1, \beta_0 = -\beta_1$ | $\Delta y_t = \beta_0 \Delta x_t + \varepsilon_t$ |
| 5. Leading Indicator | $\beta_0 = \phi_1 = 0$ | $y_t = \beta_1 x_{t-1} + \varepsilon_t$ |
| 6. Partial Adjustment | $\beta_1 = 0$ | $y_t = \beta_0 x_t + \phi_1 y_{t-1} + \varepsilon_t$ |
| 7. Common Factor | $\beta_1 = -\beta_0 \phi_1$ | $y_t = \beta_0 x_t + \varepsilon_t, \varepsilon_t = \beta_1 \varepsilon_{t-1} + u_1$ |
| 8. Finite Distributed Lag | $\phi_1 = 0$ | $y_t = \beta_0 x_t + \beta_1 x_{t-1} + \varepsilon_t$ |
| 9. Dead Start | $\beta_0 = 0$ | $y_t = \beta_1 x_{t-1} + \phi_1 y_{t-1} + \varepsilon_t$ |
| 10. Error Correction | None | $\Delta y_t = \beta_0 \Delta x_t + (\beta_1 - 1)(y - Kx)_{t-1} + \varepsilon_t$ |

Note: The constant term $\alpha$ is omitted for simplicity.
Source: This table is adapted from Hendry (1995, p. 232).

With certain restrictions imposed on the parameters in Equation (4.3), a number of econometric models may be derived, and these models have been widely used in empirical studies. The models are presented in Table 4.1.

## 4.2.1   Static Model

The static model states that the lagged dependent and lagged independent variables do not influence the dependent variable, that is, the restrictions imposed on the coefficients of the general model are $\beta_1 = \phi_1 = 0$. Many early tourism demand models, such as Gray (1966), Artus (1972), Kwack (1972) and Loeb (1982), were static models in which the current value of tourism demand is related only to the current values of the explanatory variables. However, the error terms in static tourism demand models have generally been found to be highly autocorrelated, and this indicates that the demand relationships are likely to be spurious and that the normal $t$ and $F$ statistics are invalid. In attempting to solve the problem of spurious correlation, some researchers and practitioners, such as Witt (1980a, 1980b) and Little (1980), began to introduce dynamic effects, such as lagged values of the dependent and independent variables, into tourism demand models. Static regression has recently become popular again in the application of the Engle and Granger (1987) two-stage cointegration analysis to tourism demand modelling and forecasting (see Kulendran and Witt, 1997, Kim and

Song, 1998, Song *et al.*, 2000 and Song and Witt, 2003). The Engle-Granger two-stage cointegration approach requires that the static long-run equilibrium relationship is estimated first, and the disequilibrium errors are then incorporated into the corresponding short-run error correction model (this approach will be discussed in detail in the following two chapters).

### 4.2.2   Autoregressive (AR) Model

Lagged dependent variables, but no independent variables, are involved in the AR model. The AR(1) process in Table 4.1 is a special case of the Box and Jenkins (1976) autoregressive integrated moving average (ARIMA) representation. Such univariate time series models have been widely used for *ex ante* tourism demand forecasting, and they have been shown by researchers, such as Witt and Witt (1992), Kulendran (1996) and Kulendran and King (1997), to be powerful competitors to econometric forecasting. However, univariate time series analysis is not useful for understanding the causal relationships between tourism demand and its determinants. Indeed, the nature of univariate time series extrapolation makes policy evaluation impossible. However, when the data on tourism demand are limited, autoregressive modelling may be a very useful alternative for tourism demand forecasting.

### 4.2.3   Growth Rate Model

The growth rate specification requires that the following hypothesis regarding the coefficients in the general model hold: $\phi_1 = 1, \beta_0 = -\beta_1$. This type of model is an early attempt to deal with the problem of nonsensical correlation caused by trended economic variables (see, for example, Witt, 1980a). However, although the growth rate model overcomes the problem of spurious regression results, the long-run properties of the economic model are lost due to data differencing.

### 4.2.4   Leading Indicator Model

In the case of the leading indicator model, the restrictions on the general model are: $\beta_0 = \phi_1 = 0$. The leading indicator model is a useful tool for macroeconomic forecasting. The model does not normally have behavioural underpinning, and the inclusion of leading indicators in the regression model is usually determined by trial and error. Turner *et al.* (1997) and Kulendran and Witt (2003b) employed the leading indicator model to forecast tourism demand to Australia. One of the important conditions for accurate forecasts is that the coefficients of the leading indicators should be constant. If this condition is violated, the leading indicator model tends to produce poor forecasts, especially in periods of rapid economic change when accurate forecasts are crucial.

## 4.2.5   Partial Adjustment Model

The restrictions on the coefficients in the general model in the case of the partial adjustment model are: $\beta_1 = 0$. The partial adjustment model has been widely used in modelling macroeconomic activities that involve habit persistence and adaptive expectations processes, such as the consumption function based on the permanent income hypothesis, the demand for durable goods and aggregate investment determination. In tourism demand analysis, the partial adjustment model has also been used extensively in situations which involve habit persistence and the influences of social factors, such as cultural status, personal preferences and expectations. It has also been used to accommodate supply constraints. Tourism demand studies which use the partial adjustment model include Witt (1980a, 1980b), Kliman (1981) and Martin and Witt (1988).

## 4.2.6   Common Factor (COMFAC) Model

In order to meet the requirements of a *COMFAC* model, the coefficients of the general model have to satisfy: $\beta_1 = -\beta_0\phi_1$. The common factor model is also called the autoregressive error model. It is similar to the static model, but with an autoregressive error term. The *COMFAC* model is a statistical model without a well-established economic-theory basis (Hendry, 1995, p. 267). The tourism demand model developed by Lee *et al.* (1996) is a *COMFAC* model.

## 4.2.7   Finite Distributed Lag Model

Lagged dependent variables do not enter the regression in finite distributed lag models. Although the lag length of the finite distributed lag model presented in Table 4.1 is equal to 1, in practice the model could be specified with current values of the explanatory variables, and as many lagged explanatory variables as the data permit. There is little evidence to suggest that tourism demand can be represented by a finite distributed lag process.

## 4.2.8   Dead Start Model

In the dead start model, all current values of the independent variables are assumed to be irrelevant to the dependent variable. The dead start model is a partial adjustment type model. The model could arise for two possible reasons in tourism demand modelling. First, the model is a structural model that represents the decision-making process of economic agents. Second, the model derivation may be based on a given hypothesis; for example, in macroeconomic modelling the Hall (1978) consumption model utilises the permanent income hypothesis together with rational expectations. Since the structure of the dead start model is similar to the partial adjustment process, and also incorporates leading indicators in the estimation, it is likely that this model will be a good contender in the model selection process in tourism demand analysis.

## 4.2.9    Error Correction Model

In the subsequent chapters, we shall show that not only does the error correction model avoid the problem of spurious regression, but it also avoids the problems associated with the use of the simple growth rate model. In particular, the inclusion of the error correction term in Model 9 in Table 4.1 ensures that no information on the levels variables is ignored. The error correction model has been used successfully in many areas of economics since the mid-1980s. However, this type of model started to appear in the tourism literature much later. Tourism demand studies which use the error correction model include Kulendran (1996), Kulendran and King (1997), Kulendran and Witt (1997), Kim and Song (1998), Song *et al.* (2000) and Song *et al.* (2003a, 2003b and 2003c).

In order to decide which specification of the above models is appropriate in modelling tourism demand, statistical tests on the parameters of the general regression model (4.3) have to be carried out. These tests are known as restriction tests.

## 4.3    TESTS OF RESTRICTIONS ON REGRESSION PARAMETERS

In some cases, the tests of restrictions on parameters in the general model (4.3) are straightforward, while in other cases they are much more complicated. The null hypothesis of the restriction tests is that the restrictions imposed on the coefficients of the general model are true, that is, these restrictions cannot be rejected at a given level of significance.

If a general tourism demand ADLM version of Equation (4.3) is specified with the dependent variable $y_t$ being a measure of tourism demand and the explanatory variable $x_t$ being, say, income, then the parameter restrictions in cases 6, 8 and 9 in Table 4.1 can be tested easily using the $t$ statistic, while an $F$ statistic would be appropriate for testing the restrictions in cases 2, 3, 4 and 5. For example, in order to test whether tourism demand may be modelled by a static process (case 2 in Table 4.1) against the general ADLM, the $F$ test is carried out as follows:

1. Estimate both the unrestricted general model (4.3) and the restricted static model using OLS.
2. Obtain the residual sum of squares, $SSR_0$, from the general model, and the residual sum of squares, $SSR_1$, from the restricted (static) model. It should be noted that $SSR_0$ is normally smaller than $SSR_1$, since the unrestricted model (which has more explanatory variables) is likely to

explain more variations in the dependent variable than the restricted models.

3. Calculate the *F* statistic based on

$$F(r, n-k) = \frac{(SSR_1 - SSR_0)/r}{SSR_0/(n-k)} \tag{4.4}$$

where *r* is the number of restrictions, *n* is the number of observations, and *k* is the number of explanatory variables (including the constant term) in the unrestricted equation.

If the restrictions are valid, that is, $\beta_1 = 0$, $\phi_1 = 0$ in this case, $SSR_1$ would not be significantly larger than $SSR_0$, and the calculated *F* statistic should approach zero.

4. Decide whether the restrictions should be rejected or accepted by comparing the calculated *F* statistic with $(r, n-k)$ degrees of freedom with the critical value. If the calculated *F* statistic is greater than the critical value, then the null hypothesis that the restrictions are true should be rejected. The *F* test can be carried out easily in most econometric packages (for example, Eviews 5.1 and Microfit 4.0).

The *F* test loses its power when the restrictions are more complicated or non-linear, such as in case 7 in Table 4.1. Alternative tests have been developed for both linear and non-linear restrictions. Three of the commonly used tests are the Wald, Likelihood Ratio (LR) and Lagrange Multiplier (LM) tests. (Detailed descriptions of these tests are given in Thomas (1997, pp. 355–60).) The inference procedure for each of these tests is the same as that for the *F* test; that is, the calculated statistic based on the sample data is compared with the critical value of the statistic at a certain level of significance, with a larger value leading to rejection of the null hypothesis.

The error correction model is a re-parameterisation of the general ADLM, and it incorporates both short-run and long-run relationships in the modelling process. To test for the existence of an error correction mechanism, the presence of a long-run cointegration relationship needs to be tested for first. These topics are discussed in the next chapter.

## 4.4   DIAGNOSTIC CHECKING

Restriction tests are useful in selecting the model type, but the final model will have had to be subject to rigorous statistical checking in order to determine its statistical acceptability. In practice, the final model used for policy evaluation and forecasting should not exhibit autocorrelation, heteroscedasticity or structural instability. The final model should also be correctly specified in terms of functional form, and the independent variables should be exogenous. Moreover, the final model should be able to compete with all rival models, that is, the final model should encompass all other models which have been used to explain the same variables. If any of these conditions is not met, the model is mis-specified and should not be used for policy evaluation and forecasting. Diagnostic statistics for testing model specification are available in most econometric and forecasting packages. The most commonly used diagnostic statistics are now described.

## 4.4.1    Testing for Autocorrelation

*(a) The Durbin-Watson (DW) Statistic.* The DW statistic is the most widely used test for detecting the problem of autocorrelation in the regression residuals. The statistic is defined as

$$DW = \frac{\sum_{t=2}^{n} (\hat{\varepsilon}_t - \hat{\varepsilon}_{t-1})^2}{\sum_{t=1}^{n} \hat{\varepsilon}_t^2} \tag{4.5}$$

where $\hat{\varepsilon}_t$ is the residual from the estimated regression equation.

The statistic can be used to test for the presence of first-order autocorrelation in the regression. If there is no autocorrelation, the value of the DW statistic should be approximately 2. A DW statistic of 0 would suggest perfect positive autocorrelation, while a DW value of 4 would indicate perfect negative autocorrelation. Although the DW statistic is standard output for all regression programs, it has severe limitations. The first limitation is the inconclusive region, which varies according to the size of the sample. The second is its inability to detect higher order autocorrelation. The third limitation is that the DW statistic is biased towards 2 when a lagged dependent variable is included as an explanatory variable in the model.

*(b) The Lagrange Multiplier (LM) Test.* This is also known as the Breusch-Godfrey test and was developed by Breusch (1978) and Godfrey (1978). The LM statistic is not limited to testing for the presence of first-order autocorrelation, and it is still valid even if a lagged dependent variable is present on the right-hand side of the regression model. Due to these two important characteristics, the LM test is far more generally applicable than the DW test. The calculation of the test is based on an auxiliary equation of the form

$$\begin{aligned} \hat{\varepsilon}_t &= \alpha + \beta_1 X_{1t} + \beta_2 X_{2t} + ... + \beta_k X_{kt} + \rho_1 \hat{\varepsilon}_{t-1} \\ &\quad + \rho_2 \hat{\varepsilon}_{t-2} + ... + \rho_p \hat{\varepsilon}_{t-p} + u_t \end{aligned} \tag{4.6}$$

where the $X_{it}$s are explanatory variables, the $\beta_i$s and $\rho_i$s are parameters, and the $\hat{\varepsilon}_{t-j}$s are the lagged residuals from the estimated regression model.

Under the null hypothesis of no autocorrelation, $H_0: \rho_1 = \rho_2 = ... = \rho_p = 0$, the test statistic is $nR^2$, where $n$ is the sample size and $R^2$ is calculated from

Equation (4.6). In large samples, the statistic has a $\chi^2$ distribution with $p$ degrees of freedom. If the value of $nR^2$ exceeds the critical value of $\chi^2$, this suggests the existence of autocorrelation.

## 4.4.2  Testing for Heteroscedasticity

*(a) The Goldfeld-Quandt Test.* This test was developed by Goldfeld and Quandt (1965). The underlying null hypothesis is that the residuals are homoscedastic, and this is tested against the alternative that the variance of the residuals increases as the values of one of the explanatory variables increase. The test is carried out as follows:

(i)  Identify the explanatory variable that is related to the variance of the residuals and re-order the observations of the explanatory variable from the largest value to the smallest one.
(ii)  Divide the re-ordered observations into two equal-sized subsamples by omitting $c$ *central* observations.
(iii)  Calculate the OLS regression for each of the subsamples and obtain the residual sum of squares from each of these two regressions.

The Goldfeld-Quandt statistic is an $F$ statistic based on the ratio

$$F[(n-c)/2-k, (n-c)/2-k] = \frac{\sum \hat{\varepsilon}_1^2}{\sum \hat{\varepsilon}_2^2} \tag{4.7}$$

where $\sum \hat{\varepsilon}_1^2$ is the residual sum of squares from the subsample containing the larger values of the explanatory variable and $\sum \hat{\varepsilon}_2^2$ is the residual sum of squares from the subsample containing the smaller values of the explanatory variable. The numbers in the square brackets are the degrees of freedom. If there is no heteroscedasticity in the residuals, the calculated $F$ statistic should not exceed the critical value at the appropriate level of significance.

A limitation of the Goldfeld-Quandt test is that different choices of the number of central observations may lead to different results.

*(b) The White Test.* This test was developed by White (1980). Suppose that we have a multiple regression model with two explanatory variables of the form

$$Y_t = \beta_1 + \beta_2 X_{1t} + \beta_3 X_{2t} + \varepsilon_t \tag{4.8}$$

In order to test whether the residual $\varepsilon_t$ has constant variance or not, the following auxiliary equation is estimated:

$$\hat{\varepsilon}_t^2 = \alpha_1 + \alpha_2 X_{1t} + \alpha_3 X_{2t} + \alpha_4 X_{1t}^2 + \alpha_5 X_{2t}^2 + \alpha_6 X_{1t} X_{2t} + u_t \tag{4.9}$$

where $\hat{\varepsilon}_t$ is the estimated residual from Equation (4.8). If the regression model has more than two explanatory variables, the $\hat{\varepsilon}_t^2$ should be regressed against all the explanatory variables together with their squares and cross-products.

The test statistic is equal to $nR^2$, where $R^2$ is calculated from the OLS estimation of Equation (4.9). The statistic has a $\chi^2$ distribution, with degrees of freedom equal to the number of regressors excluding the intercept. The null hypothesis that there is no heteroscedasticity is rejected if the calculated White statistic exceeds the critical value of $\chi^2$.

*(c) Testing for an Autoregressive Conditional Heteroscedasticity (ARCH) Process.* This test was developed by Engle (1982). Instead of relating $\hat{\varepsilon}_t^2$ to a vector of explanatory variables, as in the White test, $\hat{\varepsilon}_t^2$ is assumed to depend on past squared errors, $\hat{\varepsilon}_{t-1}^2, \hat{\varepsilon}_{t-2}^2, \ldots, \hat{\varepsilon}_{t-p}^2$. The ARCH process is autoregressive in the second moment, and the ARCH test is calculated using an auxiliary equation of the form

$$\hat{\varepsilon}_t^2 = \alpha_0 + \alpha_1 \hat{\varepsilon}_{t-1}^2 + \alpha_2 \hat{\varepsilon}_{t-2}^2 + \ldots + \alpha_p \hat{\varepsilon}_{t-p}^2 + u_t \qquad (4.10)$$

The test statistic has a $\chi^2$ distribution with $p$ degrees of freedom. The most common form of the ARCH test is the first-order autoregressive model in which $p = 1$.

### 4.4.3 Testing for Normality

The Jarque-Bera (J-B) test. The normality test was developed by Jarque and Bera (1980). If the normality assumption regarding the residuals does not hold, $t$ and $F$ statistics are invalid in small samples. The J-B test shows that the normality property may be tested using the statistic

$$n\left[\frac{\mu_3^2}{6\mu_2^3} + \frac{(\mu_4/\mu_2^2 - 3)^2}{24}\right] \qquad (4.11)$$

where $\mu_2 = \sum_{t=1}^{n} \hat{\varepsilon}_t^2 / n$, $\mu_3 = \sum_{t=1}^{n} \hat{\varepsilon}_t^3 / n$ and $\mu_4 = \sum_{t=1}^{n} \hat{\varepsilon}_t^4 / n$ are the second, third and fourth moments of the residuals, respectively.

The J-B statistic has a $\chi^2$ distribution with two degrees of freedom. Under the null hypothesis of normally distributed residuals, the third and fourth moments, $\mu_3$ and $\mu_4$, should take certain specified values. If the moments of the residuals depart sufficiently far from the expected values, that is, the calculated J-B statistic exceeds the critical $\chi^2$ value, then the hypothesis of normally distributed residuals is rejected.

### 4.4.4 Testing for Mis-specification

*The Ramsey RESET Test.* The Ramsey (1969) regression equation specification error test (RESET) is designed to test for model mis-specification due to either the omission of important explanatory variables or incorrect choice of functional form. Consider a regression model with two explanatory variables as an example. The test involves three steps. The first step is to estimate the proposed regression model using OLS and to retain the estimated values of $Y_t$ from Equation (4.12):

$$\hat{Y}_t = \hat{\beta}_1 + \hat{\beta}_2 X_{1t} + \hat{\beta}_3 X_{2t} \tag{4.12}$$

and the second step is to estimate the augmented equation of the form

$$Y_t = \beta_1 + \beta_2 X_{1t} + \beta_3 X_{2t} + \alpha_1 \hat{Y}_t^2 + \alpha_2 \hat{Y}_t^3 + \alpha_3 \hat{Y}_t^4 + u_t \tag{4.13}$$

Finally, the significance of the $\alpha$ parameters is tested using a standard restriction test, such as the $F$ or Wald test. In carrying out the functional form test, we introduce, one-by-one, the estimated dependent variables with various powers into regression model (4.13) with the lowest powered variable first. If only $\hat{Y}_t^2$ is included, the significance of its coefficient may be tested using the $t$ statistic. It should be noted that the RESET test is a general misspecification test. The null hypothesis is that the model is correctly specified, but there is no specific alternative hypothesis. Therefore, rejection of the null hypothesis is merely an indication that the model is incorrectly specified, but how the model is mis-specified is beyond the concern of this test.

### 4.4.5    Testing for Structural Instability

For an econometric model to be able to produce accurate forecasts, the structure of the model should be constant over time, that is, the values of the parameters of the model that represents the economic relationship should be the same for both the sample period and the forecasting period. This assumption is often violated by regime shifts, such as changes in economic policy, evolution of consumers' tastes, oil crises and political unrest. Another potential source of structural instability is model mis-specification, such as the omission of important explanatory variables and incorrect specification of the functional form. If structural instability is caused by one of the above factors, then the model has to be re-specified and tested until a stable specification is reached. Testing for structural stability may be carried out using two tests developed by Chow (1960), and also a recursive least squares procedure.

*(a) The Chow Parameter Constancy Test (or Breakpoint Test).* This test examines whether there is a statistically significant difference between the OLS regression residuals from two sub-samples, and the statistic is calculated as follows:

$$F_{Chow1} = \frac{(SSR_0 - SSR_1 - SSR_2)/k}{(SSR_1 + SSR_2)/(n_1 + n_2 - 2k)} \sim F(k, n_1 + n_2 - 2k) \tag{4.14}$$

where $SSR_0$ is the residual sum of squares for the whole sample period, $SSR_1$ and $SSR_2$ are the residual sums of squares for the two sub-samples, and $n_1$ and $n_2$ are the numbers of observations in the first and second sub-sample periods, respectively.

If the calculated $F$ statistic is larger than the critical value, the null hypothesis of parameter constancy between the two sub-sample periods is rejected. In performing this test, the break point is assumed to be known.

*(b) The Chow Predictive Failure Test.* In this second Chow test of structure instability, the equation which was estimated using the first $n_1$ observations is used to forecast the dependent variable for the remaining $n_2$ data points. If the differences between the predicted values and the actual values are large, this suggests that the structure of the model in the estimation period is not the same as that in the forecast period. The test is calculated from the OLS residuals using the following formula:

$$F_{Chow2} = \frac{(SSR_0 - SSR_1)/n_2}{SSR_1/(n_1 - k)} \sim F(n_2, n_1 - k) \tag{4.15}$$

The null hypothesis of structural stability between the two sub-samples is rejected if the test statistic (4.15) exceeds the critical $F$ value. The difference between the Chow parameter constancy test and the Chow predictive failure test is that the latter does not involve estimating the regression for the second sub-sample. This can sometimes be useful when the second sub-sample is too short, such as when we evaluate the *ex post* forecasting performance of a regression model in which only a small number of observations are reserved for forecasting comparison purposes.

*(c) The Recursive Least Squares Procedure.* A critical feature of the two Chow tests is that we have to know exactly at which point we suspect the structural break takes place, but sometimes this is impossible as the change in structure may not happen suddenly, but rather evolve gradually over time. In such situations the Chow tests are not very useful. An alternative way of looking at structural instability is to employ the recursive least squares procedure.

In recursive least squares, the parameters of the model are first estimated using OLS with a small sub-sample of observations, $t = 1,2,3,\ldots,m$, where $m > k$. The sample period is then extended to $t = 1,2,3,\ldots,m+1$ observations and the model is re-estimated. The procedure is repeated until all the sample observations are used up. At each step, the values of the estimated parameters are noted, and these values are plotted against time at the end of the estimation process. Under the assumption of constant structure, the plotted estimates should converge to a constant value. Any significant divergence of the recursive estimates from their mean values suggests structural instability of the model.

## 4.4.6   Testing for Exogeneity

Although a more detailed discussion of exogeneity will take place in Chapter 7, when we examine the vector autoregressive (VAR) modelling approach, a brief introduction to the exogeneity test within a single equation framework is now provided. The test was developed by Wu (1973) and subsequently modified by Hausman (1978).

Consider a regression equation with two explanatory variables:

$$Y_t = \beta_0 + \beta_1 X_{1t} + \beta_2 X_{2t} + u_t \tag{4.16}$$

Suppose we suspect that $X_{2t}$ also depends on the current value of $Y_t$, that is, $X_{2t}$ is not exogenous to $Y_t$. If this is the case, the variable $X_{2t}$ will be correlated with the error term $u_t$. Testing the null hypothesis that there is no correlation between $X_{2t}$ and $u_t$ is therefore a test of the exogeneity of the variable $X_{2t}$. The test is carried out as follows. First, regress $X_{2t}$ against a number of instrumental variables (normally lagged $Y_t$, $X_{1t}$ and $X_{2t}$):

$$X_{2t} = \alpha_0 + \sum_{i=1}^{p} \alpha_i X_{2t-i} + \sum_{i=1}^{p} \gamma_i X_{1t-i} + \sum_{i=1}^{p} \lambda_i Y_{t-i} + \varepsilon_t \tag{4.17}$$

Then estimate:

$$Y_t = \beta_0' + \beta_1' X_{1t} + \beta_2' X_{2t} + \beta_3' \hat{\varepsilon}_t + u_t \tag{4.18}$$

where $\hat{\varepsilon}_t$ is the estimated error term from Equation (4.17).

The hypothesis $\beta_3' = 0$ in Equation (4.18) is then tested using the $t$ statistic. Rejection of the null hypothesis suggests that the variable $X_{2t}$ is endogenous.

If it is suspected that two or more explanatory variables in a multiple regression model are endogenous, these variables should be regressed individually against the instrumental variables. The estimated residuals are then collected from each of these models and introduced into the proposed multiple regression model. In this case, the appropriate test is whether the variables in question are jointly exogenous, and a standard restriction test such as the $F$ or Wald test can be used.

### 4.4.7   Encompassing Test

The concept of encompassing is associated with Mizon and Richard (1986). Encompassing tests are particularly useful when a researcher has to choose only one model for policy evaluation and forecasting from a number of competing models. Encompassing means that 'a model should not just be able to explain existing data. It should also be able to explain why previous models could or could not do so. In particular, if different researchers using different models have come to different conclusions, a preferred model should be able to explain why this is the case' (Thomas, 1997, p. 362). For simplicity, we shall concentrate on the case where there are only two competing models, M1 and M2. M1 is said to encompass M2 if M1 can explain all the results of M2. For example, suppose a tourism demand model M1 contains a variable that captures some irregular movements in the dependent variable due to, say, policy changes. If an alternative model M2 does not include this variable, structural instability may occur in this second model, and M1 will be able to predict the structural instability of M2. If this is the case, we say that M1 encompasses M2.

Although a number of encompassing tests are available in the literature, only two of them are introduced here. Suppose we are interested in choosing one model from the following two competing models:

$$\text{M1:} \quad Y_t = \alpha_0 + \alpha_1 X_{1t} + \alpha_2 X_{2t} + \alpha_3 X_{3t} + u_t \tag{4.19}$$

$$\text{M2:} \quad Y_t = \beta_0 + \beta_1 X_{1t} + \beta_2 Z_{1t} + \beta_3 Z_{2t} + e_t \tag{4.20}$$

The first test is known as the J-Test. This test is developed by Davidson and MacKinnon (1981) and can be carried out as follows. First estimate M1 and M2 using OLS, and save the estimated values of $\hat{Y}_t$ from the models. Next, the following two models are estimated using OLS:

$$Y_t = \alpha_0' + \alpha_1' X_{1t} + \alpha_2' X_{2t} + \alpha_3' X_{3t} + \alpha_4' \hat{Y}_{M2t} + u_t' \tag{4.21}$$

$$Y_t = \beta_0' + \beta_1' X_{1t} + \beta_2' Z_{1t} + \beta_3' Z_{2t} + \beta_4' \hat{Y}_{M1t} + e_t' \tag{4.22}$$

where $\hat{Y}_{M2t}$ and $\hat{Y}_{M1t}$ are the estimated $Y_t$s from Equations (4.20) and (4.19), respectively.

If the calculated $t$ statistic associated with $\alpha_4'$ in Equation (4.21) is insignificant, we say that M1 encompasses M2 (or M2 is nested in M1). If the calculated $t$ statistic of $\beta_4'$ in Equation (4.22) is insignificant, this suggests that M2 encompasses M1 (or M1 is nested in M2). Although there is a possibility that the results will suggest that both M1 encompasses M2 and vice versa, in practice this is unlikely to happen.

The second test is simply termed Encompassing test. In the case of whether M1 encompasses M2, the test involves computing the $F$ statistic for testing the restrictions $\gamma_1 = \gamma_2 = 0$ in the following equation:

$$Y_t = \alpha_0 + \varphi X_{1t} + \alpha_2 X_{2t} + \alpha_3 X_{3t} + \gamma_1 Z_{1t} + \gamma_2 Z_{2t} + u_t \tag{4.23}$$

where $\varphi = \alpha_1 + \beta_1$, and $Z_{1t}$ and $Z_{2t}$ are variables that cannot be expressed as exact linear combinations of the regressors of M1.

Equation (4.23) combines the common variable, $X_{1t}$, in M2 and M1 as $\varphi X_{1t}$. Rejection of the null hypothesis suggests that M1 encompasses M2. The test of whether M2 encompasses M1 involves testing the restrictions $\alpha_2 = \alpha_3 = 0$ in Equation (4.23).

## 4.5   MODEL SELECTION

In summary, the general-to-specific modelling approach involves the following steps. First, a general demand model that has a large number of explanatory variables, including the lagged dependent and lagged explanatory variables, is constructed in the form of an ADLM. Economic theory suggests the possible variables to be included, and the nature of the data suggests the lag length. Second, the *t*, *F*, and Wald (or LR or LM as appropriate) statistics are used to test various restrictions in order to achieve a simple but statistically significant specification. Third, the normal diagnostic tests, such as those for autocorrelation, heteroscedasticity, functional form and structural instability, are carried out to examine whether the final model is statistically acceptable or not. Fourth, the final model can be used for policy evaluation or forecasting.

Thomas (1993) has summarised the various criteria for model selection within the framework of general-to-specific modelling. The criteria are: *consistent with economic theory, data coherency, parsimony, encompassing, parameter constancy and exogeneity*. The first criterion for model selection is that the final model should be consistent with economic theory. This is very important; for example, in general we cannot use a demand model for policy evaluation and forecasting if the model has a negative income elasticity. Although such a model may be acceptable according to the diagnostic statistics, it should still be rejected because it invalidates a law of economics. The data coherency criterion ensures that economic data also have a role to play in the determination of the structure of the final model. It implies that the preferred model should have been subject to rigorous diagnostic checking for mis-specification. The parsimony criterion states that simple specifications are preferred to complex ones. In the case of modelling tourism demand, if two equations have similar powers in terms of explaining the variation in the dependent variable, but one has six explanatory variables while the other has only two, the latter should be chosen as the final model. This is because we gain very little by including more variables in the model, and moreover large numbers of explanatory variables tend to result in inadequate degrees of freedom and imprecise estimation. The encompassing principle requires that the preferred model should be able to encompass all, or at least most, of the models developed by previous researchers in the same field. The encompassing criterion does not necessarily conflict with that of parsimony; the preferred model may be structurally simpler than other models, but still encompasses them. The parameter constancy criterion is particularly important when we use econometric models to forecast. In order to generate accurate forecasts, the parameters of the model should be constant over time. The final criterion for selecting a model is that the explanatory variables should be exogenous, that is they should not be contemporaneously correlated with the error term in the regression.

In modelling tourism demand, the final preferred model should ideally satisfy all of the above criteria. However, this can sometimes be very difficult due to various reasons, such as data limitations, errors in variables and insufficient knowledge of the demand system. Any of these may result in the above criteria not being satisfied. Even if we find a demand model that satisfies all the criteria, it should be borne in mind that the model can still only serve as an approximation of the complex behaviour of tourists, and it is possible that the decision-making process of tourists will change due to changes in expectations, tastes and economic regimes. Therefore, we should be always prepared to revise our model to take account of such changes.

## 4.6    A WORKED EXAMPLE

In this section we illustrate the general-to-specific modelling approach using the example of outbound tourism demand from the UK to Spain. We start with the construction of a general demand model. Various restrictions on the parameters are tested to determine which type of model is appropriate, and diagnostic checking is then carried out in the model selection process.

### 4.6.1    The Data

The data are annual and cover the period 1966 to 1994. The following variables are included in the model: the number of holidays in Spain taken by UK residents (VSP), UK real personal disposable income (PDI), the implicit deflator of UK consumer expenditure (which is calculated by dividing total consumer expenditure in current prices by consumer expenditure in constant prices) (PUK), an exchange rate index of the UK pound against the US dollar (EXUK), the consumer price index in Spain (CPISP), an exchange rate index of Spanish pesetas against the US dollar (EXSP), and the UK population (POP). The data on VSP are obtained from *Social Trends* (various issues); the PDI, PUK and POP series are complied from *Economic Trends* (1996); and the data on EXUK, EXSP and CPISP are obtained from the *IMF International Financial Statistics Yearbook* (1995). The data are given in Table A4.1 in Appendix 4.1.

In modelling UK outbound tourism demand to Spain, the dependent variable VSP and the independent variable PDI are first transformed into per capita terms. In order to examine the influence of tourism prices on tourism demand, a relative cost of tourism variable is created using the following formula:

$$RCSP = \frac{(CPISP / EXSP)}{(PUK / EXUK)} \tag{4.24}$$

This is a relative price variable adjusted by exchange rates. The demand equation is assumed to be a double-log function. Since annual data are used, a general tourism demand model is specified with one lag for each variable:

$$
\begin{aligned}
LPVSP_t = {} & \alpha_0 + \alpha_1 LPVSP_{t-1} + \alpha_2 LPPDI_t + \alpha_3 LPPDI_{t-1} \\
& + \alpha_4 LRCSP_t + \alpha_5 LRCSP_{t-1} + \varepsilon_t
\end{aligned} \tag{4.25}
$$

where *LPVSP* is the logarithm of per capita holiday visits to Spain; *LPPDI* is the logarithm of per capita personal disposable income, and the *LRCSP* is the logarithm of living costs in Spain relative to UK living costs adjusted by the exchange rate.

## 4.6.2    Estimated General Model

Equation (4.25) is estimated using OLS based on data for the period 1966 to 1994:

$$LPVSP_t = \underset{(3.268)}{-8.018} + \underset{(0.133)}{0.648}\,LPVSP_{t-1} + \underset{(1.288)}{1.249}\,LPPDI_t$$
$$- \underset{(1.185)}{0.429}\,LPPDI_{t-1} - \underset{(0.266)}{0.470}\,LRCSP_t \qquad (4.26)$$
$$- \underset{(0.284)}{0.440}\,LRCSP_{t-1}$$

$$R^2 = 0.938 \quad \sigma = 0.1304 \quad SSR = 0.374 \quad \chi^2_{Auto}(2) = 0.150$$

$$\chi^2_{Norm}(2) = 1.705 \quad \chi^2_{ARCH}(1) = 0.083 \quad \chi^2_{White}(18) = 18.515$$

$$\chi^2_{RESET}(2) = 4.213 \quad F_{Forecast}(4,18) = 0.520$$

where $\sigma$ is the standard error of the regression; SSR is the sum squared residuals; $\chi^2_{Auto}(2)$ is the Breusch-Godfrey LM test for autocorrelation; $\chi^2_{Norm}(2)$ is the Jarque-Bera normality test; $\chi^2_{ARCH}(1)$ is the Engle test for autoregressive conditional heteroscedasticity; $\chi^2_{White}(18)$ is the White test for heteroscedasticity; $\chi^2_{RESET}(2)$ is the Ramsey test for omitted variables/functional form; and $F_{Forecast}(4,18)$ is the Chow predictive failure test (when calculating this test, 1991 was chosen as the starting point for forecasting). The figures in parentheses under the estimated coefficients are standard errors, and this is the case throughout this chapter.

The diagnostic statistics show that the general model passes all but one of the tests. The model only fails the RESET test for model mis-specification.

## 4.6.3    Tests for Restrictions

The model reduction process can be started by performing various restriction tests. This process aims to determine a parsimonious specification that can be used to model the demand by UK residents for holidays to Spain. Since the demand model involves two explanatory variables, the restrictions on the coefficients are slightly more complicated than is the case in the single explanatory variable model (4.3). However, the restrictions can still be easily tested using either the $F$ test, or the Wald (or LR or LM) statistic.

*(a) Testing for the Static Model.* The null hypothesis is that $\alpha_1 = \alpha_3 = \alpha_5 = 0$, so there are three restrictions on the regression coefficients of model (4.25). In order to test these restrictions we also need to estimate the restricted static model (4.27):

$$LPVSP_t = \alpha_0 + +\alpha_2 LPPDI_t + \alpha_4 LRCSP_t + u_t \qquad (4.27)$$

OLS estimation of Equation (4.27) gives

$$LPVSP_t = \underset{(1.887)}{-23.050} + \underset{(0.220)}{2.369}\, LPPDI_t \underset{(0.339)}{-0.861}\, LRCSP_t$$

$$R^2 = 0.819 \quad \sigma = 0.220 \quad SSR = 1.261$$

Since 28 observations are used in estimating the unrestricted general model (4.26) and there are three restrictions involved, the $F$ statistic can be calculated as

$$F(r, n-k) = \frac{(SSR_1 - SSR_0)/r}{SSR_0/(n-k)} = \frac{(1.126 - 0.374)/3}{0.374/(28-6)} = 14.75$$

The critical value of the $F$ statistic with [3, 22] degrees of freedom at the 5% significance level is 3.05. As the calculated $F$ value exceeds this critical value, the restrictions should not be accepted, that is, the static model is not an appropriate specification for modelling the demand by UK residents for tourism in Spain.

*(b) Testing for the Autoregressive Model.* The restrictions in this case are $\alpha_2 = \alpha_3 = \alpha_4 = \alpha_5 = 0$. The $F$ statistic is calculated in the same way as in (a), but the degrees of freedom are [4,22], as there are now four restrictions instead of three. The estimated restricted model is

$$LPVSP_t = \underset{(0.173)}{-0.184} + \underset{(0.061)}{0.914}\, LPVSP_{t-1}$$

$$R^2 = 0.896 \quad \sigma = 0.155 \quad SSR = 0.625$$

and the restriction test statistic is

$$F(r, n-k) = \frac{(SSR_1 - SSR_0)/r}{SSR_0/(n-k)} = \frac{(0.625 - 0.374)/4}{0.374/(28-6)} = 3.69$$

Since the critical value of $F[4,22]$ is 2.84, the autoregressive model cannot be accepted.

*(c) Testing for the Growth Rate Model.* The growth rate model requires that the coefficients in the general model satisfy $\alpha_1 = 1, \alpha_2 = -\alpha_3$ and $\alpha_4 = -\alpha_5$, that is, the demand model may be rewritten as

$$\Delta LPVSP_t = \alpha_0 + \alpha_2 \Delta LPPDI_t + \alpha_4 \Delta LRCSP_t + u_t \qquad (4.28)$$

OLS estimation of Equation (4.28) yields

$$\Delta LPVSP_t = \underset{(0.043)}{-0.061} - \underset{(1.430)}{0.045 \Delta LPPDI_t} - \underset{(0.306)}{0.107 \Delta LRCSP_t}$$

$$R^2 = 0.01 \quad \sigma = 0.163 \quad SSR = 0.668$$

The results show that this restricted model fits the data badly. The income coefficient has the 'wrong' sign and all the coefficients are statistically insignificant. These empirical results indicate that the growth rate model cannot be accepted. This is confirmed by the $F$ test, with the calculated $F[3, 22]$ statistic (5.77) exceeding the critical value (3.05).

*(d) Testing for the Leading Indicator Model.* In the leading indicator model, the lagged dependent variable and the current values of independent variables do not enter the equation. The null hypothesis for the tourism demand model is, therefore, $\alpha_2 = \alpha_3 = \alpha_5 = 0$. The estimated leading indicator model is

$$LPVSP_t = \underset{(1.80)}{-22.73} + \underset{(0.210)}{2.333 LPPDI_{t-1}} - \underset{(0.309)}{1.331 LRCSP_{t-1}}$$

$$R^2 = 0.832 \quad \sigma = 0.201 \quad SSR = 1.006$$

The calculated value of the $F[3,22]$ statistic is 12.392, which clearly suggests rejection of the leading indicator model.

*(e) Testing for the Partial Adjustment Process.* The restrictions on the coefficients of the general model are $\alpha_4 = \alpha_6 = 0$. The estimated restricted model is

$$LPVSP_t = \underset{(3.001)}{-5.247} + \underset{(0.122)}{0.755 LPVSP_{t-1}} + \underset{(0.314)}{0.534 LPPDI_t} - \underset{(0.212)}{0.666 LRCSP_t}$$

$$R^2 = 0.927 \quad \sigma = 0.134 \quad SSR = 0.435$$

The $F$ statistic is given by

$$F(r, n-k) = \frac{(SSR_1 - SSR_0)/r}{SSR_0/(n-k)} = \frac{(0.435 - 0.374)/2}{0.374/(28-6)} = 1.974$$

This calculated $F[2, 22]$ value is lower than the critical value (3.44), which suggests that the goodness of fit does not deteriorate much when the restrictions for a partial adjustment process are imposed. Since this model involves fewer variables than the general model and has more degrees of freedom, the partial adjustment model is preferred to the general demand model. The various diagnostic statistics for the partial adjustment model are as follows:

$$\chi^2_{Auto}(2) = 1.899 \quad \chi^2_{Norm}(2) = 2.229 \quad \chi^2_{ARCH}(1) = 0.018$$

$$\chi^2_{White}(9) = 4.647 \quad \chi^2_{RESET}(2) = 1.394 \quad F_{Forecast}(4, 20) = 0.527.$$

The model passes all the diagnostic tests, and in particular the Ramsey RESET statistic now does not suggest a model mis-specification problem in terms of omitted explanatory variables or incorrect functional form. An important implication of rejecting the general model is that the error correction model should also be rejected, since it can be shown that the error correction model is a reparameterisation of the ADLM process (Chapter 6).

*(f) Testing for the COMFAC Model.* The restrictions for the COMFAC model in the present example are $\alpha_3 = -\alpha_2\alpha_1$ and $\alpha_5 = -\alpha_4\alpha_1$. Since the restrictions are non-linear, the Wald test is employed. The calculated Wald statistic is $\chi^2(2) = 12.554$[1], which suggests that the restrictions cannot be accepted, that is, the COMFAC specification is not appropriate.

*(g) Testing for the Finite Distributed Lag Model.* In this case, the restriction is $\alpha_1 = 0$ and the estimated restricted model is

$$LPVSP_t = -22.910 + 4.144\,LPPDI_t - 1.801\,LPPDI_{t-1}$$
$$\phantom{LPVSP_t = }{\scriptstyle(1.659)}\phantom{+4.144}{\scriptstyle(1.615)}\phantom{LPPDI_t-}{\scriptstyle(1.625)}$$
$$\phantom{LPVSP_t =} -0.534\,LRCSP_t - 0.789\,LRCSP_{t-1}$$
$$\phantom{LPVSP_t = -}{\scriptstyle(0.376)}\phantom{LRCSP_t-}{\scriptstyle(0.388)}$$

$$R^2 = 0.869 \quad \sigma = 0.184 \quad SSR = 0.779$$

The calculated $F[2,22]$ value is 23.83, so clearly the restriction $\alpha_1 = 0$ is not valid.

*(h) Testing for the Dead Start Model.* The restrictions in this case are $\alpha_2 = \alpha_4 = 0$. The estimated dead start model is

$$LPVSP_t = -7.139 + 0.677\,LPVSP_{t-1} + 0.731\,LPPDI_{t-1} - 0.748\,LRCSP_{t-1}$$
$$\phantom{LPVSP_t =}{\scriptstyle(2.989)}\phantom{+}{\scriptstyle(0.119)}\phantom{LPVSP}{\scriptstyle(0.314)}\phantom{LPPDI}{\scriptstyle(0.230)}$$

$$R^2 = 0.929 \quad \sigma = 0.134 \quad SSR = 0.438$$

The calculated $F[2,22]$ statistic is 1.585, which is smaller than the corresponding critical value (3.44), and therefore we cannot reject the restrictions at the 5% level. The dead start model is preferred to the general demand model. The diagnostics are as follows:

$$\chi^2_{Auto}(2) = 0.016 \quad \chi^2_{Norm}(2) = 1.806 \quad \chi^2_{ARCH}(1) = 0.085 \quad \chi^2_{White}(9) = 12.718$$

$$\chi^2_{RESET}(2) = 2.504 \quad F_{Forecast}(4,20) = 0.852$$

From the diagnostic statistics we can see that the model is well specified and the coefficients of all the variables have 'correct' signs and are statistically significant at the 5% level. These results imply that there are two specific models that we can choose from—the partial adjustment model and the dead start model. Apart from the fact that both models pass all the diagnostic tests, the values of $R^2$ and the standard errors of regression for the two models are almost identical. The decision between these two models therefore has to be based on other criteria, such as the encompassing test.

In order to choose which is the better model—the partial adjustment model (M1) or the dead start model (M2)—we carry out the two encompassing tests explained in the previous section. The J-Test is based on the following two regressions:

$$LPVSP_t = \alpha'_0 + \alpha'_1 LPVSP_{t-1} + \alpha'_2 LPPDI_t + \alpha'_3 LRCSP_t$$
$$+ \alpha'_4 \overline{LPVSP}_{M2t} + u'_t \tag{4.29}$$

$$LPVSP_t = \beta'_0 + \beta'_1 LPVSP_{t-1} + \beta'_2 LPPDI_{t-1} + \beta'_3 LRCSP_{t-1}$$
$$+ \beta'_4 \overline{LPVSP}_{M1t} + e'_t \tag{4.30}$$

where $\overline{LPVSP}_{M2t}$ is the estimated $LPVSP$ from the dead start model and $\overline{LPVSP}_{M1t}$ is the estimated $LPVSP$ from the partial adjustment model.

The statistics concerned are the $t$ ratios for $\alpha'_4$ and $\beta'_4$. If the coefficient $\alpha'_4$ is not significantly different from zero, we say that the dead start model (M2) is nested in the partial adjustment model (M1), and if the coefficient $\beta'_4$ is not significantly different from zero, we say that M1 is nested in M2. After estimating the partial adjustment and the dead start models the estimated values of $LPVSP$ are saved as $\overline{LPVSP}_{M1t}$ and $\overline{LPVSP}_{M2t}$, respectively. These two variables are then included in Equations (4.30) and (4.29), and OLS estimation of these equations gives:

$$LPVSP_t = \underset{(1.602)}{-4.092} + \underset{(0.065)}{0.787} LPVSP_{t-1} + \underset{(0.168)}{0.412} LPPDI_t - \underset{(0.116)}{0.431} LRCSP_t$$
$$+ \underset{(0.113)}{0.891} \overline{LPVSP}_{M2t}$$

$$LPVSP_t = \underset{(3.578)}{-3.658} + \underset{(0.301)}{0.218} LPVSP_{t-1} + \underset{(0.371)}{0.376} LPPDI_{t-1} - \underset{(0.274)}{0.482} LRCSP_{t-1}$$
$$+ \underset{(0.382)}{0.631} \overline{LPVSP}_{M1t}$$

The calculated $t$ statistic for $\alpha'_4$ in Equation (4.29) is $\dfrac{\hat{\alpha}'_4}{SE(\hat{\alpha}'_4)} = \dfrac{0.891}{0.113} =$ 7.869, so $\alpha'_4$ is highly significant. This suggests that the partial adjustment model (M1) does not encompass the dead start model (M2). The calculated $t$ statistic for $\beta'_4$ in Equation (4.30) is (0.631/0.382) = 1.647, so $\beta'_4$ is not significantly different from zero even at the 10% level. The dead start model (M2) therefore encompasses the partial adjustment model (M1).

The second encompassing test based on Equation (4.23) is exactly the same as testing for the partial adjustment model and dead start model as described in (e) and (h). Therefore, the encompassing statistics are $F[2,22]$ = 1.974 and $F[2,22]$ = 1.585, respectively. These two statistics suggest that the dead start model does not encompass the partial adjustment model and also that the partial adjustment model does not encompass the dead start model.

Although the J-Test suggests that the dead start model is better than the partial adjustment model, this is not confirmed by the second encompassing test. Therefore, further criteria, such as the *ex post* forecasting performance, should be used to assist in model selection. (The forecasting performance criteria will be fully discussed in Chapter 11.)

Using the Wu-Hausman test, the exogeneity of the explanatory variables $LPPDI_t$ and $LRCSP_t$ can be tested. In the following example we explain the Wu-Hausman test using the dead start model. The test procedure is as follows. First, estimate the two auxiliary equations in which $LPPDI_t$ and $LRCSP_t$ are regressed against all the lagged variables in the general model (4.25). The results are given as

$$LPPDI_t = \underset{(0.508)}{1.230} + \underset{(0.053)}{0.875}\,LPPDI_{t-1} + \underset{(0.020)}{0.055}\,LPVSP_{t-1} - \underset{(0.039)}{0.013}\,LRCSP_{t-1} \quad (4.31)$$

$$R^2 = 0.986 \quad \sigma = 0.023 \quad SSR = 0.012$$

$$LRCSP_t = \underset{(2.450)}{1.398} + \underset{(0.189)}{0.622}\,LRCSP_{t-1} - \underset{(0.258)}{0.140}\,LPPDI_{t-1} + \underset{(0.864)}{0.097}\,LPVSP_{t-1} \quad (4.32)$$

$$R^2 = 0.372 \quad \sigma = 0.109 \quad SSR = 0.288$$

Second, the estimated residuals from these two models are saved as $u_{LPPDI_t}$ and $u_{LRCSP_t}$, respectively. Third, the terms $u_{LPPDI_t}$ and $u_{LRCSP_t}$ are introduced into the dead start specification, and the resultant model is estimated using OLS:

$$LPVSP_t = \underset{(2.919)}{-7.140} + \underset{(0.116)}{0.677}\,LPVSP_{t-1} + \underset{(0.307)}{0.731}\,LPPDI_{t-1} - \underset{(0.225)}{0748}\,LRCSP_{t-1}$$

$$+ \underset{(1.288)}{1.249}\,u_{LPPDI_t} - \underset{(0.267)}{0.670}\,u_{LRCSP_t} \quad (4.33)$$

$$R^2 = 0.923 \quad \sigma = 0.130 \quad SSR = 0.374$$

The Wu-Hausman statistic is calculated by imposing the restriction that the coefficients of $u_{LPPDI_t}$ and $u_{LRCSP_t}$ are jointly equal to zero. The $F$ version of the Wu-Hausman statistic is calculated as

$$F(r, n-k) = \frac{(SSR_1 - SSR_0)/r}{SSR_0/(n-k)} = \frac{(0.438 - 0.374)/2}{0.374/(28-6)} = 1.882$$

where $SSR_0$ is the sum of squared residuals from Equation (4.33) and $SSR_1$ is the sum of squared residuals from the estimated dead start model.

The calculated $F[2,22]$ statistic is 1.882, which is less than the critical value of 3.44, indicating that the coefficients of $u_{LPPDI_t}$ and $u_{LRCSP_t}$ are jointly equal to zero. Therefore, we can conclude that the variables $LPPDI_t$ and $LRCSP_t$ are exogenous to $LPVSP_t$. The same conclusion is reached if the partial adjustment process is used as the base model.

**APPENDIX 4.1**

Table A4.1  Worked Example: Data Used in Estimation

| Year | VSP | PDI | PUK | EXUK | POP | CPISP | EXSP |
|------|-----|-----|-----|------|-----|-------|------|
| 1966 | 1.282300 | 201207.0 | 0.134250 | 0.485709 | 54.64300 | 0.096155 | 0.435193 |
| 1967 | 1.271800 | 204171.0 | 0.137742 | 0.563200 | 54.95900 | 0.102310 | 0.505549 |
| 1968 | 1.537000 | 207772.0 | 0.144298 | 0.568364 | 55.21600 | 0.107425 | 0.506419 |
| 1969 | 1.950100 | 209684.0 | 0.152272 | 0.564515 | 55.46100 | 0.109823 | 0.508160 |
| 1970 | 1.830000 | 217675.0 | 0.161250 | 0.566155 | 55.63200 | 0.113580 | 0.505694 |
| 1971 | 2.612600 | 220344.0 | 0.175189 | 0.576441 | 55.92800 | 0.122852 | 0.519910 |
| 1972 | 3.153500 | 238744.0 | 0.186568 | 0.626625 | 56.07900 | 0.133083 | 0.500617 |
| 1973 | 3.060100 | 254329.0 | 0.202143 | 0.703709 | 56.22300 | 0.148190 | 0.498295 |
| 1974 | 2.596600 | 252360.0 | 0.236360 | 0.706515 | 56.23600 | 0.170490 | 0.498295 |
| 1975 | 2.881500 | 253814.0 | 0.292056 | 0.784033 | 56.22600 | 0.200623 | 0.507580 |
| 1976 | 2.151400 | 253012.0 | 0.337778 | 0.924894 | 56.21600 | 0.235952 | 0.575470 |
| 1977 | 2.544000 | 247695.0 | 0.387586 | 0.863692 | 56.19000 | 0.293742 | 0.712845 |
| 1978 | 2.860200 | 265925.0 | 0.424315 | 0.867812 | 56.17800 | 0.351930 | 0.662508 |

| 1979 | 2.861500 | 281084.0 | 0.482226 | 0.802721 | 56.24000 | 0.407082 | 0.632045 |
| 1980 | 2.924900 | 285411.0 | 0.560568 | 0.724715 | 56.33000 | 0.470626 | 0.733154 |
| 1981 | 3.582000 | 283176.0 | 0.623576 | 0.826736 | 56.35200 | 0.539365 | 0.822732 |
| 1982 | 4.451100 | 281722.0 | 0.677889 | 0.925951 | 56.31800 | 0.538406 | 1.004932 |
| 1983 | 5.404900 | 289204.0 | 0.710628 | 0.978113 | 56.37700 | 0.604108 | 1.189962 |
| 1984 | 6.104200 | 299756.0 | 0.712308 | 1.148640 | 56.50600 | 0.672368 | 1.232828 |
| 1985 | 5.427200 | 309821.0 | 0.785876 | 1.030533 | 56.68500 | 0.731596 | 1.228113 |
| 1986 | 6.305600 | 323622.0 | 0.817104 | 1.124233 | 56.85200 | 0.795940 | 1.174585 |
| 1987 | 6.400000 | 334702.0 | 0.852381 | 1.027294 | 57.00900 | 0.837343 | 1.121564 |
| 1988 | 6.720000 | 354627.0 | 0.894970 | 1.007860 | 57.15800 | 0.877548 | 1.107348 |
| 1989 | 5.880000 | 371676.0 | 0.947763 | 1.109298 | 57.35800 | 0.937175 | 1.045840 |
| 1990 | 4.637000 | 378325.0 | 1.000000 | 1.000000 | 57.56100 | 1.000000 | 1.000000 |
| 1991 | 4.428300 | 377969.0 | 1.073715 | 1.036266 | 57.80800 | 1.058988 | 1.003191 |
| 1992 | 4.648000 | 386804.0 | 1.124222 | 1.232419 | 58.00600 | 1.121493 | 1.143178 |
| 1993 | 5.866800 | 393125.0 | 1.163626 | 1.256732 | 58.19100 | 1.173048 | 1.416842 |
| 1994 | 7.216700 | 396181.0 | 1.192823 | 1.266178 | 58.39500 | 1.228119 | 1.394937 |

# 5 Cointegration

## 5.1 SPURIOUS REGRESSION

Many tourism demand variables (dependent and explanatory), such as aggregate tourism expenditure, total tourist arrivals, tourism costs in the destination countries and income in the tourism generating country, are often trended, that is, the variables are non-stationary. This can be a potential problem for tourism demand analysis. We tend to obtain a high $R^2$ and significant $t$ statistics for the regression coefficients if all the variables in the demand model have a common deterministic trend, but this does not necessarily mean that these variables are actually related, in other words, the regression may be spurious.

A typical spurious correlation is illustrated in the following example. The implicit deflator of consumer expenditure for the UK and the consumer price index (CPI) for Spain are plotted in Figure 5.1. The figure shows that both variables are upward trended.

Although there is no reason for us to believe that inflation in the UK determines inflation in Spain or vice versa, the correlation between these two variables is very high since both series exhibit a similar trend over the same period. This can be shown by examining the ordinary least squares (OLS) estimates of the regression of the log of the Spanish consumer price index on the log of the implicit deflator of UK consumer expenditure (the equivalent CPI for the UK). The apparent correlation between the two price variables as measured by the extremely high value of $R^2$ (0.99) in Equation (5.1) is clearly spurious.

$$\log(CPI)_{Spain} = \underset{(0.016)}{0.041} + \underset{(0.014)}{1.171} \log(CPI)_{UK} \tag{5.1}$$

$R^2 = 0.990 \quad DW = 0.565 \quad \chi^2_{Auto}(2) = 16.42\,*** \quad \chi^2_{Norm}(2) = 4.712\,*$

$\chi^2_{ARCH}(1) = 4.700\,** \quad \chi^2_{White}(2) = 3.675 \quad \chi^2_{RESET}(2) = 22.82\,***$

where figures in parentheses are standard errors and *, ** and *** denote significant at 10%, 5% and 1% levels, respectively.

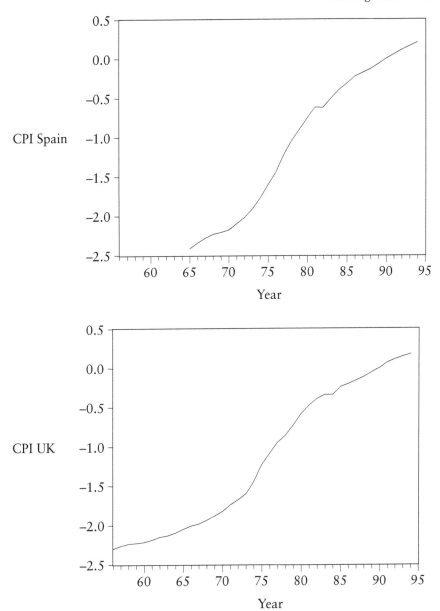

*Figure 5.1* Consumer price indices of Spain and the UK (log).

Even if there is a weak linkage between Spanish inflation and the UK price level due to the spill-over effect caused by imports and exports between these two countries, the estimated standard errors (or $t$ statistics) for the regression coefficients and the $R^2$ values are likely to be very much exaggerated. Moreover, all diagnostic statistics apart from the White heteroscedasticity test statistic are violated, implying that the model is unacceptable statistically (the Chow breakpoint test was also performed using 1973, 1979 and 1982 as breakpoints; model stability was rejected in all cases).

Until recently very little attention was paid to the spurious regression problem by tourism forecasters and practitioners. Early attempts to solve the problem used differenced variables in the regression model. However, by doing this, important information concerning the long-run equilibrium relationship among the economic variables is lost. The cointegration technique developed by Engle and Granger (1987), coupled with the error correlation mechanism, has proved to be a useful tool for solving the problem of spurious correlation when non-stationary time series are used in econometric modelling. This chapter is devoted to examining the concept of and tests for cointegration.

## 5.2   THE CONCEPT OF COINTEGRATION

According to Engle and Granger (1987), if a pair of non-stationary economic variables, $x_t$ and $y_t$, belongs to the same economic system, such as tourism demand and income, there should be an *attractor* or *cointegration relationship* that prevents these two time series from drifting away from each other; that is, there exists a *force of equilibrium* that keeps the two variables, $x_t$ and $y_t$, moving together in the long run. More formally, if $x_t$ and $y_t$ move together in the long run, they can be modelled by a long-run equilibrium model of the form:

$$y_t = \beta_0 + \beta_1 x_t \tag{5.2}$$

The disequilibrium error of Equation (5.2) is

$$\varepsilon_t = y_t - \beta_0 - \beta_1 x_t \tag{5.3}$$

Engle and Granger (1987) state that if the long-run equilibrium relationship (5.2) exists, the disequilibrium error (5.3) should 'rarely drift far from zero'. This means that if the long-run equilibrium regression (5.2) is estimated using OLS, the residuals of the model should follow a stationary process and fluctuate around the value of zero over time, that is, the two non-stationary variables, $x_t$ and $y_t$, are cointegrated.

A non-stationary time series is also called an integrated process. The order of integration for a series is determined by the number of times the series must be differenced to achieve a stationary process. Therefore, a stationary variable is a series that is integrated of order zero, or $I(0)$ for short. A series is said to be integrated of order 1, or $I(1)$ if it becomes stationary after taking first differences. In general, if a time series needs to be differenced $d$ times before achieving stationarity, then the series is said to be integrated of order $d$, or $I(d)$.

Cointegration may be defined as follows: $x_t$ and $y_t$ are said to be cointegrated of order $d, b$, denoted by $(x_t, y_t) \sim CI\,(d, b)$, if $x_t$ and $y_t$ are integrated of order $d$ and there exists a vector of parameters $(\beta_0, \beta_1)$ such that the linear combination $y_t = \beta_0 + \beta_1 x_t$ is integrated of order $(d - b)$, where $b > 0$. The vector $(\beta_0, \beta_1)$ is called the cointegration vector. Although this definition refers to the two-variable case, it can be extended to a *k-variable* cointegration system.

The following points need to be made regarding this definition. First, all variables in the cointegration regression must be integrated of the same order (although some of the recent cointegration literature allows for different orders of integration). This pre-condition for a cointegration relationship does not necessarily mean that all economic variables that have the same integration order are cointegrated. For example, the consumer price indices in the UK and Spain may be integrated of the same order, but they are clearly not cointegrated. Second, in a two-variable cointegration equation, the cointegration vector $(\beta_0, \beta_1)$ is unique. However, if there are $k$ variables in the system, there may be as many as $k - 1$ cointegration relationships. In Chapter 7 we will look at multiple cointegration relationships within a vector autoregressive (VAR) modelling framework. Third, most of the empirical literature on cointegration concentrates on the model in which all variables are integrated of order one, that is, the variables are $CI(1,1)$. Our subsequent discussions of cointegration also follow this tradition.

The cointegration relationship may be tested using the OLS residuals, $\hat{\varepsilon}_t$, from Equation (5.2). The aim is to test whether $\hat{\varepsilon}_t$ is a stationary process or not. If the $\hat{\varepsilon}_t$ term from the OLS estimation of (5.2) is found to be stationary, we will say that $x_t$ and $y_t$ are cointegrated. On the other hand if the residuals are found to be non-stationary, the conclusion would be that the two variables concerned are not cointegrated. The discussion on how to test for cointegration will be given in section 5.5. Since the cointegration relationship requires that the variables in the cointegration regression are integrated of order one, we need to test for the integration order of each individual time series in the long-run equilibrium model before the cointegration test can be carried out. The tests used for identifying the order of integration are called the Dickey and Fuller (1981) tests and they are presented in the following section.

## 5.3    TEST FOR ORDER OF INTEGRATION

### 5.3.1    Stationary and Non-stationary Time Series

We begin with the definition of a stationary series. *A time series is said to be stationary if its mean, variance and covariance remain constant over time,* that is:

$$E(y_t) = \mu \tag{5.4}$$

$$E[(y_t - \mu)^2] = Var(y_t) = \sigma^2 \tag{5.5}$$

$$E[(y_t - \mu)(y_{t-p} - \mu)] = Cov(y_t - y_{t-p}) = \Omega_p \tag{5.6}$$

Equations (5.4) and (5.5) state that the time series, $y_t$, has a constant mean, $\mu$, and a constant variance, $\sigma^2$, respectively, while Equation (5.6) indicates that the covariance between any two values from the time series depends only on the time interval, $p$, between those two values and not on time itself. If a time series violates any of the above conditions, it is regarded as a non-stationary series. Figure 5.2 shows the log of per capita holiday visits by UK residents to Spain ($LPVSP_t$) and the same variable expressed in first differences ($\Delta LPVSP_t$). It is clear that $LPVSP_t$ is a non-stationary variable since its mean increases over time, while $\Delta LPVSP_t$ fluctuates around a mean value of 0.06, suggesting that it is likely to be a stationary variable. (This will be confirmed by the standard test statistics in section 5.3.7.)

## 5.3.2    Non-stationary Series and Unit Roots

A non-stationary time series is also known as a series that has unit roots. The number of unit roots contained in the series is equal to the number of times the series must be differenced in order to achieve a stationary series. For example, if the time series $y_t$ becomes stationary after taking first differences, we say that $y_t$ has one unit root, denoted as $y_t \sim I(1)$, or is integrated of order one. If $y_t$ needs to be differenced twice in order to become a stationary process, then it has two unit roots, that is, $y_t$ is an $I(2)$ series. Therefore an $I(d)$ series means that the series has $d$ unit roots.

A non-stationary series can always be represented by an autoregressive process of order $p$ (AR(p)):

$$y_t = \beta_0 + \beta_1 y_{t-1} + \beta_2 y_{t-2} + \ldots + \beta_p y_{t-p} + e_t \tag{5.7}$$

where $e_t$ is an error term which is assumed to have a zero mean and constant variance.

The condition for $y_t$ to be a non-stationary series is: $\beta_1 + \beta_2 + \ldots + \beta_p = 1$. If the order of the AR process is $p = 1$, Equation (5.7) becomes

$$y_t = \beta_0 + \beta_1 y_{t-1} + e_t \tag{5.8}$$

and if $y_t$ is a non-stationary series, $\beta_1 = 1$, that is,

$$y_t = \beta_0 + y_{t-1} + e_t \tag{5.9}$$

Equation (5.9) is also called a random walk with drift (RWD). If the constant term equals zero in (5.9), the process is termed a random walk (RW). To test for stationarity is therefore to test either that $\beta_1 + \beta_2 + \ldots + \beta_p = 1$ or $\beta_1 = 1$ in Equations (5.7) and (5.8), respectively, and this can be accom-

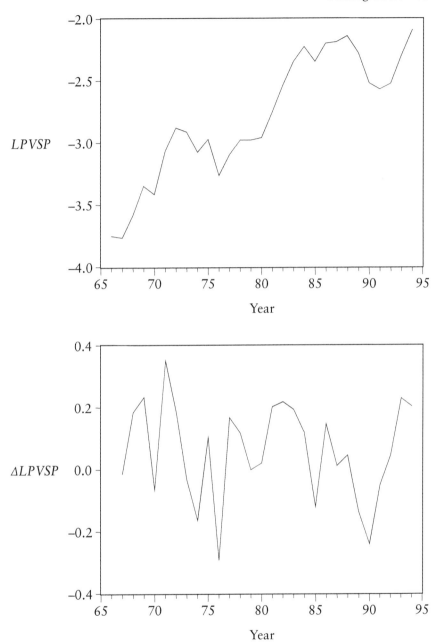

*Figure 5.2* Comparison of stationary and non-stationary time series.

plished by using the Dickey-Fuller (DF) and the augmented Dickey-Fuller (ADF) tests (Dickey and Fuller, 1981).

### 5.3.3 The DF and ADF Tests for Unit Roots

#### 5.3.3.1 DF Test

Let us assume that the time series can be modelled by an AR(1) process, as in Equation (5.8). Our objective is to test the null hypothesis, $H_0 : \beta_1 = 1$, against the alternative, $H_1 : \beta_1 < 1$. An obvious way of testing for $\beta_1 = 1$ is to look at the $t$ ratio:

$$t = \frac{\hat{\beta}_1 - 1}{SE(\hat{\beta}_1)} \tag{5.10}$$

However, instead of testing $\beta_1 = 1$ directly, Dickey and Fuller (1979) transformed (5.8) into (5.11):

$$\Delta y_t = \beta_0 + \phi y_{t-1} + e_t \tag{5.11}$$

This is done by subtracting $y_{t-1}$ from both sides of Equation (5.8). In Equation (5.11) $\Delta y_t = y_t - y_{t-1}$ and $\phi = \beta_1 - 1$. Note that testing for $H_0 : \beta_1 = 1$ against $H_1 : \beta_1 < 1$ in (5.8) is exactly the same as testing $H_0 : \phi = 0$ against $H_1 : \phi < 0$ in (5.11). The commonly used test for $\phi = 0$ is of course the $t$ ratio: $\hat{\phi}/[SE(\hat{\phi})]$. However, under the null hypothesis of non-stationarity, the $t$ ratio has a non-standard distribution, and therefore the conventional critical values for the $t$ statistic are not applicable. Dickey and Fuller obtained critical values based on Monte Carlo simulations, and a selection of these critical values is presented in Table 5.1 under the column $\tau_\mu$. If the calculated $t$ value is lower than the critical value of $\tau_\mu$, the null hypothesis that the series is non-stationary should be rejected. Acceptance of the null hypothesis means that the time series has at least one unit root. The test is therefore repeated on the differenced series of $y_t$ if the levels variable is found to be non-stationary. The DF regression now becomes

$$\Delta^2 y_t = \beta_0 + \phi \Delta y_{t-1} \tag{5.12}$$

where $\Delta^2 y = \Delta y_t - \Delta y_{t-1}$.

If $\phi = 0$ in Equation (5.12) is rejected, then the time series $y_t$ is said to be $I(1)$, or has one unit root. However, if we still cannot reject the null, then the DF test must be carried out again, now with the dependent variable expressed in third difference form and the explanatory variable in second difference form. This process is repeated until the null hypothesis of non-stationarity is rejected.

The DF test explained so far is based on the assumption that the time series can be represented by an AR(1) process as in Equation (5.8). There

*Table 5.1* Critical Values for the DF Tests

| Sample Size | Critical Value of $\tau$ | | | Critical Value of $\tau_\mu$ | | | Critical Value of $\tau_\tau$ | | |
|---|---|---|---|---|---|---|---|---|---|
| | Significance Level | | | | | | | | |
| | 0.01 | 0.05 | 0.10 | 0.01 | 0.05 | 0.10 | 0.01 | 0.05 | 0.10 |
| 25 | −2.66 | −1.95 | −1.60 | −3.75 | −3.00 | −2.63 | −4.38 | −3.60 | −3.24 |
| 50 | −2.62 | −1.95 | −1.61 | −3.58 | −2.93 | −2.60 | −4.15 | −3.50 | −3.18 |
| 100 | −2.60 | −1.95 | −1.61 | −3.51 | −2.89 | −2.58 | −4.04 | −3.45 | −3.15 |

Source: Fuller (1976).
Notes: If the DF or ADF regression does not have constant and trend terms, $\tau$ is applicable. If the DF or ADF regression has a constant term but no trend, $\tau_\mu$ is relevant. If both trend and constant terms are present, $\tau_\tau$ should be used.

are other variants of the DF tests, and these are based on the following two equations:

$$\Delta y_t = \phi y_{t-1} + e_t \tag{5.13}$$

$$\Delta y_t = \beta_0 + \lambda T + \phi y_{t-1} + e_t \tag{5.14}$$

where $T$ is a time trend variable.

The null hypothesis is still $\phi = 0$, and the critical values for the DF tests are given in Table 5.1 under the columns $\tau$ and $\tau_\tau$, corresponding to Equation (5.13) and Equation (5.14), respectively. Regression (5.13) is only valid when the overall mean of the series is zero, while regression (5.14) relates to a series that has a deterministic trend. Equation (5.14) encompasses both (5.11) and (5.13). The DF test therefore normally starts from the general specification of (5.14), and restrictions may then be imposed on the coefficients $\beta_0$ and $\lambda$ to decide whether Equation (5.11) or Equation (5.13) is preferred.

### 5.3.3.2  ADF Test

If a simple AR(1) DF regression is used, when in fact the time series $y_t$ follows an AR($p$) process, then the error term will be autocorrelated and this will invalidate the DF statistics. To avoid the problem of autocorrelation in the residuals, the DF regressions may be augmented by including lagged dependent variables. Corresponding to the three DF regressions (5.11), (5.13) and (5.14), the three ADF models are, respectively:

$$\Delta y_t = \beta_0 + \phi y_{t-1} + \sum_{i=1}^{p-1} \gamma_i \Delta y_{t-i} + e_t \tag{5.15}$$

$$\Delta y_t = \phi y_{t-1} + \sum_{i=1}^{p-1} \gamma_i \Delta y_{t-i} + e_t \tag{5.16}$$

$$\Delta y_t = \beta_0 + \lambda T + \phi y_{t-1} + \sum_{i=1}^{p-1} \gamma_i \Delta y_{t-i} + e_t \tag{5.17}$$

To test the null hypothesis, we again calculate the DF $t$ statistic, $\hat{\phi}/[SE(\hat{\phi})]$, which is compared with the corresponding critical values in Table 5.1. It is important to select the appropriate lag length for the dependent variable. Too few lags may result in over-rejection of the null hypothesis when it is true, while too many lags may reduce the power of the test due to loss of degrees of freedom. The criteria for selecting the lag length are $\bar{R}^2$, the Akaike information criterion (AIC) and the Schwarz Bayesian criterion (SBC). The preferred lag length in the ADF regression should maximise $\bar{R}^2$ and minimise both the AIC and SBC.

Although the idea of testing for unit roots is simple, the test procedure is not a straightforward process. In the following subsection, the procedure is illustrated using examples.

### 5.3.4   Phillips-Perron Tests

The distribution theory supporting the Dickey-Fuller tests assumes that the error term in the DF (ADF) regression is identical and independently distributed (IID). In order to use the Dickey-Fuller tests, there should therefore be no autocorrelation or heteroscedasticity present in the estimated residuals, but these assumptions are rather restrictive. Phillips and Perron (1988) have developed a generalisation of the Dickey-Fuller procedure that relaxes these assumptions. The expressions of the Phillips-Perron tests are extremely complex and are beyond the scope of this book. However, many econometric software packages provide standard print-outs of the Phillips-Perron statistics, and the critical values are exactly the same as those of the Dickey-Fuller tests.

### 5.3.5   The Unit Root Testing Procedure

The unit root test starts from the general specification of Equation (5.17), since this encompasses all other testing models, and a test down procedure is then followed to decide on the final DF (ADF) regression from which the DF or ADF statistic is calculated.

*Step 1* Estimate the general AR($p$) model (5.17) using OLS or the Phillips-Perron procedure. The lag length for the dependent variable is determined by $\bar{R}^2$, AIC and SBC.

*Step 2* Test the joint hypothesis (restrictions) that $\lambda = \phi = 0$ using the $F$ statistic. However, since the distribution of the calculated $F$ statistic based on

Table 5.2  Critical Values of the Dickey-Fuller $\Phi_3$ Statistic

|                    | Significance Level | | |
| Sample Size: n | 0.01 | 0.05 | 0.10 |
| --- | --- | --- | --- |
| 25  | 10.61 | 7.42 | 5.91 |
| 50  | 9.31  | 6.73 | 5.61 |
| 100 | 8.73  | 6.49 | 5.47 |
| 500 | 8.34  | 6.30 | 5.36 |

Source: Dickey and Fuller (1981)

the ADF regression is not standard, the critical values of the conventional $F$ statistic cannot be used. Dickey and Fuller (1981) derived the critical values of the $F$ statistic ($\Phi_3$ in Dickey and Fuller, 1981, p. 1063) based on Monte Carlo simulations. Selected critical values of $\Phi_3$ are presented in Table 5.2:

If the joint hypothesis $H_0 : \lambda = \phi = 0$ is accepted in accordance with the critical values in Table 5.2, then go to Step 4.

Step 3  If the null hypothesis in Step 2 is rejected, this suggests that the trend variable is statistically significant and the standard $t$ statistic, $\hat{\phi}/[SE(\hat{\phi})]$, can then be used to test that $\phi = 0$ instead of using the DF $\tau_\tau$ statistic. If the standard $t$ statistic indicates that $\phi = 0$, we conclude that the series is a nonstationary process with a deterministic trend; otherwise we conclude that the series is a trended stationary series.

Step 4  Since the joint null hypothesis $H_0 : \lambda = \phi = 0$ is not rejected in Step 2, this means that the series is a non-stationary series without trend, but with possible drift. This conclusion may be confirmed by looking at the calculated $t$ statistic in Equation (5.17) and comparing it with the corresponding critical value $\tau_\tau$ in Table 5.1. The test is usually terminated at this stage, since the main aim of the DF and ADF tests is to find out whether or not a series is stationary. However, occasionally, we may wish to test whether a non-stationary series is a random walk or random walk with drift. In this case, further tests may be required. Interested readers are referred to Dickey and Fuller's $\Phi_2$ and $\Phi_1$ statistics (Dickey and Fuller, 1981).

### 5.3.6    Seasonal Unit Roots

If seasonal time series are used in tourism demand modelling, testing for seasonal unit roots and seasonal cointegration is necessary. Seasonal unit root tests are much more complicated than the simple unit root tests, since seasonal time series tend to have different unit roots, such as quarterly, semi-annual and annual. If any of these unit roots are present in the time series, then the relevant differencing strategy is needed to achieve stationarity; for example, in the case of a quarterly time series, annual unit roots require annual differencing ($\Delta_4 y_t = y_t - y_{t-4}$) while semi-annual unit roots need semi-annual differencing ($\Delta_2 y_t = y_t - y_{t-2}$). There are a number of seasonal unit root tests available, such as Dickey *et al.* (1984), Osborn *et al.* (1988) and Hylleberg, Engle, Granger and Yoo (HEGY) (1990), but here we only present the HEGY seasonal unit root test. Our discussion focuses on quarterly seasonal data.

The simplest HEGY seasonal unit root test uses the following regression:

$$\Delta_4 y_t = \sum_{i=1}^{4} \pi_i Y_{it-1} + e_t \tag{5.18}$$

where the $Y_{i,t}$s are new series generated from the following:

$$Y_{1t} = y_t + y_{t-1} + y_{t-2} + y_{t-3}$$
$$Y_{2t} = -y_t + y_{t-1} - y_{t-2} + y_{t-3}$$
$$Y_{3t} = -y_t + y_{t-2}$$
$$Y_{4t} = -y_{t-1} + y_{t-3}$$

The HEGY regression may be estimated by OLS. The null hypothesis of seasonal unit roots implies that: $\pi_1 = \pi_2 = \pi_3 = \pi_4 = 0$. Alternatively, we say that the series does not have any unit roots or it is stationary if the null hypothesis is rejected. However, if some of the $\pi$s are zero while others are not, the interpretations will be different. In particular, if only $\pi_1 = 0$, then the series only has normal unit roots, as discussed above. If $\pi_2 = 0$, this suggests that there are semi-annual seasonal unit roots, and $\pi_3 = \pi_4 = 0$ indicates that annual unit roots are present. Testing for $\pi_1 = 0$ and $\pi_2 = 0$ may be achieved by looking at the $t$ statistics, while $\pi_3 = \pi_4 = 0$ can be tested using the $F$ statistic. However, the $t$ and $F$ statistics from the HEGY regression are non-standard. The critical values have to be generated from Monte Carlo simulations, and they can be found in HEGY (1990).

The HEGY test may be generalised by including a constant term and/or deterministic seasonality such that:

$$\Delta_4 y_t = \pi_0 + \sum_{i=1}^{4} \pi_i Y_{it-1} + e_t \tag{5.19}$$

$$\Delta_4 y_t = \sum_{i=1}^{4} \pi_i Y_{it-1} + \sum_{i=1}^{4} b_i Q_{it} + e_t \tag{5.20}$$

where the $Q_{it}$s are seasonal dummies.

The critical values for the HEGY tests where there is either an intercept or deterministic seasonal components are different from those of the simplest

HEGY test relevant to Equation (5.18), and they can also be found in HEGY (1990).

The above HEGY regressions can also be augmented by lagged dependent variables to ensure that the residuals from the HEGY regressions do not exhibit autocorrelation. As in the case of the ADF test, the inclusion of the lagged dependent variables does not affect the distribution of the statistics, and the critical values are the same as those for the model without the augmented terms.

## 5.3.7    Examples of Unit Root Tests

Although most econometric packages have built-in options to test for unit roots, in this subsection we give a step-by-step guide to testing for unit roots. We use the three tourism demand series introduced in Chapter 4 for illustrative purposes. The variables that we wish to test for unit roots are: the log of per capita holiday visits to Spain by UK residents, $LPVSP_t$; the log of UK per capita personal disposable income, $LPPDI_t$; and the log of living costs in Spain relative to UK living costs, adjusted by the corresponding exchange rate, $LRCSP_t$. We present a step-by-step unit root testing procedure for the variable $LPVSP_t$, but for the variables $LPPDI_t$ and $LRCSP_t$ we only report the results, with the intermediate steps omitted.

In Step 1, the general ADF regression corresponding to Equation (5.17) is constructed:

$$\Delta LPVSP_t = \beta_0 + \lambda T + \phi LPVSP_{t-1} + \sum_{i=1}^{p-1} \gamma_i \Delta LPVSP_{t-i} + e_t \qquad (5.21)$$

There are 28 observations available for the estimation of Equation (5.21). We use OLS to estimate the equation, first with five lagged dependent variables, and then we reduce by one lag at a time in order to see what is the appropriate lag length according to $\overline{R}^2$, AIC and SBC. The results are reported in Table 5.3.

Since the ADF regression with four lagged dependent variables maximises $\overline{R}^2$ and minimises the AIC (although lag one minimises the SBC), we set the lag length equal to 4 when we conduct the ADF test.

The second step is to test the joint hypothesis that $\lambda = \phi = 0$ in Equation (5.17). First, let us examine the estimated ADF regression:

$$\Delta LPVSP_t = \underset{(-3.425)}{-3.134} + \underset{(3.169)}{0.047\,T} - \underset{(-3.571)}{0.866\,LPVSP_{t-1}} + \underset{(2.600)}{0.568\,\Delta LPVSP_{t-1}}$$
$$+ \underset{(2.447)}{0.571\,\Delta LPVSP_{t-2}} + \underset{(1.795)}{0.432\,\Delta LPVSP_{t-3}} + \underset{(1.414)}{0.333\,\Delta LPVSP_{t-4}} \qquad (5.22)$$

$$\overline{R}^2 = 0.286 \quad AIC = -3.736 \quad SBC = -3.393 \quad SSR = 0.31$$

The figures in parentheses are $t$ ratios. The ADF statistic in this case is $-3.571$. To test for $\lambda = \phi = 0$, the $F$ test for restrictions discussed in Chapter

Table 5.3 Empirical Results for General ADF Regression (5.17)

| Statistics | Lag Length | | | | |
|---|---|---|---|---|---|
| | 5 | 4 | 3 | 2 | 1 |
| ADF | −2.661 | −3.570 | −3.031 | −2.879 | −2.649 |
| $\overline{R}^2$ | 0.171 | 0.286 | 0.162 | 0.165 | −0.159 |
| AIC | −3.676 | −3.736 | −3.329 | −3.657 | −3.699 |
| SBC | −3.281 | −3.393 | −3.336 | −3.415 | −3.507 |

4, section 3 may be used. In calculating the $F$ statistic we need to estimate both the unrestricted model (5.21) and the restricted model (5.23) below, and obtain the SSRs from both equations.

$$\Delta LPVSP_t = \beta_0 + \sum_{i=1}^{p-1} \gamma_i \Delta LPVSP_{t-i} + e_t \tag{5.23}$$

Here we do not report the estimated results for Equation (5.23), but the sum of squared residuals from (5.22) and the estimated model (5.23) are 0.3194 and 0.5688, respectively. The $F$ statistic is therefore

$$F(r, n-k) = \frac{(SSR_1 - SSR_0)/r}{SSR_0/(n-k)} = \frac{(0.5688 - 0.3194)/2}{0.3194/(24-7)} = 6.636$$

The critical value of the ADF $F$ statistic ($\Phi_3$) with 25 observations in Table 5.2 is 7.24. As the calculated $F$ value is lower than the critical value, this suggests that we should accept the joint hypothesis that $\lambda = \phi = 0$. This result means that the time series $LPVSP_t$ is non-stationary with a possible drift.

Since the restriction that $\lambda = \phi = 0$ cannot be rejected, the next step is to compare the calculated ADF statistic, −3.571, with the corresponding critical value of $\tau_\tau$ in Table 5.1. We can see that the critical values of $\tau_\tau$ with 25 degrees of freedom at the 1% and 5% significance levels are −4.38 and −3.60, respectively. The calculated ADF statistic is higher than these two values, indicating that the series is likely to be non-stationary.

Since the variable $LPVSP_t$ is non-stationary in levels, we need to perform the ADF test based on the differenced series, and the ADF regression now becomes

$$\Delta^2 LPVSP_t = \beta_0 + \lambda T + \phi \Delta LPVSP_{t-1} + \sum_{i=1}^{p-1} \gamma_i \Delta^2 LPVSP_{t-i} + e_t \tag{5.24}$$

where $\Delta^2 LPVSP_t = \Delta LPVSP_t - \Delta LPVSP_{t-1}$.

Equation (5.24) is estimated with different numbers of lagged dependent variables, and the values of $\overline{R}^2$ and AIC and SBC are reported in Table 5.4.

According to the results given in Table 5.4, we can see that the ADF model with no lagged dependent variable, that is, the DF regression, should be used, and the estimated model is presented below:

$$\Delta^2 LPVSP_t = 0.095 - 0.025\ T - 0.906\ \Delta LPVSP_{t-1} \qquad (5.25)$$
$$\phantom{\Delta^2 LPVSP_t = }(1.321)\quad (-0.617)\qquad (-4.382)$$

$$\overline{R}^2 = 0.398 \quad \text{AIC} = -3.507 \quad \text{SBC} = -3.363 \quad \text{SSR} = 0.648$$

Now the joint hypothesis that $\lambda = \phi = 0$ is tested again using the $F$ statistic. After estimating the restricted model with only the constant term in the ADF regression, the value 1.167 is obtained for the SSR. Since we already know the SSR from the unrestricted DF regression (5.25), the $F$ statistic can be calculated as

$$F(r, n-k) = \frac{(SSR_1 - SSR_0)/r}{SSR_0/(n-k)} = \frac{(1.167 - 0.648)/2}{0.648/(27-3)} = 9.611$$

Comparing this $F[2,24]$ statistic with the corresponding critical value of the Dickey-Fuller $F$ statistic ($\Phi_3$) in Table 5.2, we can see that the null hypothesis $\lambda = \phi = 0$ is rejected at the 5% significance level. This suggests that the variable $\Delta LPVSP_t$ is a stationary series without trend but with a possible drift, and this is confirmed by the ADF value of $-4.382$, which is lower than the critical value of the ADF test as given in Table 5.1. If we look at the estimated parameters in Equation (5.25) we can see that the trend variable is insignificant. If the variable $T$ is dropped from the ADF regression, the ADF statistic becomes $-4.395$, and this value is compared with the critical value under the column $\tau_\mu$ in Table 5.1. We can see that the null hypothesis of non-stationarity is clearly rejected, and therefore we conclude that the variable $\Delta LPVSP_t$ is a stationary series.

*Table 5.4* Empirical Results for ADF Regression (5.24)

| Statistics | Lag Length | | | | | |
|---|---|---|---|---|---|---|
| | 5 | 4 | 3 | 2 | 1 | 0 |
| ADF | −2.054 | −2.570 | −2.403 | −2.359 | −2.852 | −4.380 |
| $\overline{R}^2$ | 0.267 | 0.318 | 0.309 | 0.351 | 0.359 | 0.398 |
| AIC | −3.259 | −3.376 | −3.260 | −3.314 | −3.401 | −3.507 |
| SBC | −2.863 | −3.031 | −2.965 | −3.070 | −3.207 | −3.363 |

Table 5.5 ADF Test Results for $LPPDI_t$, $LRCSP_t$ and $LPVSP_t$

| Variable | ADF Statistic | Critical Value | | Lag Length | T and $\beta_0$[1] |
|----------|---------------|------|------|------------|-----------------------|
| | | 0.01 | 0.05 | | |
| $LPPDI_t$ | −3.630 | −4.38 | −3.60 | 1 | T & $\beta_0$ |
| $\Delta LPPDI_t$ | −4.195 | −3.75 | −3.00 | 1 | $\beta_0$ |
| $LRCSP_t$ | −2.226 | −3.75 | −3.00 | 4 | $\beta_0$ |
| $\Delta LRCSP_t$ | −7.212 | −2.66 | −1.95 | 0 | — |
| $LPVSP_t$ | −3.571 | −4.38 | −3.60 | 4 | T & $\beta_0$ |
| $\Delta LPVSP_t$ | −4.395 | −3.75 | −3.00 | 0 | $\beta_0$ |

Note: 1. The tests for the presence of trend and constant terms in the ADF regression are carried out using the ADF, $\Phi_2$ and $\Phi_1$ statistics (Dickey and Fuller, 1981).

The ADF tests are performed in the same way for the other two variables $LPPDI_t$ and $LRCSP_t$. The results are summarised in Table 5.5. Although the test on $LPPDI_t$ shows that the calculated ADF statistic (just) leads to rejection of the null hypothesis of non-stationarity at the 5% level, we are reluctant to conclude that the per capita disposable income variable is a trend stationary variable, due to the small sample size. We can see from the ADF test results that all three variables appear to be integrated of order one.

## 5.4    TEST FOR COINTEGRATION

Once the order of integration of a time series has been identified, we can test for cointegration. The approach followed in this section is that developed by Engle and Granger (1987).

As has already been mentioned in section 5.2, the cointegration relationship requires that all variables in the cointegration regression should be integrated of order one (although stationary series, such as event dummies and a time trend, could also be included). The variables that are integrated of higher orders therefore need to be differenced in order to reduce the order of integration. For example, if a variable is an $I(2)$ series, then the first difference of the variable will be an $I(1)$ series.

Suppose that two variables, $x_t$ and $y_t$, are found to be $I(1)$ series. The cointegration relationship can be tested by first running the following long-run static regression:

$$y_t = \beta_0 + \beta_1 x_t + \varepsilon_t \tag{5.26}$$

The ADF statistic is then employed to test whether the estimated residual, $\hat{\varepsilon}_t$, is stationary or not based on

$$\Delta\hat{\varepsilon} = \phi^*\hat{\varepsilon}_{t-1} + \sum_{i=1}^{p}\gamma_i^*\Delta\hat{\varepsilon}_{t-i} + u_t \qquad (5.27)$$

Note that neither constant nor trend terms should be included in Equation (5.27). The null hypothesis is that the estimated error term in the long-run static model (5.26) is a non-stationary process, that is, $\hat{\varepsilon}_t$ has unit roots. The test statistic is the $t$ value of the estimated coefficient, $\phi^*$. However, the critical values for the Dickey-Fuller tests presented in Table 5.1 cannot be used for the following reasons. First, the OLS estimator tends to minimise the sum of squared residuals from Equation (5.26), which makes the error term $\hat{\varepsilon}_t$ appear to be stationary even if the variables are not cointegrated. Second, the distribution of the $t$ statistic under the null of non-cointegration is affected by the number of variables included in the long-run static model. Therefore, the use of the ADF critical values in Table 5.1 tends to over-reject the null hypothesis of non-cointegration. Using Monte Carlo simulations, MacKinnon (1991) re-calculated the critical values of the ADF regression for differing numbers of $I(1)$ variables included in the long-run static model. Table 5.6 presents some of the critical values calculated from the MacKinnon (1991) simulation.

If the calculated $t$ statistic of the coefficient $\phi^*$ in the ADF regression (5.27) is lower than the critical value in Table 5.6, the null hypothesis of non-cointegration is rejected.

The example considered here is the model of demand for tourism to Spain by UK residents. Suppose we want to test whether a long-run equilibrium (cointegration) relationship exists between the three tourism demand

*Table 5.6* Critical Values for Cointegration ADF Test

| | Sample Size/Significance Level | | | | | | | |
|---|---|---|---|---|---|---|---|---|
| | 25 | | 50 | | 100 | | ∞ | |
| $m^1$ | 0.05 | 0.10 | 0.05 | 0.10 | 0.05 | 0.10 | 0.05 | 0.10 |
| 2 | −3.59 | −3.22 | −3.46 | −3.13 | −3.39 | −3.09 | −3.90 | −3.05 |
| 3 | −4.10 | −3.71 | −3.92 | −3.58 | −3.83 | −3.51 | −3.74 | −3.45 |
| 4 | −4.56 | −4.15 | −4.31 | −3.98 | −4.21 | −3.89 | −4.10 | −3.81 |
| 5 | −5.41 | −4.96 | −5.05 | −4.69 | −4.88 | −4.56 | −4.70 | −4.42 |

Note: 1. $m$ is the number of $I(1)$ variables in the long-run static model.
Source: Calculated from MacKinnon (1991).

variables: $LPVSP_t$, $LPPDI_t$ and $LRCSP_t$. The estimated long-run static model would be

$$LPVSP_t = -23.010 + 2.369\ LPPDI_t - 0.861\ LRCSP_t \tag{5.28}$$

$$R^2 = 0.82 \quad DW = 0.66$$

Notice that the standard errors for the estimated cointegration parameters are omitted. This is because the variables in the static model are non-stationary. Although the OLS estimators are still consistent under the assumption of cointegration, the standard errors are non-standard, and therefore the estimated standard errors cannot be used in significance testing. The diagnostic statistics, apart from the DW statistic, are also not reported, since they are not relevant in the estimation of the long-run static model. The DW statistic can be used as an informal criterion for cointegration; Engle and Granger (1987) called it the Cointegration Durbin-Watson (CIDW). If the value of the CIDW is significantly greater than zero (normally larger than the $R^2$ from the long-run static model), then the error term from the static model is likely to be a stationary process.

The residuals from the above estimated long-run regression are now tested for stationarity. The ADF regressions with different lag lengths are estimated, and the best model is chosen based on $\bar{R}^2$, AIC and SBC. The results are presented below:

$$\Delta\hat{\varepsilon} = \underset{(-3.453)}{-0.842}\ \hat{\varepsilon}_{t-1} + \underset{(1.473)}{0.337}\ \Delta\hat{\varepsilon}_{t-1} + \underset{(2.239)}{0.488}\ \Delta\hat{\varepsilon}_{t-2}$$
$$+ \underset{(2.612)}{0.548}\ \Delta\hat{\varepsilon}_{t-3} + \underset{(0.955)}{0.197}\ \Delta\hat{\varepsilon}_{t-4} \tag{5.29}$$

$$\bar{R}^2 = 0.33 \quad AIC = -3.639 \quad SBC = -3.394$$

where the figures in parentheses are $t$ values.

As we can see from Equation (5.29), the calculated ADF $t$ statistic is $-3.453$[1]. If we compare this value with the critical value where $m = 3$ and with a sample size of 25 in Table 5.6, we can see that this value is greater than the corresponding critical values at the 5% and also 10% levels. We therefore conclude that there is no cointegration relationship between $LPCSP_t$, $LPPDI_t$ and $LRCSP_t$. This conclusion is also supported by the CIDW statistic. The failure to find a cointegration relationship between these variables may well be an indication that some important variables are missing. This is also consistent with the early results in Chapter 4, where we found that the demand for tourism to Spain can best be modelled by a dead start or partial adjustment process.

To summarise, the procedure for testing for a cointegration relationship involves the following two steps:

(1) Test for the order of integration of all the variables in the long-run static model using the ADF test. The cointegration regression requires

that all the explanatory variables are integrated of order one, so variables that have a higher order of integration should be differenced in order to yield $I(1)$ series. Since most tourism demand variables are likely to be integrated of order one, we will find in most cases that the long-run cointegration relationship only relates to $I(1)$ variables.

(2) Use OLS to estimate the long-run static regression of the form

$$y_t = \beta_0 + \beta_1 x_{1t} + \beta_2 x_{2t} + \ldots + \beta_m x_{mt} + \varepsilon_t \tag{5.30}$$

The estimated residuals from Equation (5.30) are then tested for stationarity using the ADF statistic. The calculated $t$ ratio of the coefficient $\phi^*$ with $n$ degrees of freedom in (5.27) is compared with the MacKinnon critical values presented in Table 5.6. If the calculated $t$ value is lower than the corresponding MacKinnon critical value, the null hypothesis of non-cointegration is rejected. Moreover, the Cointegration Durbin-Watson (CIDW) statistic can also be used as a rough guide for cointegration.

# 6 Error Correction Model

## 6.1 COINTEGRATION AND ERROR CORRECTION MECHANISM

Engle and Granger (1987) show that cointegrated variables can always be transformed into an error correction mechanism (ECM) and vice versa. This bi-directional transformation is often called the 'Granger Representation Theorem' and implies that there is some adjustment process that prevents economic variables from drifting too far away from their long-run equilibrium time path. The cointegration and error correction models are very useful in situations where both long-run equilibrium and short-run disequilibrium behaviour are of interest. In tourism demand analysis, the long-run equilibrium behaviour of tourists is expected to be a major concern of policy makers and planners whilst the short-run dynamics are likely to provide useful information for short-term business forecasting and managerial decisions.

This chapter explores how cointegration and error correction are linked, and the ways in which error correction models are estimated within a single equation framework.

### 6.1.1 From ADLM to Error Correction Model

We started in Chapter 4 with the general ADLM of the form

$$y_t = \alpha + \sum_{j=1}^{k}\sum_{i=0}^{p} \beta_{ji} x_{jt-i} + \sum_{i=1}^{p} \phi_i y_{t-i} + \varepsilon_t \tag{6.1}$$

Equation (6.1) can be reparameterised into an ECM of the form

$$\Delta y_t = (current\ and\ lagged\ \Delta x_{jt}s, lagged\ \Delta y_t s)$$

$$-(1-\phi_1)[y_{t-1} - \sum_{j=1}^{k} \xi_j x_{jt-1}] + \varepsilon_t \tag{6.2}$$

We shall demonstrate this in the case of an ADLM(1,1) model, but the derivation can be extended to a general ADLM($p,q$) process. The ADLM(1,1) model takes the form

$$y_t = \alpha + \beta_0 x_t + \beta_1 x_{t-1} + \phi_1 y_{t-1} + \varepsilon_t \tag{6.3}$$

Subtracting $y_{t-1}$ from both sides of Equation (6.3) yields

$$\Delta y_t = \alpha + \beta_0 x_t + \beta_1 x_{t-1} - (1 - \phi_1)y_{t-1} + \varepsilon_t$$

or $\quad \Delta y_t = \alpha + \beta_0 \Delta x_t + (\beta_0 + \beta_1)x_{t-1} - (1 - \phi_1)y_{t-1} + \varepsilon_t. \tag{6.4}$

Equation (6.4) can be further reparameterised to give

$$\Delta y_t = \beta_0 \Delta x_t - (1 - \phi_1)[y_{t-1} - k_0 - k_1 x_{t-1}] + \varepsilon_t \tag{6.5}$$

where $k_0 = \alpha / (1 - \phi_1)$, $k_1 = (\beta_0 + \beta_1)/(1 - \phi_1)$.

The parameter $\beta_0$ is called the impact parameter, $(1 - \phi_1)$ is the feedback effect, $k_0$ and $k_1$ are the long-run response coefficients, and the combination of the terms in the square brackets is called the error correction mechanism. Since the coefficient $\phi_1$ is less than 1 and greater than 0, the coefficient of the error correction term, $-(1 - \phi_1)$, is greater than $-1$ and less than 0. This implies that the system will adjust itself toward equilibrium by removing $(1 - \phi_1)$ of a unit from the error made in the previous period. Although Equations (6.3) and (6.5) are different in their functional forms, they actually represent the same data generating process.

Equation (6.5) has the following advantages over Equation (6.3):

First, Equation (6.5) reflects both the long-run and short-run effects in a single model. The specification indicates that changes in $y_t$ depend on changes in $x_t$ and the disequilibrium error in the previous period.

Second, Equation (6.5) overcomes the problem of spurious correlation by employing differenced variables. It can be easily shown that the term $[y_{t-1} - k_0 - k_1 x_{t-1}]$ is a stationary process if $y_t$ and $x_t$ are cointegrated. Therefore, it is unlikely that the residuals in (6.5) will be correlated. Moreover, the use of (6.5) avoids the problems associated with the growth rate model in which only differenced data are used.

Third, the ECM fits in well with the general-to-specific methodology. Since the ECM is another way of writing the general ADLM, acceptance of the ADLM is equivalent to acceptance of the error correction model.

Fourth, the estimation of Equation (6.5) reduces the problem of data mining, since in the model reduction process one is permitted to eliminate the differenced variables according to statistical significance. However, the elimination of lagged levels variables is not permitted since they represent the cointegration relationship. For example, suppose that a cointegration relationship is found between the variables $y_t$, $x_t$ and $z_t$. In the estimation of the ECM in which both differenced and lagged levels forms of $y$, $x$ and $z$ are involved, the researcher is free to eliminate $\Delta y$, $\Delta x$ and/or $\Delta z$, but the lagged levels variables $y$, $x$ and $z$ should always appear in the final ECM.

Finally, estimation of the general ADLM (6.3), which involves a large number of explanatory variables, tends to suffer from the problem of multicollinearity, that is, several of the explanatory variables are likely to be highly correlated, which will result in abnormally large standard errors and hence the calculated $t$ statistics cannot be used as a reliable criterion for hypothesis testing. However, the corresponding variables in the ECM are less likely to be highly correlated. In fact, Engle and Granger (1987) show that the explanatory variables in the ECM are almost orthogonal (that is, the correlation is almost zero). This is a desirable property, as the $t$ statistics provide a reliable guide for the elimination of differenced variables. Consequently, it is easier for a researcher to arrive at a sufficiently parsimonious final preferred model using the testing down procedure of the general-to-specific methodology.

### 6.1.2   From ECM to Cointegration Regression

Engle and Granger (1987) demonstrate that if a pair of economic variables is cointegrated, they can always be represented by an ECM and vice versa. This can be shown by the following transformation. The long-run steady state suggests that $y_t = y_{t-1}$ and $x_t = x_{t-1}$, that is, $\Delta y_t = \Delta x_t = 0$. Therefore, the ECM (6.5) becomes

$$0 = -(1 - \phi_1)[y_t - k_0 - k_1 x_t]$$

$$\text{i.e.,} \quad y_t = k_0 + k_1 x_t \tag{6.6}$$

Equation (6.6) is the long-run cointegration regression with $k_0$ and $k_1$ being the long-run cointegration coefficients. Now $k_0 = \alpha / (1 - \phi_1)$ and $k_1 = (\beta_0 + \beta_1)/(1 - \phi_1)$, and therefore the long-run cointegration coefficients (vector) can be obtained from the estimates of the general ADLM model (6.1).

### 6.2   ESTIMATING THE ECM

Various procedures for estimating the single equation ECM have been proposed. In this section three estimation methods are explained: the Engle-Granger two-stage, the Wickens-Breusch one-stage and the ADLM procedures.

### 6.2.1   Engle-Granger Two-Stage Approach

In their seminal paper Engle and Granger (1987) suggest testing for the long-run equilibrium relationship between a set of economic variables and modelling their short-run dynamics via an ECM in a two-step procedure. The first step is to test for a cointegration relationship between the two $I(1)$ variables, $y_t$ and $x_t$, based on the static long-run equilibrium regression:

$$y_t = k_0 + k_1 x_t + \varepsilon_t \tag{6.7}$$

If the estimated residual term is a stationary process, $y_t$ and $x_t$ are said to be cointegrated. According to Stock (1987) if $y_t$ and $x_t$ are cointegrated, OLS estimates of the cointegration vector $(k_0, k_1)$ will be 'super-consistent'.

After confirming the acceptance of a cointegration relationship, the second step is to estimate the ECM

$$\Delta y_t = \sum_{i=0}^{p} \beta_i \Delta x_{t-i} + \sum_{j=1}^{p} \phi_j \Delta y_{t-j} - \lambda \hat{\varepsilon}_{t-1} + u_t \tag{6.8}$$

where $\hat{\varepsilon}_{t-1} = y_{t-1} - \hat{k}_0 - \hat{k}_1 x_{t-1}$ is the OLS residuals from (6.7).

As we can see, the error correction equation (6.8) consists of differenced variables with appropriate lags, and the lag structure is determined by experimentation. In this stage the short-run parameters are obtained. According to Engle and Granger (1987), the estimates of the short-run parameters are consistent and efficient. The estimated standard errors of the parameters in the second stage are the true standard errors, and therefore the model can be used for forecasting and policy evaluation.

One of the concerns about the Engle and Granger two-stage approach is its first step. As we already know that the variables in the cointegration regression are $I(1)$ variables, the estimated standard errors of the cointegration coefficients are not standard normal. That is why many researchers do not even bother to report them in their empirical studies. Moreover, the Engle-Granger two-stage approach does not prove that the cointegration regression is really a long-run one. This is an assumption and cannot be tested statistically. Researchers therefore have to have a good justification that the variables in the cointegration regression represent the long-run equilibrium relationship, and normally the justification is the relevant economic theory. Another problem associated with the Engle-Granger method is that it tends to produce biased estimates of the long-run coefficients in small samples.

## 6.2.2 Wickens-Breusch One-Stage Approach

It has been shown by Wickens and Breusch (1988) that although the estimates of the short-run ECM of the Engle-Granger two-stage approach are consistent and efficient in large samples, they are biased in small samples. An alternative estimation method which overcomes this problem has been suggested by Wickens and Breusch, and involves estimating both the long-run and short-run parameters in a single step using OLS. The estimation is based on

$$\Delta y_t = \alpha + \sum_{i=0}^{p-1} \beta_i \Delta x_{t-i} + \sum_{i=1}^{p-1} \phi_i \Delta y_{t-i} + \lambda_1 y_{t-1} + \lambda_2 x_{t-1} + u_t \tag{6.9}$$

Again the lag lengths of the differenced variables are determined by the statistical significance of the estimated coefficients in (6.9). After estimating (6.9), the long-run cointegration parameters may be derived from

$$y_t = -\frac{\hat{\alpha}}{\hat{\lambda}_1} - \frac{\hat{\lambda}_2}{\hat{\lambda}_1} x_t$$

or   $y_t = k_0^* + k_1^* x_t$ $\qquad (6.10)$

where $k_0^* = -\hat{\alpha}/\hat{\lambda}_1$ and $k_1^* = -\hat{\lambda}_2/\hat{\lambda}_1$.

Wickens and Breusch (1988) show that the OLS estimates of both the long-run and short-run parameters in Equation (6.9) are consistent, efficient and unbiased.

## 6.2.3    ADLM Approach

This method of estimating the ECM was developed by Pesaran and Shin (1995), and involves estimating both the long-run cointegration relationship and the short-run ECM based on a general ADLM. Our discussion of this estimation approach is based on Equation (6.3), but the principle is the same for the more general form of the ADLM, as given in Equation (6.1).

The ADLM approach first estimates Equation (6.3) with extended lag structure using OLS.

$$y_t = \alpha + \beta_0 x_t + \beta_1 x_{t-1} + \ldots + \beta_p x_{t-P} + \phi_1 y_{t-1} + \phi_2 y_{t-2} + \ldots + \phi_P y_{t-P} + \varepsilon_t \tag{6.11}$$

The optimal lag structure of the ADLM from which the ECM is derived is determined by the following criteria: $\bar{R}^2$, *AIC* and *SBC* as described in Chapter 4. The long-run cointegration regression is $y_t = \hat{k}_0 + \hat{k}_1 x_t$, where

$$\hat{k}_1 = \frac{\hat{\beta}_0 + \hat{\beta}_1 + \ldots + \hat{\beta}_p}{1 - \hat{\phi}_1 - \hat{\phi}_2 - \ldots - \hat{\phi}_p} \tag{6.12}$$

and   $$\hat{k}_0 = \frac{\hat{\alpha}}{1 - \hat{\phi}_1 - \hat{\phi}_2 - \ldots - \hat{\phi}_p} \tag{6.13}$$

The corresponding short-run ECM may be derived from Equation (6.11). Since

$$\Delta y_t = y_t - y_{t-1}$$
$$y_t = \Delta y_t + y_{t-1}$$
Also   $x_t = \Delta x_t + x_{t-1}$

Substituting these relationships into Equation (6.11) and rearranging the terms gives the following ECM representation:

$$\Delta y_t = \sum_{i=0}^{p-1} \beta_i^* \Delta x_{t-i} + \sum_{i=1}^{p-1} \phi_i^* \Delta y_{t-i} - \lambda EC_{t-1} + \varepsilon_t \tag{6.14}$$

where $\lambda = 1 - \hat{\phi}_1 - \hat{\phi}_2 - \ldots - \hat{\phi}_{p-1}$, $EC_{t-1} = y_{t-1} - \alpha - \beta_1 x_{t-1}$, which is the error correction term, and the coefficients $\beta_i^*$ and $\phi_i^*$ are calculated from:

$$\beta_0^* = \hat{\beta}_p + \hat{\beta}_{p-1} + \ldots + \hat{\beta}_2 + \hat{\beta}_1$$
$$\beta_1^* = \hat{\beta}_p + \hat{\beta}_{p-1} + \ldots + \hat{\beta}_2$$
$$\vdots$$
$$\beta_{p-1}^* = \hat{\beta}_p$$

and
$$\phi_1^* = \hat{\phi}_p + \hat{\phi}_{p-1} + \ldots + \hat{\phi}_3 + \hat{\phi}_2$$
$$\phi_2^* = \hat{\phi}_p + \hat{\phi}_{p-1} + \ldots + \hat{\phi}_3$$
$$\vdots$$
$$\phi_{p-1}^* = \hat{\phi}_p$$

The $\hat{\beta}_i$s and $\hat{\phi}_i$s are the estimated parameters from the ADLM (6.11). The standard errors of these estimated coefficients can be calculated using the formula provided by Bewley (1979).

As noted by Pesaran and Shin (1995), however, the ADLM approach also tends to suffer from small-sample bias, although the consistency improves with increasing sample size.

## 6.3    WORKED EXAMPLES

In this section we use inbound tourism demand data for South Korea to illustrate the error correction modelling procedure. The demand for tourism to Korea by two major tourism-generating countries, the UK and USA, is examined. The total number of tourist arrivals by country ranging from 1962 to 1994 (33 observations) is used as the dependent variable and the data are obtained from the Korea National Tourism Corporation (KNTC) Annual Statistical Report jointly published by KNTC and the Ministry of Culture and Sports. Since the tourist arrivals variable includes both business and leisure travellers, the gross domestic product (GDP) of the tourism-generating country is used as the income variable, rather than personal disposable income. To reflect the influence of business activities on tourism demand, a trade volume variable measured by the sum of total imports and exports between Korea and the tourist-generating country is also included in the model. The tourism price variable is measured by the relative consumer price index (CPI) of Korea to that of the tourism-generating country, adjusted by the corresponding exchange rate (see Equation (6.16)). The data are provided in Table A6.1 in Appendix 6.1.

### 6.3.1 Testing for Cointegration

The proposed long-run demand model is of the form

$$\ln TA_{it} = \alpha_0 + \alpha_1 \ln GDP_{it} + \alpha_2 \ln TV_{it} + \alpha_3 \ln RCPI_{it} + u_t \qquad (6.15)$$

where $TA_{it}$ is total tourist arrivals in South Korea from country $i$ ($i = 1$ represents UK and $i = 2$ represents USA) in year $t$; $GDP_{it}$ is the index of the real gross domestic product of origin $i$ in year $t$; $TV_{it}$ is real trade volume measured by total imports and exports between South Korea and country $i$ in year $t$; $RCPI_{it}$ is the tourism price variable calculated from

$$RCPI_{it} = \frac{CPI_{Korea,t} / EX_{Korea/i,t}}{CPI_{it}} \qquad (6.16)$$

This takes into account the effects of both relative inflation and the exchange rate on the demand for tourism to Korea.

The null hypothesis is that the variables in Equation (6.15) are cointegrated. The integration orders (or the numbers of unit roots) of the variables are examined prior to the cointegration test. In testing for unit roots, the Dickey-Fuller and Phillips-Perron tests discussed in Chapter 5 are used. The results of these tests show that all the series (in logarithms) are likely to be $I(1)$ with the possibility that the USA GDP is a trended stationary process. Since a trended stationary series still needs to be differenced to get rid of the trend, the inclusion of this variable in the cointegration regression is not unjustified.

The long-run cointegration regressions are estimated using OLS as

$$\text{UK:} \quad \ln TA_{1t} = -4.257 + 2.097 \ln GDP_{1t} + 0.473 \ln TV_{1t} \\ - 0.213 \ln RCPI_{1t} \qquad (6.17)$$

$$R^2 = 0.995 \quad CIDW = 1.516$$

$$\text{USA:} \quad \ln TA_{2t} = -6.158 + 1.655 \ln GDP_{2t} + 0.576 \ln TV_{2t} \\ - 0.861 \ln RCPI_{2t} \qquad (6.18)$$

$$R^2 = 0.971 \quad CIDW = 0.490$$

As a rough guide, if there is a cointegration relationship between a set of variables, the CIDW statistic in the cointegration regression should be

*Table 6.1* Dickey-Fuller (DF)
and Phillips-Perron (PP) Test Results

| Tests | UK | USA |
| --- | --- | --- |
| DF | –4.733(0) | –3.490(3) |
| PP | –4.707(3) | –3.188(3) |

*Note:* Figures in parentheses are the lag lengths
used in the tests.

greater than its R-squared value. According to this criterion the variables in
the UK model are likely to be cointegrated whilst those in the USA model
are not. This can be further confirmed by the Dickey-Fuller and Phillips-
Perron tests on the OLS residuals from Equations (6.17) and (6.18). The
results are presented in Table 6.1.

The critical value for non-cointegration with four $I(1)$ variables in the
long-run model with 25 degrees of freedom is –4.56 at the 5% level and
–4.15 at the 10% level. The results in Table 6.1 show that the tourism
demand variables are cointegrated in the UK model, but not in the USA
equation.

The long-run equations (6.17 and 6.18) show that all the demand elasticities are correctly signed and significant at the 5% level. The income elasticities are positive and greater than 1 suggesting that travelling to South Korea
is a luxury for tourists from the UK and USA. However, since the variables
in the USA long-run model are not cointegrated, the estimated long-run
elasticities are biased.

The significance of the trade volume variable is not surprising since a
relatively large proportion (about 20%) of tourist arrivals in South Korea
is related to business travel. According to Lee *et al.* (1996), business travellers dominated Korean inbound tourism in the 1960s, and they paved
the way for the surge of pleasure tourists to South Korea since the early
1970s.

The relative price elasticity in the UK and USA long-run models is less
than 1. This indicates that tourism demand is price inelastic.

### 6.3.2 Error Correction Models

This section presents the Engle and Granger two-stage, the Wickens and
Breusch one-stage and the ADLM procedures for ECM estimation. Although
a cointegration relationship does not exist in the USA model, we still try to
model the short-run dynamics using the ECM. This will allow us to compare
the consequences of ECMs with and without cointegrated variables.

### 6.3.2.1    *Engle-Granger Two-Stage Approach*

As mentioned earlier, if a set of variables is found to be cointegrated, the cointegration regression can always be transformed into an error correction model of the form

$$\Delta \ln TA_{it} = \beta_0 + \beta_1 \Delta \ln GDP_{it} + \beta_2 \Delta \ln TV_{it} + \beta_3 \Delta \ln RCPI_{it} + \delta \hat{u}_{t-1} + \varepsilon_t \quad (6.19)$$

where $\hat{u}_{t-1}$ is the estimated error term obtained from the cointegration regression Equation (6.15) and $\Delta$ is the first difference operator. The coefficient of $\hat{u}_{t-1}$ is expected to be negative and significant. In estimating Equation (6.19) lagged dependent and independent variables are also included and a 'test-down' procedure is employed repeatedly until the most parsimonious specification is achieved.

The initial estimates of the general ECMs for the UK and USA are given in Equations (6.20) and (6.21):

UK:   $\Delta \ln TA_{1t} = \underset{(1.736)}{0.048} - \underset{(-0.349)}{0.072} \Delta \ln TA_{1t-1} + \underset{(1.645)}{0.718} \Delta \ln GDP_{1t}$

$\qquad + \underset{(0.220)}{0.126} \Delta \ln GDP_{1t-1} + \underset{(4.837)}{0.340} \Delta \ln TV_{1t}$

$\qquad + \underset{(0.993)}{0.074} \Delta \ln TV_{1t-1} + \underset{(0.417)}{0.055} \Delta \ln RCPI_{1t}$ $\qquad (6.20)$

$\qquad - \underset{(2.201)}{0.280} \Delta \ln RCPI_{1t-1} - \underset{(-1.891)}{0.384} \hat{u}_{1t-1}$

$R^2 = 0.608 \quad \sigma = 0.082$

USA:   $\Delta \ln TA_{2t} = \underset{(-0.411)}{-0.017} + \underset{(1.450)}{0.224} \Delta \ln TA_{2t-1} - \underset{(-0.419)}{0.431} \Delta \ln GDP_{2t}$

$\qquad + \underset{(0.488)}{0.561} \Delta \ln GDP_{2t-1} + \underset{(3.168)}{0.858} \Delta \ln TV_{2t}$

$\qquad + \underset{(0.368)}{0.092} \Delta \ln TV_{2t-1} - \underset{(-1.827)}{0.665} \Delta \ln RCPI_{2t}$ $\qquad (6.21)$

$\qquad - \underset{(-0.067)}{0.026} \Delta \ln RCPI_{2t-1} - \underset{(-3.056)}{0.561} \hat{u}_{2t-1}$

$R^2 = 0.610 \quad \sigma = 0.105$

The values in parentheses are $t$ ratios. The insignificant variables judged by the $t$ values are eliminated one by one starting with the most insignificant ones until all remaining coefficients are statistically significant. The final ECMs for the UK and USA are given as below:

UK:   $\Delta \ln TA_{1t} = \underset{(2.595)}{0.052} + \underset{(1.887)}{0.752} \Delta \ln GDP_{1t} + \underset{(5.553)}{0.341} \Delta \ln TV_{1t}$

$\qquad - \underset{(-2.176)}{0.239} \Delta \ln RCPI_{1t-1} - \underset{(-2.976)}{0.468} \hat{u}_{1t-1}$ $\qquad (6.22)$

$$R^2 = 0.584 \qquad \sigma = 0.078 \qquad \chi^2_{Auto}(2) = 1.467$$

$$\chi^2_{Norm}(2) = 0.952 \quad \chi^2_{ARCH}(1) = 0.049 \qquad \chi^2_{White}(14) = 15.720$$

$$\chi^2_{RESET}(2) = 1.388 \quad F_{Forecast}(5,21) = 0.260$$

$$\text{USA:} \quad \Delta \ln TA_{2t} = \underset{(-0.357)}{-0.013} + \underset{(1.530)}{1.356 \Delta \ln GDP_{2t-1}} + \underset{(4.195)}{0.823 \Delta \ln TV_{2t}}$$
$$\underset{(-2.142)}{- 0.666 \Delta \ln RCPI_{2t}} - \underset{(-3.155)}{0.440 \, \hat{u}_{2t-1}} \tag{6.23}$$

$$R^2 = 0.554 \qquad \sigma = 0.104 \qquad \chi^2_{Auto}(2) = 3.340$$

$$\chi^2_{Norm}(2) = 8.843 ** \qquad \chi^2_{ARCH}(1) = 0.585 \qquad \chi^2_{White}(14) = 24.440 **$$

$$\chi^2_{RESET}(2) = 23.292 *** \quad F_{Forecast}(5,21) = 0.886$$

** and *** denote that the statistics are significant at the 5% and 1% levels, respectively. The diagnostic statistics are explained in Chapter 4.

The estimation results given in Equations (6.22) and (6.23) show that the UK short-run ECM passes all the diagnostic statistics whilst the USA equivalent fails the normality, homoscedasticity and the functional form tests. This is not surprising since no cointegration relationship was found in the USA long-run model based on the Engle-Granger procedure. In practice, if a cointegration relationship does not exist between a set of economic variables, the ECM specification should not be used. The solution to this problem is either to try an alternative modelling strategy or to re-specify the long-run model in terms of a different functional form and/or inclusion of new explanatory variables based on economic theory.

The estimated coefficients in the short-run error correction model are short-run demand elasticities. Since the USA ECM is not statistically acceptable, there is no point in trying to interpret the economic meanings of the coefficients. However, the estimated demand elasticities in the UK ECM are unbiased, efficient and consistent, and therefore economic interpretations of the estimated coefficients are possible. The short-run income and trade elasticities in Equation (6.22) are lower than those in the long-run model, as expected on the base of economic theory, but the short-run price elasticity of the demand for Korean tourism by UK residents remains more or less the same as that in the long-run model. This suggests that the relative cost of living for UK tourists in Korea has a similar influence on both long-run and short-run decision making for UK residents. The coefficient of the error correction term in the UK ECM is correctly signed and significant at the 1% level as expected.

### 6.3.2.2   Wickens-Breusch One-Stage Approach

The general tourism demand models are first estimated using the Wickens-Breusch method, based on the same data set, and the results are given below:

UK:   $\Delta \ln TA_{1t} = \underset{(-0.939)}{-1.339} - \underset{(-0.689)}{0.146} \Delta \ln TA_{1t-1} + \underset{(1.230)}{0.638} \Delta \ln GDP_{1t}$

$\qquad \underset{(-0.220)}{- 0.021} \Delta \ln GDP_{1t-1} + \underset{(3.935)}{0.297} \Delta \ln TV_{1t}$

$\qquad \underset{(1.012)}{+ 0.080} \Delta \ln TV_{1t-1} + \underset{(0.702)}{0.115} \Delta \ln RCPI_{1t}$

$\qquad \underset{(-1.965)}{- 0.290} \Delta \ln RCPI_{1t-1} - \underset{(-1.630)}{0.342} \ln TA_{1t-1}$

$\qquad \underset{(1.414)}{+ 0.752} \ln GDP_{1t-1} + \underset{(1.369)}{0.143} \ln TV_{1t-1}$

$\qquad \underset{(-0.506)}{- 0.058} \ln RCPI_{1t-1}$

$R^2 = 0.656 \quad \sigma = 0.083$

USA:   $\Delta \ln TA_{2t} = \underset{(-2.150)}{-4.908} - \underset{(-0.164)}{0.028} \Delta \ln TA_{2t-1} - \underset{(-0.932)}{0.957} \Delta \ln GDP_{2t}$

$\qquad \underset{(0.100)}{+ 0.116} \Delta \ln GDP_{2t-1} + \underset{(2.274)}{0.634} \Delta \ln TV_{2t}$

$\qquad \underset{(-0.165)}{- 0.045} \Delta \ln TV_{2t-1} - \underset{(-0.951)}{0.353} \Delta \ln RCPI_{2t}$

$\qquad \underset{(0.652)}{+ 0.262} \Delta \ln RCPI_{2t-1} - \underset{(-3.151)}{0.561} \ln TA_{2t-1}$

$\qquad \underset{(1.313)}{+ 0.084} \ln GDP_{2t-1} + \underset{(1.701)}{0.263} \ln TV_{2t-1}$

$\qquad \underset{(-2.810)}{- 0.821} \ln RCPI_{2t-1}$

$R^2 = 0.727 \quad \sigma = 0.095$

Since some of the coefficients in the models are insignificant, a model reduction process is needed. Following the general-to-specific methodology, the insignificant variables are eliminated based on the $t$ statistic values and the final ECMs become:

UK:   $\Delta \ln TA_{1t} = \underset{(-0.837)}{-0.858} + \underset{(4.156)}{0.281} \Delta \ln TV_{1t} - \underset{(-2.669)}{0.443} \ln TA_{1t-1}$

$\qquad \underset{(1.488)}{+ 0.604} \ln GDP_{1t-1} + \underset{(2.376)}{0.208} \ln TV_{1t-1} \qquad\qquad (6.24)$

$\qquad \underset{(-2.305)}{- 0.178} \ln RCPI_{1t-1}$

$R^2 = 0.541 \qquad\qquad \sigma = 0.082 \qquad\qquad \chi^2_{Auto}(2) = 0.717$

$\chi^2_{Norm}(2) = 0.974 \quad \chi^2_{ARCH}(1) = 0.156 \qquad \chi^2_{White}(20) = 27.363$

$\chi^2_{RESET}(2) = 4.358 \quad F_{Forecast}(5, 21) = 0.137$

USA:   $\Delta \ln TA_{2t} = \underset{(-2.510)}{-4.171} + \underset{(2.209)}{0.450} \Delta \ln TV_{2t} + \underset{(1.600)}{0.135} \Delta \ln RCPI_{2t-1}$

$\qquad \underset{(-3.791)}{- 0.531} \ln TA_{2t-1} + \underset{(1.875)}{0.836} \ln GDP_{2t-1} \qquad\qquad (6.25)$

$\qquad \underset{(1.875)}{+ 0.235} \ln TV_{2t-1} - \underset{(-3.210)}{0.696} \ln RCPI_{2t-1}$

$$R^2 = 0.703 \qquad \sigma = 0.088 \qquad \chi^2_{Auto}(2) = 1.865$$

$$\chi^2_{Norm}(2) = 0.004 \qquad \chi^2_{ARCH}(1) = 2.659 \qquad \chi^2_{White}(26) = 29.438$$

$$\chi^2_{RESET}(2) = 22.235^{***} \qquad F_{Forecast}(5,19) = 0.467$$

Again, the UK model is highly satisfactory in terms of the diagnostic statistics, whereas the USA model suffers from the same problems as those in the Engle-Granger two-stage model. Although the coefficient of the variable $\Delta \ln RCPI_{2t-1}$ is not significant at the 5% level, we keep it in the final specification since the elimination of this variable will drastically reduce the explanatory power of the model. To obtain the long-run parameters, Equations (6.24) and (6.25) can be transformed to give:

UK: $\quad \Delta \ln TA_{1t} = 0.304 \Delta \ln TV_{it} - 0.443(\ln TA_{1t-1} + 1.937$
$$- 1.363 \ln GDP_{1t-1} - 0.469 \ln TV_{1t-1} \qquad (6.26)$$
$$+ 0.402 \ln RCPI_{1t-1})$$

USA: $\quad \Delta \ln TA_{2t} = 0.450 \Delta \ln TV_{2t} + 0.135 \Delta \ln RCPI_{2t-1}$
$$- 0.530(\ln TA_{2t-1} + 7.870 - 1.577 \ln GDP_{2t-1} \qquad (6.27)$$
$$- 0.443 \ln TV_{2t-1} + 1.313 \ln RCPI_{2t-1})$$

Theoretically, the Engle-Granger method and the Wickens-Breusch approach should produce similar results for large samples if the cointegration relationship exists in the levels variables. However, since the lagged levels variables in the parentheses in the UK model (6.24) represent the cointegration relationship and the combination of these levels variables tends to be stationary, the OLS estimates of the long-run parameters in this method are more reliable. In contrast, OLS estimation in the first stage of the Engle-Granger method tends to be biased and these biases are likely to be carried over to the second stage of the estimation. For the USA model, since no cointegration relationship has been found, the Wickens-Breusch ECM still suffers from similar problems to those of the corresponding Engle-Granger ECM.

The long-run relationships for the UK and USA can therefore be derived as:

UK: $\quad \ln TA_{1t-1} = -1.937 + 1.363 \ln GDP_{1t-1} + 0.469 \ln TV_{1t-1}$
$$- 0.402 \ln RCPI_{1t-1} \qquad (6.28)$$

USA: $\quad \ln TA_{2t-1} = -7.870 + 1.577 \ln GDP_{2t-1} + 0.443 \ln TV_{2t-1}$
$$- 1.313 \ln RCPI_{2t-1} \qquad (6.29)$$

Comparing Equations (6.28) and (6.29) with (6.17) and (6.18), respectively, we see that the long-run parameters estimated from the Engle-Granger method are not the same as those from the Wickens-Breusch approach for both the UK and USA models.

To conclude, the Engle-Granger and the Wickens-Breusch cointegration-ECM approaches should produce similar results for large samples. In the case of small samples, the Wickens-Breusch method is preferred due to the consistent and unbiased nature of the estimation.

### 6.3.2.3   ADLM Method

Since the data are annual, we introduce one lag for each of the variables in the general ADLM[1], that is:

$$\ln TA_{it} = \alpha + \beta_{11} \ln GDP_{it} + \beta_{12} \ln GPD_{it-1} + \beta_{21} \ln TV_{it} + \beta_{22} \ln TV_{it-1}$$
$$+ \beta_{31} \ln RCPI_{it} + \beta_{32} \ln RCPI_{it-1} + u_t \tag{6.30}$$

The estimates of the ADLM (6.30) using the UK and USA data are given below[2]:

UK:   $\ln TA_{1t} = \underset{(-1.089)}{-1.321} + \underset{(3.116)}{0.544 \ln TA_{1t-1}} + \underset{(1.217)}{0.582 \ln GDP_{1t}}$

$\qquad + \underset{(0.342)}{0.194 \ln GPD_{1t-1}} + \underset{(4.017)}{0.281 \ln TV_{1t}}$

$\qquad - \underset{(-0.956)}{0.073 \ln TV_{1t-1}} - \underset{(-0.027)}{0.004 \ln RCPI_{1t}} \tag{6.31}$

$\qquad - \underset{(-1.089)}{0.144 \ln RCPI_{1t-1}}$

$R^2 = 0.997 \qquad \sigma = 0.082 \qquad \chi^2_{Auto}(1) = 0.022$

$\chi^2_{Norm}(2) = 0.920 \qquad \chi^2_{Hetro}(1) = 1.912^3 \qquad \chi^2_{RESET}(1) = 0.886$

USA:   $\ln TA_{2t} = \underset{(-3.290)}{-5.140} + \underset{(6.238)}{0.617 \ln TA_{2t-1}} - \underset{(-0.772)}{0.644 \ln GDP_{2t}}$

$\qquad + \underset{(1.641)}{1.555 \ln GDP_{2t-1}} + \underset{(1.957)}{0.440 \ln TV_{2t}}$

$\qquad - \underset{(-1.614)}{0.334 \ln TV_{2t-1}} - \underset{(-1.434)}{0.428 \ln RCPI_{2t}} \tag{6.32}$

$\qquad - \underset{(-0.836)}{0.289 \ln RCPI_{2t-1}}$

$R^2 = 0.994 \qquad \sigma = 0.091 \qquad \chi^2_{Auto}(1) = 0.889$

$\chi^2_{Norm}(2) = 7.950** \qquad \chi^2_{Hetro}(1) = 4.279** \qquad \chi^2_{RESET}(1) = 8.914***$

The ADLM method uses the full lag structure to derive the long-run and short-run parameters, and the insignificant parameters are therefore not eliminated. However, Pesaran and Shin (1995) show that the optimal lag structure can be determined by a number of criteria such as the Akaike information criterion (AIC), Schwarz Bayesian criterion (SBC) and the Hannan-Quinn criterion (HQC). For illustrative purposes we impose the restriction that lag length equals one.

The results show that the UK model is well specified according to the diagnostics, but the USA model still appears to have problems with regard to functional form, heteroscedasticity and normality. Based on the formulae (6.12) and (6.13), we can derive the long-run static parameters. Assuming there are no dynamics in the long run, Equation (6.31) becomes

$$(1-0.544)\ln TA_{1t} = -1.321 + (0.582 + 0.194)\ln GDP_{1t} + (0.281$$
$$- 0.072)\ln TV_{1t} - (0.004 + 0.144)\ln RCPI_{1t}$$

If both sides of the above equation are divided by (1 – 0.544), we get

$$\ln TA_{1t} = -2.897 + 1.702\ln GDP_{1t} + 0.456\ln TV_{1t} - 0.322\ln RCPI_{1t} \quad (6.33)$$

This is the long-run model for the UK. Using the same procedure, the USA long-run model can be derived as follows:

$$\ln TA_{2t} = -13.425 + 2.380\ln GDP_{2t} + 0.277\ln TV_{2t} - 1.871\ln RCPI_{2t} \quad (6.34)$$

Although the standard errors (or $t$ ratios) of the coefficients in (6.33) and (6.34) are omitted, they can be calculated according to the method proposed by Bewley (1979).

The corresponding ECMs are estimated based on the estimated long-run regressions (6.33) and (6.34).

UK: 
$$\Delta \ln TA_{1t} = \underset{(-1.089)}{-1.321} + \underset{(1.216)}{0.582}\,\Delta \ln GDP_{1t} + \underset{(4.017)}{0.281}\Delta \ln TV_{1t}$$
$$\underset{(-0.026)}{-0.004}\,\Delta \ln RCPI_{1t-1} - \underset{(-2.612)}{0.456}\,E\hat{C}_{1t-1} \quad (6.35)$$

where $E\hat{C}_{1t-1} = \ln TA_{1t-1} + 2.897 - 1.702\ln GDP_{1t-1} - 0.456\ln TV_{1t-1} + 0.322\ln RCPI_{1t-1}$

USA: 
$$\Delta \ln TA_{2t} = \underset{(-3.290)}{-5.140} - \underset{(-0.772)}{0.644}\,\Delta \ln GDP_{2t} + \underset{(1.957)}{0.440}\Delta \ln TV_{2t}$$
$$- \underset{(-1.433)}{0.428}\,\Delta \ln RCPI_{2t-1} - \underset{(-3.871)}{0.383}\,E\hat{C}_{2t-1} \quad (6.36)$$

where $E\hat{C}_{2t-1} = \ln TA_{2t-1} + 13.425 - 2.379\ln GDP_{2t-1} - 0.277\ln TV_{2t-1} + 1.871\ln RCPI_{2t-1}$

Apart from the R-squared values, the other diagnostic statistics for (6.35) and (6.36) are the same as those in (6.31) and (6.32).

As can be seen, the ADLM estimation method is also a two-stage process. The advantage of this method over the Engle-Granger two-stage approach is that in the first stage the error term in the ADLM tends to be independent and identically distributed, and therefore the diagnostic statistics and the standard errors of the coefficients are standard and the normal critical values can be used for inference.

As to which method performs best, there is no clear cut answer to this question. But if the sample is sufficiently large and there is only one cointegration relationship between a number of variables, then all three methods should produce similar results. However, in the case of multi-cointegration relationships, a more advanced approach, such as the Johansen (1988) method, should be used. This approach will be discussed in the next chapter.

Another way of assessing the validity of these estimation methods is to look at the *ex post* forecasting performance. In the next sub-section we will re-estimate the ECMs using the data from 1962 to 1990 and reserve the final four observations for forecasting comparison purposes. Since the USA ECMs are badly specified for all three methods, we will not carry out the forecasting exercise for the USA.

### 6.3.2.4   Forecasting Performance of ECMs

The forecasts from 1991 to 1994 are generated from all three ECMs. The forecasting errors are calculated based on the differences between the actual and forecast values. In order to see which model performs best, two measures of forecasting performance are used: the mean absolute forecasting error (MAE) and the root mean square forecasting error (RMSE). The results are presented in Table 6.2.

The results in Table 6.2 show that the ADLM approach produces the smallest forecasting errors.

*Table 6.2* Forecast Errors Generated
from the Three UK ECMs

| Model | MAE | RMSE |
|---|---|---|
| Engle-Granger | 0.04378 | 0.04690 |
| Wickens-Breusch | 0.05928 | 0.06167 |
| ADLM | 0.03221 | 0.03633 |

**APPENDIX 6.1**

Table A6.1 Data Used in Chapter 6

| Year | UKTA | USTA | UKGDP | USGDP | UKTV | USTV | UKCPI | USCPI | KCPI | UKEXR[1] | KEXR[2] |
|------|------|------|-------|-------|------|------|-------|-------|------|---------|---------|
| 1962 | 602 | 7328 | 48.89 | 42.83 | 28.623 | 841.67 | 10.7 | 23.1 | 3.8 | 2.8 | 130 |
| 1963 | 705 | 10178 | 51.02 | 44.47 | 24.727 | 1113.80 | 10.9 | 23.4 | 4.5 | 2.8 | 130 |
| 1964 | 737 | 11530 | 53.69 | 46.54 | 35.145 | 861.232 | 11.3 | 23.7 | 5.8 | 2.8 | 213.85 |
| 1965 | 828 | 14152 | 56.05 | 50.71 | 17.266 | 877.689 | 11.8 | 24.1 | 6.6 | 2.8 | 266.4 |
| 1966 | 1052 | 30226 | 57.11 | 53.76 | 25.436 | 1218.47 | 12.2 | 24.9 | 7.5 | 2.8 | 271.34 |
| 1967 | 1522 | 39274 | 58.42 | 55.16 | 45.993 | 1542.16 | 12.5 | 25.5 | 8.3 | 2.77 | 270.52 |
| 1968 | 1924 | 41823 | 60.80 | 57.43 | 76.610 | 2331.86 | 13.1 | 26.6 | 9.3 | 2.4 | 276.65 |
| 1969 | 2564 | 49606 | 62.05 | 58.99 | 139.70 | 2824.90 | 13.8 | 28.1 | 10.4 | 2.4 | 288.16 |
| 1970 | 2680 | 55352 | 63.47 | 58.96 | 144.54 | 3076.25 | 14.7 | 29.7 | 12.1 | 2.4 | 310.56 |
| 1971 | 3029 | 58003 | 64.73 | 60.79 | 214.36 | 3689.30 | 16.1 | 31.0 | 13.7 | 2.43 | 347.15 |
| 1972 | 3671 | 63578 | 67.00 | 63.70 | 299.91 | 4121.35 | 17.2 | 32.0 | 15.3 | 2.5 | 392.89 |
| 1973 | 4980 | 77537 | 71.93 | 67.01 | 371.83 | 5744.44 | 18.8 | 34.0 | 15.8 | 2.45 | 398.32 |
| 1974 | 5345 | 80621 | 70.71 | 66.59 | 428.48 | 6941.30 | 21.8 | 37.8 | 19.6 | 2.34 | 404.47 |
| 1975 | 6446 | 97422 | 70.20 | 66.05 | 566.20 | 6794.04 | 27.1 | 41.2 | 24.6 | 2.22 | 484 |
| 1976 | 8899 | 102199 | 72.15 | 69.31 | 808.37 | 8470.53 | 31.6 | 43.6 | 28.4 | 1.81 | 484 |
| 1977 | 9970 | 113710 | 73.85 | 72.44 | 810.83 | 9991.04 | 36.6 | 46.4 | 31.3 | 1.75 | 484 |
| 1978 | 12566 | 118039 | 76.40 | 75.93 | 1004.98 | 11827.24 | 39.6 | 49.9 | 35.8 | 1.92 | 484 |

*(Continued)*

Table A6.1 Data Used in Chapter 6 (*Continued*)

| Year | UKTA | USTA | UKGDP | USGDP | UKTV | USTV | UKCPI | USCPI | KCPI | UKEXR[1] | KEXR[2] |
|------|------|------|-------|-------|------|------|-------|-------|------|----------|---------|
| 1979 | 13395 | 127355 | 78.54 | 77.84 | 1537.67 | 13282.13 | 44.9 | 55.6 | 42.3 | 2.12 | 484 |
| 1980 | 12414 | 121404 | 76.84 | 77.43 | 1134.54 | 12307.89 | 53.0 | 63.1 | 54.5 | 2.33 | 607.43 |
| 1981 | 14874 | 130402 | 75.85 | 78.79 | 1308.42 | 13924.08 | 59.3 | 69.6 | 66.1 | 2.03 | 681.03 |
| 1982 | 16140 | 151249 | 77.16 | 77.09 | 1659.30 | 14236.05 | 64.4 | 73.9 | 70.8 | 1.75 | 731.08 |
| 1983 | 18598 | 176488 | 80.00 | 80.09 | 1688.86 | 16693.46 | 67.4 | 76.2 | 73.3 | 1.52 | 775.75 |
| 1984 | 19213 | 212986 | 81.86 | 85.05 | 1699.55 | 19512.33 | 70.7 | 79.5 | 75.0 | 1.34 | 805.98 |
| 1985 | 21414 | 239423 | 94.93 | 87.75 | 1604.28 | 19552.42 | 75.0 | 82.4 | 76.8 | 1.30 | 870.02 |
| 1986 | 23481 | 284571 | 88.57 | 90.30 | 1726.22 | 23744.78 | 77.6 | 83.9 | 78.9 | 1.47 | 881.45 |
| 1987 | 24606 | 326330 | 92.83 | 93.08 | 2541.86 | 30704.75 | 80.8 | 87.0 | 81.3 | 1.64 | 822.57 |
| 1988 | 33276 | 347281 | 97.48 | 96.74 | 3129.35 | 37156.52 | 84.7 | 90.5 | 87.1 | 1.78 | 731.47 |
| 1989 | 34423 | 317133 | 99.60 | 99.19 | 2774.33 | 36902.69 | 91.3 | 94.9 | 92.1 | 1.64 | 671.46 |
| 1990 | 36054 | 325388 | 100.00 | 100.00 | 2976.00 | 36392.00 | 100.0 | 100.0 | 100.0 | 1.78 | 707.76 |
| 1991 | 35848 | 315828 | 98.04 | 98.84 | 3320.36 | 37437.13 | 105.9 | 104.2 | 109.3 | 1.77 | 733.35 |
| 1992 | 36284 | 333805 | 97.52 | 102.09 | 3159.72 | 36088.30 | 109.8 | 107.4 | 116.1 | 1.77 | 780.65 |
| 1993 | 35923 | 325366 | 99.72 | 105.27 | 2993.16 | 35255.13 | 111.5 | 110.6 | 121.7 | 1.50 | 802.67 |
| 1994 | 40999 | 332428 | 103.56 | 109.57 | 3325.29 | 40667.95 | 114.3 | 113.4 | 129.3 | 1.53 | 803.45 |

Notes: [1]Exchange rate in terms of pound sterling per US dollar.
[2]Exchange rate in terms of Korean won per US dollar.

# 7 Vector Autoregression (VAR) and Cointegration

## 7.1 INTRODUCTION

Our main focus so far in this book has been on the single equation tourism demand model, in which an endogenous tourism demand variable is related to a number of exogenous variables. The single equation approach depends heavily on the assumption that the explanatory variables are exogenous. If this assumption is invalid, a researcher would have to model the economic relationships using a system of (or simultaneous) equations method. The popularity of simultaneous equations approaches dates back to the 1950s and 1960s within the context of structural macroeconomic models which were used for policy simulation and forecasting. In estimating these structural models, restrictions were often imposed in order to obtain identified equations. Sims (1980) argued that many of the restrictions imposed on the parameters in the structural equations were 'incredible' relative to the data generating process, and hence he suggested that it would be better to use models that do not depend on the imposition of incorrect prior information. Following this argument, Sims developed a vector autoregressive (VAR) model in which all the variables, apart from the deterministic variables such as trend, intercept and dummy variables, are modelled purely as dynamic processes, that is, the VAR model treats all variables as endogenous.

More importantly, the VAR technique has been closely associated with some of the recent developments in multivariate cointegration analysis, such as the Johansen (1988) cointegration method. Although there has been increasing interest in using the VAR technique in macroeconomic modelling and forecasting, relatively little effort has been made to use this method for tourism demand analysis. Exceptions are Kulendran and King (1997), Kulendran and Witt (1997) and Song and Witt (2006), who model the demand for Australian inbound tourism and UK outbound tourism, respectively, using the cointegrated VAR system.

In this chapter we introduce the VAR modelling approach and its use in causality testing, impulse response analysis, forecasting and cointegration analysis. Although the aim of this book is to use the least complicated mathematical expressions possible, from this chapter onwards it is necessary to use matrices to cope with the complexity of the techniques involved.


## 7.2    BASICS OF VAR ANALYSIS

In order to introduce the general VAR specification, we start with two AR(1) processes:

$$y_{1t} = \pi_{11}y_{1t-1} + u_{1t}; \quad u_{1t} \sim IID(0, \sigma_{11})$$
$$y_{2t} = \pi_{22}y_{2t-1} + u_{2t}; \quad u_{2t} \sim IID(0, \sigma_{22})$$

The above equations may also be written in vector format:

$$\begin{bmatrix} y_{1t} \\ y_{2t} \end{bmatrix} = \begin{bmatrix} \pi_{11} & 0 \\ 0 & \pi_{22} \end{bmatrix} \begin{bmatrix} y_{1t-1} \\ y_{2t-1} \end{bmatrix} + \begin{bmatrix} u_{1t} \\ u_{2t} \end{bmatrix}$$

or in matrix form:

$$Y_t = \Pi_1 Y_{t-1} + U_t; \quad U_t \sim IID(0, \Sigma) \tag{7.1}$$

There are restrictions on the $\Pi_1$ matrix in Equation (7.1) that force it to be diagonal. If no restrictions were imposed on the matrix $\Pi_1$ we would obtain an unrestricted VAR model of order one, or VAR(1), which represents the following equations:

$$y_{1t} = \pi_{11}y_{1t-1} + \pi_{12}y_{2t-1} + u_{1t}; \quad u_{1t} \sim IID(0, \sigma_{11})$$
$$y_{2t} = \pi_{21}y_{1t-1} + \pi_{22}y_{2t-1} + u_{2t}; \quad u_{2t} \sim IID(0, \sigma_{22})$$

Equation (7.1) can be extended to a general VAR($p$) model:

$$Y_t = \Pi_1 Y_{t-1} + \Pi_2 Y_{t-2} + \ldots + \Pi_p Y_{t-p} + U_t; \quad U_t \sim IID(0, \Sigma) \tag{7.2}$$

An intercept vector can also be added to Equation (7.2). The above equation is known as Sims' general (unrestricted) VAR model, in which the current values of all the variables are regressed against all the lagged values of the same set of variables in the system. $U_t$ is a vector of regression errors that are assumed to be contemporaneously correlated but not autocorrelated. This indicates that each equation in the system can be individually estimated by OLS. Although the use of the seemingly unrelated regression estimator (SURE) is an alternative, it does not add much efficiency to the estimation procedure.

If a VAR model has $m$ equations, there will be $m + pm^2$ coefficients that need to be estimated (including the constant term in each equation). This suggests that an unrestricted VAR model is likely to be over-parameterised. A practical problem with estimating a VAR($p$) model is that we would like to include as much information as possible for the purposes of forecasting and policy analysis, but degrees of freedom will quickly run out as more variables are introduced. Therefore, the process of lag length selection is very important for the specification of a VAR model. If the lag length of $p$ is too small, the model cannot represent correctly the DGP; if, on the other hand, $p$ is too large, lack of degrees of freedom can be a problem and OLS estimation is biased. To determine the lag length of the VAR model, we normally begin with the longest possible lag length permitted by the sample. For example, if we have about 150 observations on five quarterly series (that is, there are five equations in the system), we may start with a lag length of 12 quarters based on the *a priori* assumption that a period of three years is sufficiently long to capture the dynamics of the system. There are 305 parameters that need to be estimated for this initial specification and this will probably lead to an over-parameterised VAR. We can then re-estimate the system with a reduced lag structure, say 11 lags, and see whether the shortening of the lag length significantly reduces the model's explanatory power.

A likelihood ratio statistic can be used to test whether the reduction in the model's explanatory power is significant:

$$LR = T(\ln |\Sigma_{11}| - \ln |\Sigma_{12}|) \tag{7.3}$$

where $T$ is the sample size and $\ln|\Sigma_{12}|$ and $\ln|\Sigma_{11}|$ are the natural logarithms of the determinants of the variance/covariance matrices in the initial and reduced VARs, respectively.

The $LR$ statistic has an asymptotic $\chi^2$ distribution with degrees of freedom equal to the number of restrictions in the system. In the example given above, we have five equations and the reduction of one lag for each equation means that we will lose 25 parameters, that is, the number of restrictions for the $LR$ static is 25. A small value for the calculated $\chi^2(25)$ statistic compared with the critical value suggests that the null hypothesis should be accepted. If this is the case, we can then test whether ten lags are appropriate by calculating the $LR$ statistic:

$$LR = T(\ln |\Sigma_{10}| - \ln |\Sigma_{11}|) \tag{7.4}$$

This process can be repeated until the smallest lag length, normally one lag, is reached.

The $LR$ statistic represented by Equation (7.3) or Equation (7.4) is useful for large sample sizes. However, in small samples, the use of this statistic tends to over-reject the null hypothesis. The degrees-of-freedom-adjusted $LR$ statistic for small samples is calculated as follows

$$LR^* = (T - q - 2 - mp)(\ln |\Sigma_r| - \ln |\Sigma_u|) \tag{7.5}$$

where $LR^*$ is the adjusted $LR$ statistic, $q$ is the number of deterministic variables, such as intercept, trend and dummies, $p$ is the order of the unrestricted VAR model and $m$ is the total number of equations in the VAR model. The statistic has a $\chi^2$ distribution with appropriate degrees of freedom.

Alternative criteria that can be used in the determination of the lag length of the VAR model are AIC and SBC, which are calculated from

$$AIC = -\frac{Tm}{2}(1 + \ln 2\pi) - \frac{T}{2}\ln|\Sigma| - (m^2 p + mq + 2m) \tag{7.6}$$

$$SBC = -\frac{Tm}{2}(1 + \ln 2\pi) - \frac{T}{2}\ln|\Sigma| - \frac{1}{2}(m^2 p + mq + 2m)\ln T \tag{7.7}$$

where $|\Sigma|$ is the determinant of the variance/covariance matrix of the estimated errors and $\pi = 3.1416$.

Unlike the single equation case discussed in Chapter 5, where the lowest values of AIC and SBC are favourable, in VAR modelling the highest AIC and SBC are preferred. This occurs because the criteria underlying Equations (7.6) and (7.7) are constructed in a slightly different way.

## 7.3    IMPULSE RESPONSE ANALYSIS

One of the advantages of VAR modelling is that the model can be used for policy simulation via impulse response analysis. In tourism demand analysis, we may want to know how 'shocks' to the price of tourism in the destination country and/or 'shocks' to the level of income in the tourism-generating country would affect the demand for tourism in the destination.

In order to investigate how impulse response analysis can be used for policy evaluation, let us consider a simple VAR(1) model:

$$Y_t = \Pi_1 Y_{t-1} + U_t \tag{7.8a}$$

$$\text{or} \quad \begin{bmatrix} y_{1t} \\ y_{2t} \end{bmatrix} = \begin{bmatrix} \pi_{11} & \pi_{12} \\ \pi_{21} & \pi_{22} \end{bmatrix} \begin{bmatrix} y_{1t-1} \\ y_{2t-1} \end{bmatrix} + \begin{bmatrix} u_{1t} \\ u_{2t} \end{bmatrix} \tag{7.8b}$$

Lagging the above equation by one period and substituting for $Y_{t-1}$ in Equation (7.8a) yields

$$Y_t = \Pi_1(\Pi_1 Y_{t-2} + U_{t-1}) + U_t$$
$$= \Pi_1^2 Y_{t-2} + U_t + \Pi_1 U_{t-1}$$

If this process is repeated $n$ times we end up with

$$Y_t = \sum_{i=0}^{n} \Pi_1^i U_{t-i} + \Pi_1^{n+1} Y_{t-n+1} \tag{7.9}$$

If the time series is stationary, that is, $0 < |\Pi_1| < 1$, then $\lim_{n \to \infty} \Pi_1^n = 0$ (this is called the stability condition), and Equation (7.9) becomes

$$Y_t = \sum_{i=0}^{\infty} \Pi_1^i U_{t-i} \tag{7.10}$$

Equation (7.10) is called a *vector moving average* (VMA) process since the vector of the dependent variables is represented by an infinite sum of lagged random errors weighted by an exponentially diminishing coefficient.

In the case of a VAR(1) system with only two variables, Equation (7.10) becomes

$$\begin{bmatrix} y_{1t} \\ y_{2t} \end{bmatrix} = \sum_{i=0}^{\infty} \begin{bmatrix} \pi_{11} & \pi_{12} \\ \pi_{21} & \pi_{22} \end{bmatrix}^i \begin{bmatrix} u_{1t-i} \\ u_{2t-i} \end{bmatrix} \tag{7.11}$$

Equation (7.11) suggests that the variables $y_{1t}$ and $y_{2t}$ can be expressed by sequences of 'shocks' to the system. The formula indicates what would be the impacts of unitary changes in the error terms (shocks) on the dependent variables, which is what policy makers are interested in. However, due to the fact that the error terms $u_{1t}$ and $u_{2t}$ are correlated, the impact of each shock from the two equations cannot actually be separated. To solve this problem, we need to transform Equation (7.11) into a form in which the error terms $u_{1t}$ and $u_{2t}$ are not correlated, and this process is known as orthogonalisation.

According to the assumptions made regarding the error terms in Equation (7.8b) we know that $E(u_{1t}) = 0, E(u_{2t}) = 0, Var(u_{1t}) = E(u_{1t}^2) = \sigma_{11}, Var(u_{2t}) = E(u_{2t}^2) = \sigma_{22}$, and $Cov(u_{1t}, u_{2t}) = \sigma_{12}$. One way of orthogonalising this VAR(1) model is to subtract the result of multiplying the first row of Equation (7.8b) by a constant term $\delta = \dfrac{\sigma_{12}}{\sigma_{11}}$ from the second row in Equation (7.8b). The resulting model is

$$\begin{bmatrix} y_{1t} \\ y_{2t} - \delta y_{1t} \end{bmatrix} = \begin{bmatrix} \pi_{11} & \pi_{12} \\ \pi'_{21} & \pi'_{22} \end{bmatrix} \begin{bmatrix} y_{1t-1} \\ y_{2t-1} \end{bmatrix} + \begin{bmatrix} u_{1t} \\ u'_{2t} \end{bmatrix} \tag{7.12}$$

where $\pi'_{21} = (\pi_{21} - \delta\pi_{11})$, $\pi'_{22} = (\pi_{22} - \delta\pi_{12})$, and $u'_{2t} = (u_{2t} - \delta u_{1t})$. The error terms in Equation (7.12) are no longer correlated since

$$Cov(u_{1t}, u'_{2t}) = E(u_{1t} * u'_{2t}) = E[(u_{1t} * u_{2t}) - (\sigma_{12} / \sigma_{11})E(u_{1t}^2)]$$
$$= \sigma_{12} - \sigma_{12} = 0$$

Now, substituting $u'_{2t-i} + \delta u_{1t-i}$ for $u_{2t-i}$ in Equation (7.11), we get

$$\begin{bmatrix} y_{1t} \\ y_{2t} \end{bmatrix} = \sum_{i=0}^{\infty} \begin{bmatrix} \pi_{11} & \pi_{12} \\ \pi_{21} & \pi_{22} \end{bmatrix}^i \begin{bmatrix} 1 & 0 \\ \delta & 1 \end{bmatrix} \begin{bmatrix} u_{1t-i} \\ u'_{2t-i} \end{bmatrix} \tag{7.13}$$

If we denote $\phi_i = \begin{bmatrix} \Pi_1^i \end{bmatrix} \begin{bmatrix} 1 & 0 \\ \delta & 1 \end{bmatrix}$, Equation (7.13) becomes

$$\begin{bmatrix} y_{1t} \\ y_{2t} \end{bmatrix} = \sum_{i=0}^{\infty} \begin{bmatrix} \phi_{11}(i) & \phi_{12}(i) \\ \phi_{21}(i) & \phi_{22}(i) \end{bmatrix} \begin{bmatrix} u_{1t-i} \\ u'_{2t-i} \end{bmatrix} \tag{7.14}$$

or more compactly,

$$Y_t = \sum_{i=0}^{\infty} \phi_i U'_{t-i} \tag{7.15}$$

where $U'_t = \begin{bmatrix} u_{1t} \\ u'_{2t} \end{bmatrix}$ and the $\phi_i$ matrices are termed the *impulse response functions* since they represent the behaviour of the time series $y_{1t}$ and $y_{2t}$ in response to the shocks $U'_t$.

When $i = 0$, the four elements in the $\phi_i$ matrix, $\phi_{11}(0), \phi_{12}(0), \phi_{21}(0)$ and $\phi_{22}(0)$ are called the impact multipliers since they represent the instantaneous impacts of unit changes in $u_{1t}$ and $u'_{2t}$ on the series $y_{2t}$ and $y_{1t}$. For example, $\phi_{12}(0)$ is the instantaneous impact of a one-unit change in $u'_{2t}$ on $y_{1t}$. Similarly, $\phi_{21}(1)$ and $\phi_{22}(1)$ represent the one-period responses of unit changes in $u_{1t-1}$ and $u'_{2t-1}$ on $y_{2t}$, respectively. The impulse response functions can also be used to look at the accumulated effects of unit changes in $u_{1t}$ and $u'_{2t}$ on the future values $y_{1t+n}$ and $y_{2t+n}$. For example, $\phi_{12}(n)$ is the effect of $u'_{2t}$ on $y_{1t+n}$, and the cumulative sum of the effects of $u'_{2t}$ after $n$ periods on $y_{1t}$ would be $\sum_{i=0}^{n}\phi_{12}(i)$. The impulse response functions can be plotted against $i$ to give a visual indication of how the series $y_{1t}$ and $y_{2t}$ would respond to various shocks.

## 7.4   FORECASTING WITH VAR AND ERROR VARIANCE DECOMPOSITION

In the single equation approach, in order to forecast the dependent variable we need to forecast the exogenous variables first. This, however, can be very difficult indeed due to limitations of the data and the understanding of the data generating processes for the exogenous variables. But there is no need to worry about the forecasts of the exogenous variables in the VAR framework since all explanatory variables are pre-determined. For example, if we want to make $n$-period-ahead forecasts for the variable $Y_t$, given the estimated coefficient matrix $\Pi_1$ in Equation (7.8a), using the information up to period $t$, the forecasts and their errors can be updated in the following ways.

For one-period-ahead forecasts, since $Y_{t+1} = \Pi_1 Y_t + U_t$, the forecasts can be generated by taking the conditional expectation of $Y_{t+1}$, that is, $\hat{Y}_{t+1} = E_t(Y_{t+1}) = \Pi_1 Y_t$. The forecasting error is $Y_{t+1} - \hat{Y}_{t+1} = U_{t+1}$. In the same way, two-period-ahead forecasts can be generated from $\hat{Y}_{t+2} = \Pi_1^2 Y_t$, and the forecasting error now becomes $U_{t+2} + \Pi_1 U_{t+1}$. More generally, the $n$-period-ahead forecast is

$$\hat{Y}_{t+n} = \Pi_1^n Y_t \tag{7.16}$$

and the corresponding forecasting error is

$$U_{t+n} + \Pi_1 U_{t+n-1} + \Pi_1^2 U_{t+n-2} + \dots + \Pi_1^{n-1} U_{t+1} \tag{7.17}$$

In fact, the forecasts and forecasting errors can also be generated from the VMA process of Equation (7.15). From Equation (7.15), we have

$$Y_{t+n} = \sum_{i=0}^{\infty} \phi_i U'_{t+n-i} \tag{7.18}$$

Based on Equation (7.18) the one-period-ahead forecast $\hat{Y}_{t+1} = E(\sum_{i=0}^{\infty} \phi_i U'_{t+1-i})$ and the corresponding one-period-ahead forecast error is $Y_{t+1} - \hat{Y}_{t+1} = \phi_0 U'_{t+1}$. Following the same procedure, we could obtain the $n$-period-ahead forecast:

$$Y_{t+n} - \hat{Y}_{t+n} = \sum_{i=0}^{n-1} \phi_i U'_{t+n-i} \tag{7.19}$$

As far as the variable $y_{1t}$ is concerned, the $n$-period-ahead forecasting error is measured by

$$y_{1t+n} - \hat{y}_{1t+n} = \phi_{11}(0)u_{1t+n} + \phi_{11}(1)u_{1t+n-1} + ... + \phi_{11}(n-1)u_{1t+1}$$
$$+ \phi_{12}(0)u'_{2t+n} + \phi_{12}(1)u'_{2t+n-1} + ... + \phi_{12}(n-1)u'_{2t+1}$$

and the error variance of the $n$-period-ahead forecast is therefore

$$\begin{aligned} var(y_{1t+n} - \hat{y}_{1t+n}) &= \sigma^2_{y_{1t}}[\phi^2_{11}(0) + \phi^2_{11}(1) + ... + \phi^2_{11}(n-1)] \\ &+ \sigma^2_{y_{2t}}[\phi^2_{12}(0) + \phi^2_{12}(1) + ... + \phi^2_{12}(n-1)] \end{aligned} \tag{7.20}$$

Equation (7.20) shows that the forecasting variance increases as the forecasting horizon lengthens.

Equation (7.20) can also be decomposed to show the shares of the $n$-period-ahead forecasting error variance resulting from separate shocks in $u_{1t}$ and $u'_{2t}$. For example, the shares of the $n$-period-ahead forecasting error variance in the series $y_{1t}$ caused by $u_{1t}$ and $u'_{2t}$ are

$$\sigma^2_{y_{1t}}[\phi^2_{11}(0) + \phi^2_{11}(1) + ... + \phi^2_{11}(n-1)] / Var(y_{1t+n} - \hat{y}_{1t+n})$$

and

$$\sigma^2_{y_{2t}}[\phi^2_{12}(0) + \phi^2_{12}(1) + ... + \phi^2_{12}(n-1)] / Var(y_{1t+n} - \hat{y}_{1t+n})$$

respectively. The forecasting error variance decomposition shows the share of the variation in a time series that is due to it own 'shocks' and also the shocks from the other variables. In the two-variable case above, if $u'_{2t}$ cannot explain the forecasting error variance of $y_{1t}$ at all forecasting horizons, then $y_{1t}$ is said to be an exogenous series. On the other hand, if $u'_{2t}$ explains all the forecasting error variance of $y_{1t}$, we say that $y_{1t}$ is completely endogenous. In this respect, the forecasting error variance decomposition can be used as a tool to test for exogeneity of a time series within a VAR framework.

## 7.5   TESTING FOR GRANGER CAUSALITY AND EXOGENEITY

In this section, we will introduce the concept of Granger causality, followed by some tests for it.

### 7.5.1   The Concept of Granger Causality

In practice, a researcher may wish to know whether the past values of a time series $y_{2t}$ would help to forecast the current and future values of another series $y_{1t}$. This problem is known as Granger causality and is defined as:

*$y_{2t}$ fails to Granger cause $y_{1t}$ if for all $n > 0$ the mean squared error (MSE) of a forecast of $y_{1t+n}$ based on $(y_{1t}, y_{1t-1}, y_{1t-2}, \ldots)$ is the same as the MSE of a forecast of $y_{1t+n}$ that uses both $(y_{1t}, y_{1t-1}, y_{1t-2}, \ldots)$ and $(y_{2t}, y_{2t-1}, y_{2t-2}, \ldots)$.*

Or, more formally, *$y_{2t}$ fails to Granger cause $y_{1t}$ if*

$$MSE[E(\hat{y}_{1t} \mid y_{1t}, y_{1t-1}, y_{1t-2}, \ldots)]$$
$$= MSE[E(\hat{y}_{1t} \mid y_{1t}, y_{1t-1}, y_{1t-2}, \ldots, y_{2t}, y_{2t-1}, y_{2t-2}, \ldots)] \tag{7.21}$$

where $\hat{y}_{1t+n}$ is the $n$-period-ahead forecast for $y_{1t}$ and '|' stands for 'conditional on'.

We can also say that $y_{1t}$ is *exogenous* with respect to $y_{2t}$ if Equation (7.21) holds. As can be seen from the definition, the concept of Granger causality is not the same as that used in everyday life. The causality here only refers to the predictability of the time series. The rationale behind this concept is given by Granger (1969). He believes that if an event $y_2$ is the cause of another event $y_1$, then the former should precede the latter. Although this argument has its philosophic base, quite often we may find this concept difficult to implement with regard to aggregate economic time series, since many of these time series are compiled in a discontinuous way in which the detailed dynamics are 'averaged' out. For example, in tourism demand analysis many researchers use annual data, but the response of tourists' choices of holiday destinations to changes in, say, exchange rates may be more frequent than an annual span.

### 7.5.2   Tests for Granger Causality

In the bivariate VAR model case, testing for Granger causality is straightforward. The normal tests for restrictions discussed in Chapter 4, such as the $F$ (or $LR$) tests, can be used. The tests can be based on the auxiliary equation proposed by either Granger (1969) or Sims (1972).

The Granger test is based on

$$y_{1t} = \alpha + \sum_{i=1}^{n} \beta_i y_{1t-i} + \sum_{i=1}^{n} \gamma_i y_{2t-i} + u_t \qquad (7.22)$$

The two variables in Equation (7.22) are normally assumed to be stationary. The restrictions imposed are $\gamma_1 = \gamma_2 = \ldots = \gamma_n = 0$. If these restrictions are accepted according to the $F$ or $LR$ statistic, we conclude that $y_{2t}$ does not Granger-cause $y_{1t}$. In estimating Equation (7.22), deterministic variables such as dummies and trend can also be included, if necessary.

The Sims (1972) test is based on

$$y_{1t} = \alpha + \sum_{i=1}^{n} \beta_i y_{1t-i} + \sum_{i=-k}^{m} \gamma_i y_{2t-i} + u_t \quad i \neq 0 \qquad (7.23)$$

In Equation (7.23) both the lagged and lead values of $y_{2t}$ are included, but not the current value of $y_{2t}$. The restrictions now imposed are $\gamma_{-m} = \gamma_{-m+1} = \ldots = \gamma_{-1} = 0$. If these restrictions are accepted, this suggests that future values of $y_2$ cannot be used to forecast the current value of $y_1$, and therefore $y_1$ does not Granger-cause $y_2$. However, if the restrictions are rejected the conclusion would be that $y_1$ does Granger-cause $y_2$.

Since either Equation (7.22) or Equation (7.23) is only one equation within a bivariate VAR system, each of the tests has to be carried out twice, with the dependent variable changed. The final conclusion has to be drawn on the basis of all of the test statistics.

The above tests are related to a two-variable VAR model. If there are more than two variables, the *block Granger causality* test (sometimes also referred as the *block exogeneity* test) should be used. The block Granger causality test examines whether a lagged variable would Granger-cause other variables in the system. For example, suppose we have three variables, $y_1$, $y_2$ and $y_3$, and we want to look at whether $y_3$ Granger-causes $y_1$ and/or $y_2$. What the test does is impose the restrictions that all of the coefficients of the lagged $y_3$ variables in the system are zero. These restrictions can be tested using the $LR$ statistic of Equation (7.5). The test is carried out as follows: first, estimate the $y_{1t}$ and $y_{2t}$ equations with $n$ lagged values of $y_{1t}$, $y_{2t}$ and $y_{3t}$ as regressors and calculate $|\Sigma_u|$; then, re-estimate the two equations excluding the lagged $y_{3t}$ values and calculate $|\Sigma_r|$; and finally, calculate the $LR$ statistic using

$$LR = (T - c)(\ln |\Sigma_r| - \ln |\Sigma_u|)$$

We already know that this statistic is distributed as $\chi^2$ with degrees of freedom equal to the total number of restrictions. $T$ is the total number of observations for each variable, and $c$ is the total number of parameters in the unrestricted equations. In this case, the degrees of freedom are equal to $2n$ since $n$ lagged $y_{3t}$s are excluded from two equations, and $c$ equals $2(3n + 1)$ since there are two unrestricted equations and each equation contains a constant term. If the calculated $LR$ is greater than the corresponding critical value $\chi^2(2n)$, the restrictions imposed should be rejected, and this suggests that $y_{3t}$ does Granger-cause $y_{1t}$ and $y_{2t}$.

## 7.6 AN EXAMPLE OF VAR MODELLING

The data set on inbound tourism demand to South Korea used in Chapter 6 is used again to illustrate the procedure of VAR modelling. Two VAR models are created based on the demand for tourism by UK and USA residents, respectively. The variables included in each VAR model are tourist arrivals in Korea from the origin country, $\ln TA_{it}$, the GDP of the origin country, $\ln GDP_{it}$, the trade value between Korea and the origin country, $\ln TV_{it}$, and the relative price variable, $\ln RCPI_{it}$.

In terms of the integration order of the variables, normally the variables included in the model should be $I(0)$. However, Sims (1980) and Doan *et al.* (1984) suggest that the variables in the VAR system should not be differenced since the aim of the VAR model is to determine the interrelationships between economic variables, and not just the estimates of the parameters. The use of differenced variables in a VAR model results in the loss of useful information related to the co-movement of the time series. Moreover, according to Geweke (1984, pp. 1139–40), various hypothesis tests, such as the Granger causality tests, are still valid if the data are transformed into logarithms, as is the case with our data. Therefore, in this section we will use the levels variables (in logarithmic form) in the construction and analysis of the VAR model.

### 7.6.1 Order Selection of VAR Model

Since annual data are used, we initially specify a VAR(4) model for each of the two tourism-generating countries as

$$Y_t = \Pi_0 + \sum_{i=1}^{4} \Pi_i Y_{t-i} \tag{7.24}$$

where $Y_t = (\ln TA_{it}, \ln GDP_{it}, \ln TV_{it}, \ln RCPI_{it})'$, $\Pi_0$ is a $1 \times 4$ vector and the $\Pi_i$s are $4 \times 4$ matrices.

The $LR$ statistic of Equation (7.5) is calculated in a pairwise fashion, that is, order four against order three, order three against order two, and so on. The AIC and SBC are also calculated using Equations (7.6) and (7.7) for each of the orders from one to four. Tables 7.1 and 7.2 are the computer printouts (Microfit 4.0) of the test results for the VAR order selection.

The results in Tables 7.1 and 7.2 show that, as expected, the values of log-likelihood increase with increases in the lag length. In the case of the UK

Table 7.1  Choice Criteria for Selecting the Order of the VAR Model (UK)

Based on 29 observations from 1966 to 1994. Order of VAR = 4

List of variables included in the unrestricted VAR:

LTAUK   LGDPUK   LTVUK   LRCPIUK

List of deterministic and/or exogenous variables:

INPT

| Order | LL | AIC | SBC | LR Test | | Adjusted LR Test |
|---|---|---|---|---|---|---|
| 4 | 176.2106 | 108.2106 | 61.7226 | — | | — |
| 3 | 162.9013 | 110.9013 | 75.3516 | CHSQ(16) = | 26.6186[.046] | 11.0146[.809] |
| 2 | 149.4026 | 113.4026 | 88.7913 | CHSQ(32) = | 53.6161[.010] | 22.1860[.902] |
| 1 | 137.8001 | 117.8001 | 104.1271 | CHSQ(48) = | 76.8211[.005] | 31.7881[.966] |
| 0 | 20.1782 | 16.1782 | 13.4436 | CHSQ(64) = | 312.0648[.000] | 129.1303[.000] |

Note: LTAUK = $\ln TA_{1t}$, LGDPUK = $\ln GDP_{1t}$, LTVUK = $\ln TV_{1t}$, and LRCPIUK = $\ln RCPI_{1t}$

*Table 7.2* Choice Criteria for Selecting the Order of the VAR Model (USA)

Based on 29 observations from 1966 to 1994. Order of VAR = 4

List of variables included in the unrestricted VAR:

LTAUS   LGDPUS   LTVUS   LRCPIUS

List of deterministic and/or exogenous variables:

INPT

| Order | LL | AIC | SBC | LR Test | Adjusted LR Test |
|---|---|---|---|---|---|
| 4 | 256.4243 | 188.4243 | 141.9362 | — | — |
| 3 | 237.3447 | 185.3447 | 149.7950 | CHSQ(16) = 38.1590[.001] | 15.7899[.468] |
| 2 | 221.9148 | 185.9148 | 161.3035 | CHSQ(32) = 69.0189[.000] | 28.5595[.641] |
| 1 | 205.2028 | 185.2028 | 171.5299 | CHSQ(48) = 102.4429[.000] | 42.3902[.701] |
| 0 | 78.1155 | 74.1155 | 71.3809 | CHSQ(64) = 356.6175[.000] | 147.5658[.000] |

Note: LTAUS = $\ln TA_{2t}$, LGDPUS = $\ln GDP_{2t}$, LTVUS = $\ln TV_{2t}$, and LRCPIUS = $\ln RCPI_{2t}$

VAR model, the AIC and SBC indicate order one and this is confirmed by the *LR\** (adjusted *LR*) statistic. For the USA VAR model, the SBC and *LR\** suggest order one whilst the AIC points to order four. However, based on all three criteria we prefer a VAR(1) specification for both the UK and USA models.

## 7.6.2    Block Granger Causality Test

Since our prime interest is in whether $\ln GDP_{it}$, $\ln TV_{it}$ and $\ln RCPI_{it}$ cause $\ln TA_{it}$, the block Granger causality test is conducted to see whether the lagged values of $\ln GDP_{it}$, $\ln TV_{it}$ and $\ln RCPI_{it}$ help to predict the tourism demand variable $\ln TA_{it}$. Tables 7.3 and 7.4 present the computer printout results of this test for the two tourism-generating countries, UK and USA. The null hypothesis is that $\ln GDP_{it}$, $\ln TV_{it}$ and $\ln RCPI_{it}$ do not jointly Granger-cause $\ln TA_{it}$.

The first section of the tables presents the variables included in the unrestricted VAR(4) model. The maximum log-likelihood value of the estimated VAR(4) model is also reported here. The second section of the tables gives a list of the variables that we have assumed to be useful in predicting $\ln TA_{it}$. The maximised value of the log-likelihood of the estimated VAR(4) model

*Table 7.3* LR Test of Block Granger Non-causality in the VAR Model (UK)

| |
|---|
| Based on 29 observations from 1966 to 1994. Order of VAR = 4 |
| List of variables included in the unrestricted VAR: |
| LTAUK   LGDPUK   LTVUK   LRCPIUK |
| List of deterministic and/or exogenous variables: |
| INPT |
| Maximised value of log-likelihood = 176.2106 |

| |
|---|
| List of variable(s) assumed to be 'non-causal' under the null hypothesis: |
| LGDPUK   LTVUK   LRCPIUK |
| Maximized value of log-likelihood = 161.2347 |

| |
|---|
| LR test of block non-causality, CHSQ(12) = 29.9519[.003] |
| The above statistic is for testing the null hypothesis that the coefficients |
| of the lagged values of: |
| LGDPUK   LTVUK   LRCPIUK |
| in the block of equations explaining the variable(s): |
| LTAUK |
| are zero. The maximum order of the lag(s) is 4. |

*Table 7.4* LR Test of Block Granger Non-causality in the VAR Model (USA)

Based on 29 observations from 1966 to 1994. Order of VAR = 4

List of variables included in the unrestricted VAR:

LTAUS   LGDPUS   LTVUS   LRCPIUS

List of deterministic and/or exogenous variables:

INPT

Maximized value of log-likelihood = 256.4243

List of variable(s) assumed to be 'non-causal' under the null hypothesis:

LGDPUS   LTVUS   LRCPIUS

Maximized value of log-likelihood = 220.2853

LR test of block non-causality, CHSQ(12) = 72.2778[.000]

The above statistic is for testing the null hypothesis that the coefficients of the lagged values of:

LGDPUS   LTVUS   LRCPIUS

in the block of equations explaining the variable(s):

LTAUS

are zero. The maximum order of the lag(s) is 4.

without these variables is also given. The next section of the tables presents the *LR* statistic of the block Granger causality test, with some explanation about the statistic. The *LR* statistics in both Tables 7.3 and 7.4 indicate that the null hypothesis of non-Granger block causality is rejected, which means that the variables $\ln GDP_{it}$, $\ln TV_{it}$ and $\ln RCPI_{it}$ do jointly Granger-cause $\ln TA_{it}$, as expected. The reader may also wish to conduct the Granger causality test to see whether there are bi-directional causal relationships among the four variables using the same procedure.

### 7.6.3   Estimating the VAR Models

Since the order selection criterion suggests that a VAR(1) model is appropriate for both the UK and USA, the two VAR(1) models are estimated. As discussed in section 7.2, equations in the VAR system can be estimated individually by OLS. Tables 7.5 through 7.8 report the estimates of the VAR(1) model for UK tourism demand to South Korea. The results for the USA VAR(1) model are omitted to save space.

The estimated results of the VAR(1) model for the UK show that all the equations fit the data well, as judged by the high *R*-squared values, although each equation fails at least one of the diagnostic statistics. Since the VAR model only relates the dependent variables to the lagged explanatory

*Table 7.5* OLS Estimation of Tourist Arrivals Equation
in the Unrestricted VAR Model

Dependent variable is LTAUK

32 observations used for estimation from 1963 to 1994

| Regressor | Coefficient | Standard Error | T Ratio[Prob] |
|---|---|---|---|
| LTAUK(–1) | .919070 | .17987 | 5.10970[.000] |
| LGDPUK(–1) | .072108 | .48931 | .14736[.884] |
| LTVUK(–1) | .003055 | .09219 | .03314[.974] |
| LRCPIUK(–1) | –.084171 | .09396 | –.89585[.378] |
| INPT | .051942 | 1.2713 | .04086[.968] |

| | | | |
|---|---|---|---|
| R-Squared | 0.9945 | R-Bar-Squared | 0.9937 |
| S.E. of Regression | 0.1036 | F-stat. F(4, 27) | 1214.0 |
| Mean of Dependent Variable | 9.0256 | S.D. of Dependent Variable | 1.3004 |
| Residual Sum of Squares | 0.2898 | Equation Log-likelihood | 29.8603 |
| Akaike Info. Criterion | 24.8603 | Schwarz Bayesian Criterion | 21.1960 |
| DW-statistic | 1.8893 | System Log-likelihood | 134.1488 |

| Diagnostic Tests | | |
|---|---|---|
| Test Statistics | LM Version | F Version |
| A: Serial Correlation: | CHSQ(1) = 0.0596[.807] | F(1, 26) = 0.0485[.827] |
| B: Functional Form: | CHSQ(1) = 6.7761[.009] | F(1, 26) = 6.9846[.014] |
| C: Normality: | CHSQ(2) = 1.3817[.501] | Not applicable |
| D: Heteroscedasticity: | CHSQ(1) = 1.7315[.188] | F(1, 30) = 1.7162[.200] |

A: Lagrange multiplier test of residual serial correlation
B: Ramsey's RESET test using the square of the fitted values
C: Based on a test of skewness and kurtosis of residuals
D: Based on the regression of squared residuals on squared fitted values

variables, the contemporaneous effects are not modelled. This may explain why in the first equation the only significant variable is lagged $\ln TA_{it}$. However, this does not necessarily mean that the variables $\ln GDP_{it}$, $\ln TV_{it}$ and $\ln RCPI_{it}$ have no role to play in the determination of UK tourism demand to South Korea. In later sections, we will see that these variables are in fact cointegrated, and the changes in tourism demand can be appropriately

*Table 7.6* OLS Estimation of GDP Equation in the Unrestricted VAR Model

Dependent variable is LGDPUK

32 observations used for estimation from 1963 to 1994

| Regressor | Coefficient | Standard Error | T Ratio[Prob] |
|---|---|---|---|
| LTAUK(–1) | 0.02269 | 0.05766 | 0.3936[0.697] |
| LGDPUK(–1) | 0.70836 | 0.15685 | 4.5162[0.000] |
| LTVUK(–1) | –0.6675E-3 | 0.02955 | –0.0226[0.982] |
| LRCPIUK(–1) | –0.05427 | 0.03012 | –1.8019[0.083] |
| INPT | 0.77736 | 0.40752 | 1.9076[0.067] |

| | | | |
|---|---|---|---|
| R-Squared | 0.9777 | R-Bar-Squared | 0.9744 |
| S.E. of Regression | 0.0332 | F-stat. F(4, 27) | 295.8493 |
| Mean of Dependent Variable | 4.3264 | S.D. of Dependent Variable | 0.2075 |
| Residual Sum of Squares | 0.0298 | Equation Log-likelihood | 66.2674 |
| Akaike Info. Criterion | 61.2674 | Schwarz Bayesian Criterion | 57.6031 |
| DW-statistic | 2.4575 | System Log-likelihood | 134.1488 |

| Diagnostic Tests | | |
|---|---|---|
| Test Statistics | LM Version | F Version |
| A: Serial Correlation | CHSQ(1) =  3.6654[0.056] | F(1, 26) = 3.3634[0.078] |
| B: Functional Form | CHSQ(1) =  0.7931[0.373] | F(1, 26) = 0.6607[0.424] |
| C: Normality | CHSQ(2) = 11.0401[0.004] | Not applicable |
| D: Heteroscedasticity | CHSQ(1) =  2.4237[0.120] | F(1, 30) = 2.4584[0.127] |

modelled by both the current (in differenced form) and lagged $\ln GDP_{it}$, $\ln TV_{it}$ and $\ln RCPI_{it}$ (as the error correction term).

### 7.6.4   Impulse Response Analysis and Forecasting Variance Decomposition

The VAR(1) models are estimated over the period 1962 to 1994. In order to look at the dynamic effects of a unitary shock measured by one standard error to a particular regression equation in the VAR(1) model on the tourism demand variables $\ln TA_{it}$, $\ln GDP_{it}$, $\ln TV_{it}$ and $\ln RCPI_{it}$, the corresponding

*Table 7.7* OLS Estimation of Trade Volume Equation
in the Unrestricted VAR Model

Dependent variable is LTVUK

32 observations used for estimation from 1963 to 1994

| Regressor | Coefficient | Standard Error | T Ratio[Prob] |
|---|---|---|---|
| LTAUK(−1) | 1.2875 | 0.4058 | 3.1724[0.004] |
| LGDPUK(−1) | −1.8913 | 1.1041 | −1.7130[0.098] |
| LTVUK(−1) | 0.2705 | 0.2080 | 1.3002[0.205] |
| LRCPIUK(−1) | 0.3346 | 0.2120 | 1.5782[0.126] |
| INPT | 3.2346 | 2.8685 | 1.1276[0.269] |

| | | | |
|---|---|---|---|
| R-Squared | 0.9829 | R-Bar-Squared | 0.9803 |
| S.E. of Regression | 0.2338 | F-stat. F(4, 27) | 387.3689 |
| Mean of Dependent Variable | 6.3559 | S.D. of Dependent Variable | 1.6671 |
| Residual Sum of Squares | 1.4756 | Equation Log-likelihood | 3.8205 |
| Akaike Info. Criterion | −1.1795 | Schwarz Bayesian Criterion | −4.8438 |
| DW-statistic | 1.5744 | System Log-likelihood | 134.1488 |

*Diagnostic Tests*

| Test Statistics | LM Version | F Version |
|---|---|---|
| A: Serial Correlation | CHSQ(1) = 1.9215[0.166] | F(1, 26) = 1.6609[0.209] |
| B: Functional Form | CHSQ(1) = 14.8842[0.000] | F(1, 26) = 22.6101[0.000] |
| C: Normality | CHSQ(2) = 2.1527[0.341] | Not applicable |
| D: Heteroscedasticity | CHSQ(1) = 1.7685[0.184] | F(1, 30) = 1.7550[0.195] |

orthogonalised impulse response functions are plotted over 20 periods. To save space we only plot the orthogonalised impulse response functions of the two equations with $\ln TA_{it}$ and $\ln GDP_{it}$ as dependent variables for each country. The same method can also be used to examine the impulse response functions in the third equation in which relative tourism prices are the dependent variable.

Figures 7.1 and 7.2 show the time path or impulse responses of $\ln TA_{it}$ to unitary 'shocks' in its own and other series for the UK and USA, respectively. Figure 7.1 suggests that the impact of a unit shock to the UK tourism demand equation tends to have a relatively large impact on trade volume

Table 7.8  OLS Estimation of Tourist Prices Equation
in the Unrestricted VAR Model

Dependent variable is LRCPIUK

32 observations used for estimation from 1963 to 1994

| Regressor | Coefficient | Standard Error | T Ratio[Prob] |
|---|---|---|---|
| LTAUK(−1) | −0.2068 | 0.2160 | −0.9574[0.347] |
| LGDPUK(−1) | 1.0610 | 0.5876 | 1.8057[0.082] |
| LTVUK(−1) | −0.0098 | 0.1107 | −0.0883[0.930] |
| LRCPIUK(−1) | 0.8223 | 0.1128 | 7.2885[0.000] |
| INPT | −3.6986 | 1.5265 | −2.4228[0.022] |

| | | | |
|---|---|---|---|
| R-Squared | 0.9458 | R-Bar-Squared | 0.9378 |
| S.E. of Regression | 0.1244 | F-stat. F(4, 27) | 117.8876 |
| Mean of Dependent Variable | −5.6288 | S.D. of Dependent Variable | 0.4989 |
| Residual Sum of Squares | 0.4179 | Equation Log-likelihood | 24.0058 |
| Akaike Info. Criterion | 19.0058 | Schwarz Bayesian Criterion | 15.3414 |
| DW-statistic | 1.2246 | System Log-likelihood | 134.1488 |

| Diagnostic Tests | | |
|---|---|---|
| Test Statistics | LM Version | F Version |
| A: Serial Correlation | CHSQ(1) = 5.3267[0.021] | F(1, 26) = 5.1923[0.031] |
| B: Functional Form | CHSQ(1) = 2.7912[0.095] | F(1, 26) = 2.4845[0.127] |
| C: Normality | CHSQ(2) = 1.2297[0.541] | Not applicable |
| D: Heteroscedasticity | CHSQ(1) = 0.0523[0.819] | F(1, 30) = 0.0491[0.826] |

and tourism demand itself for the first few periods, although the impact of the shock stabilises as the forecasting horizon increases. This makes sense, as the tourist arrivals in South Korea consist of a relatively large proportion of business travellers, and therefore there is likely to be a bi-directional causal relationship between tourism and trade—more tourists from the UK visiting Korea means more business and vice versa. This may also be observed by looking at the impulse response functions in the GDP equation (Figure 7.3). However, as expected, shocks to the demand for Korean tourism do not have much effect on the UK GDP level. This is logical because the income level in the UK (GDP) is likely to be exogenous to the tourism demand

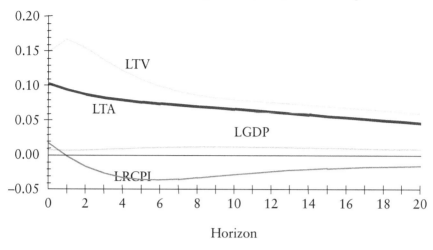

*Figure 7.1* Impulse responses to one SE shock in the UK LTA equation.

to Korea. The impulse response function in the USA model tells the same story. The policy implication from these impulse responses is that promoting tourism to South Korea will increase business opportunities and hence increase trade between Korea and the tourism-generating countries. Further examination of the income (GDP) equations for the UK and USA (Figures 7.3 and 7.4, respectively) shows that shocks to the income equations in the two tourism-generating countries tend to have large impacts on tourism demand $(\ln TA_{it})$, this being especially true for the USA.

We can also examine the forecasting error variance decomposition to determine the proportion of the movements in the time series which are due

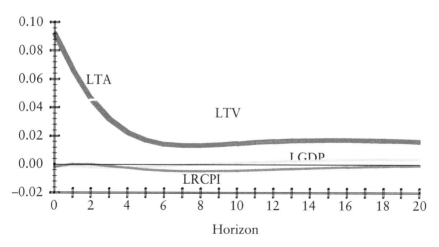

*Figure 7.2* Impulse responses to one SE shock in the US LTA equation.

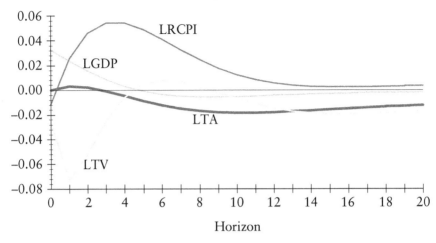

*Figure 7.3* Impulse responses to one SE shock in the UK LGDP equation.

to shocks to its own series as opposed to shocks to other variables. If shocks to one series do not explain the forecasting error variance of the other, this suggests that the former series is exogenous to the latter. Figures 7.5 and 7.6 are the plots of the forecasting error variance decomposition for the two tourist arrivals equations.

Figure 7.5 suggests that the largest proportion of the forecasting error variance in the UK tourist arrivals equation (more that 80%) is due to the shocks in the tourism arrivals series itself. The implication of this is that in order to produce better forecasts for the UK tourist arrivals series, it is crucially important to correctly utilise the information in the series itself.

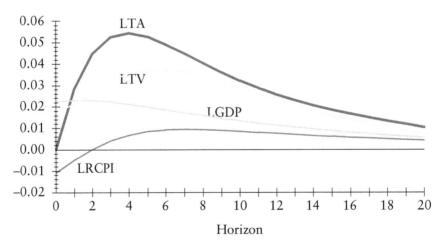

*Figure 7.4* Impulse responses to one SE shock in the US LGDP equation.

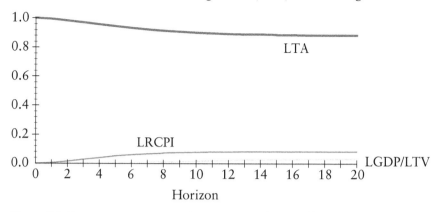

*Figure 7.5* Forecast error variance decomposition for variable LTA (UK).

For the USA tourist arrivals equation, about 50% of the forecasting errors are due to the shocks to the relative price variable. Therefore, to improve the forecasting performance of the USA tourist arrivals equation, correctly forecasting the relative price variable is very important.

### 7.6.5    Ex Post Forecasting Performance

In Chapter 6, we generated *ex post* forecasts over the period 1990 to 1994 on the log changes of the UK and USA tourist arrivals in South Korea using ECMs. To compare the forecasting performance of the VAR(1) models with that of the ECMs specified in Chapter 6, we also re-estimate our VAR(1) models over the period 1962 to 1990 and reserve four data points in order

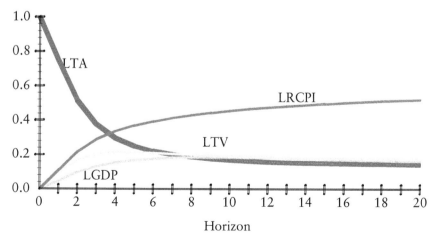

*Figure 7.6* Forecast error variance decomposition for variable LTA (US).

*Table 7.9 Ex Post* Forecast Errors of Selected Models

| Models | MAE | RMSE |
|---|---|---|
| **UK:** | | |
| VAR(1) | 0.0835 | 0.0853 |
| Engle-Granger | 0.0438 | 0.0469 |
| Wickens-Breusch | 0.0593 | 0.0617 |
| ADLM | 0.0322 | 0.0363 |
| **USA:** | | |
| VAR(1) | 0.0934 | 0.0963 |
| Engle-Granger | 0.1041 | 0.1176 |
| Wickens-Breusch | 0.1002 | 0.1170 |
| ADLM | 0.0991 | 0.1020 |

to generate the forecasts. The MAE and RMSE are then calculated from the forecasting errors and these are presented together with the MAE and RMSE for the ECMs in Table 7.9. Since we are interested in forecasts of tourist arrivals, only the forecasting results from the tourist arrivals equations are presented.

The results show that in the case of USA tourism demand forecasting, the VAR(1) model outperforms the ECMs. By contrast, the UK VAR(1) model is the poorest among the competing specifications. These results are not surprising since empirical evidence shows that ECMs tend to outperform VAR models if the variables are cointegrated (Kim and Song, 1998), as is the case with the UK series. On the other hand, if the variables are not cointegrated according to the Engle and Granger two-stage approach (as is the case with the USA series) the single ECM cannot be used for forecasting.

## 7.7    VAR MODELLING AND COINTEGRATION

In Chapter 6 we introduced the Engle-Granger two-stage approach to cointegration analysis. In this section, we will introduce a new method based on the VAR modelling framework.

### 7.7.1    Theoretical Explanation

The underlying assumption of the Engle-Granger method is that there is only one cointegration relationship among a set of economic variables.

However, this assumption is too restrictive and sometimes is unrealistic. In reality there may be more than one cointegration relationship if the long-run model involves more than two variables. What the Engle-Granger two-stage method detects is only an 'average' cointegrating vector over a number of cointegration vectors. Another serious problem with this approach is that it is based on a two-stage procedure, and any error introduced in the first stage will be carried over to the second stage. Fortunately, these problems can be overcome by the Johansen (1988) and Stock and Watson (1988) maximum likelihood estimators, which have been developed within the VAR modelling framework. Not only are these estimators less prone to estimation bias, but also they can be used to test for and estimate multiple cointegration relationships. In this section we only introduce the Johansen procedure at a basic level, but for those readers who are interested in a more advanced exposition of the Johansen procedure and/or a discussion of the Stock and Watson procedure, as well as related topics on multivariate cointegration analysis, Hamilton (1994, pp. 630–53) is a good reference.

The Johansen cointegration procedure is an extension of the univariate Dickey-Fuller test to a multivariate VAR framework. In order to understand the Johansen cointegration technique, we start by extending the univariate first-order autoregressive process $y_t = \beta y_{t-1} + u_t$ to an $m$-variable VAR(1) process:

$$Y_t = BY_{t-1} + U_t \qquad (7.25)$$

so that

$$\begin{aligned} \Delta Y_t &= (B - I)Y_{t-1} + U_t \\ &= \Phi Y_{t-1} + U_t \end{aligned} \qquad (7.26)$$

where $Y_t$ is an $(m \times 1)$ vector of variables, $U_t$ is an $(m \times 1)$ vector of errors, $I$ is an $(m \times m)$ identity matrix and $\Phi$ is an $(m \times m)$ matrix of parameters.

We shall see later that the rank of $\Phi$ equals the number of cointegrating vectors. Therefore, the cointegration test within a multivariate VAR framework is to find out the rank of the matrix $\Phi$. In order for the test statistics to be valid, the usual assumptions regarding the residual errors apply, that is, $U_t$ has to be normally distributed with zero mean and constant variance $\Sigma$. However, if the variables in $Y_t$ are $I(1)$ processes, the error terms in $U_t$ in Equation (7.26) are highly likely to be autocorrelated due to a common trend present in the data, and therefore any statistics calculated from the estimated Equation (7.26) will not be standard normal. To overcome this problem, as with the Dickey-Fuller test, Equations (7.25) and (7.26) can be generalised to allow for higher-order autoregressive processes:

$$Y_t = B_1 Y_{t-1} + B_2 Y_{t-2} + \ldots + B_p Y_{t-p} + U_t \qquad (7.27)$$

where $Y_t$ is an $(m \times 1)$ vector of m potential endogenous variables and each of the $B_i$ is an $(m \times m)$ matrix of parameters.

By allowing a higher order of autoregression, the residual term $U_t$ is more likely to be well behaved.

As with the transformation carried out in deriving the augmented Dickey-Fuller test, Equation (7.27) can also be further transformed into a more appropriate form for statistical testing. First, subtract $Y_{t-1}$ from both sides of (7.27) to yield

$$\Delta Y_t = (B_1 - I)Y_{t-1} + B_2 Y_{t-2} + B_3 Y_{t-3} + ... + B_p Y_{t-p} + U_t$$

Then, add and subtract $(B_1 - I)Y_{t-2}$ on the right hand side of the above equation to obtain

$$\Delta Y_t = (B_1 - I)\Delta Y_{t-1} + (B_1 + B_2 - I)Y_{t-2} + B_3 Y_{t-3} + ... + B_p Y_{t-p} + U_t$$

Next, add and subtract $(B_1 + B_2 - I)Y_{t-3}$ to arrive at

$$\Delta Y_t = (B_1 - I)\Delta Y_{t-1} + (B_1 + B_2 - I)\Delta Y_{t-2} + (B_1 + B_2 + B_3 - I)Y_{t-3}$$
$$+ ... + B_p Y_{t-p} + U_t$$

A similar process is repeated until eventually Equation (7.28) is obtained:

$$\Delta Y_t = \sum_{i=1}^{p-1} \Phi_i \Delta Y_{t-i} + \Phi Y_{t-p} + U_t \qquad (7.28)$$

where $\Phi_i = -(I - B_1 - B_2 - ... - B_i)$ and $\Phi = -(I - B_1 - B_2 - ... - B_p)$.

Equation (7.28) is known as a vector error correction model (VECM), and the error correction term is embodied in $\Phi Y_{t-p}$. The parameter matrices $\Phi_i$ and $\Phi$ in Equation (7.28) are short-run and long-run adjustments to the changes in $Y_t$, respectively. The $(m \times m)$ matrix $\Phi$ can be expressed as a product of two matrices:

$$\Phi = \alpha\beta'$$

where $\alpha$ represents the speed of adjustment to disequilibrium and $\beta$ is a matrix of long-run coefficients such that the term $\beta' Y_{t-p}$ represents $r \leq (m - 1)$ cointegration vectors, which ensure that $Y_t$ converges to its long-run equilibrium status.

If the variables in $Y_t$ are all $I(1)$, then $\Delta Y_{t-i}$ must be $I(0)$. For $U_t$ to be a 'white noise' process in Equation (7.28), the term $\Phi Y_{t-p}$ must satisfy one of the following three conditions. First, all the variables in $Y_t$ are stationary. This means that the spurious regression problem will not arise and a standard VAR model with levels variables would be a good strategy to model and forecast the economic relationships. Secondly, no cointegration relationships exist among the variables in $Y_t$. If this is the case, there is no need to incorporate the long-run information (levels variables) into the system, and a standard VAR model with differenced series would be appropriate. The third situation is that there are $r \le (m - 1)$ cointegration relationships. In this case, the linear combination of the $I(1)$ variables in $Y_t$ will be $I(0)$, and therefore specification (7.28) is said to be a balanced equation, that is, all the terms in Equation (7.28) are $I(0)$.

The number of cointegrating vectors can be obtained by looking at the significance of the characteristic roots of $\Phi$. From linear algebra, we know that the rank of a matrix is the same as the number of characteristic roots that are different from zero. Suppose that we have found that the matrix $\Phi$ has $r$ characteristic roots $\lambda_1, \lambda_2, \ldots, \lambda_r$, which are ranked in descending order. If the rank of $\Phi$ is zero, all the $r$ characteristic roots are also zero, and this suggests that the variables in $Y_t$ are not cointegrated.

The number of characteristic roots can be calculated from the following two statistics:

$$\lambda_{trace} = -T \sum_{i=r+1}^{m} \ln(1 - \hat{\lambda}_i) \tag{7.29}$$

$$\lambda_{max} = -T \ln(1 - \hat{\lambda}_{r+1}) \tag{7.30}$$

where $\hat{\lambda}_i$ are the estimated values of the characteristic roots or eigenvalues from the estimated $\Phi$ matrix in Equation (7.28) and $T$ is the total number of observations.

The first test is known as the trace test. The null hypothesis is that there are at most $r$ cointegrating vectors, that is, the rank of $\Phi$ is less than or equal to $r$, and the alternative hypothesis in this case is that there are more than $r$ cointegrating vectors. The second statistic, known as the maximal eigenvalue test, assumes that the rank is $r$ against the alternative that the rank is $(r + 1)$. Johansen and Juselius (1990) report the critical values for these two statistics based on a Monte Carlo simulation approach. Although interested readers can consult the original paper for the critical values, most modern econometric packages report these values against the calculated statistics.

The VECM discussed above does not include any deterministic components (such as intercept, trend or seasonal dummies). Equation (7.28) can, however, be easily extended to include these deterministic terms:

$$\Delta Y_t = \sum_{i=1}^{p-1} \Phi_i \Delta Y_{t-i} + \Phi Y_{t-p} + \Psi D_t + U_t \tag{7.31}$$

where $D_t$ is a vector of deterministic variables.

In Equation (7.31), we see that the cointegration relationship can now be represented by $\Phi Y_{t-p} + \Psi D_t$ or $\alpha \beta' Y_{t-p} + \Psi D_t$. Johansen (1995) considers five situations in which deterministic components could be incorporated in the cointegration equations. These are as follows:

*Model I:* The time series in $Y_t$ does not have deterministic trends and the long-run cointegration equations do not have intercepts:

$$\Phi Y_{t-p} + \Psi D_t = \alpha \beta' Y_{t-p} \tag{7.32}$$

This type of cointegration model normally relates to differenced data. In practice this specification is uninteresting since most economic time series are integrated. Therefore, the cointegrating equations tend to either include a trend or an intercept or sometimes both.

*Model II:* The time series in $Y_t$ does not have deterministic trends but the cointegration equations have intercepts:

$$\Phi Y_{t-p} + \Psi D_t = \alpha(\beta' Y_{t-p} + \mu) \tag{7.33}$$

where $\mu$ is an $(m \times 1)$ vector of intercepts.

This type of model normally relates to data that do not have linear trends, but may have stochastic trends (for example, financial time series such as exchange rates).

*Model III:* The time series in $Y_t$ has deterministic trends but the cointegration equations only have intercepts:

$$\Phi Y_{t-p} + \Psi D_t = \alpha(\beta' Y_{t-p} + \rho_0) + \alpha_\perp \gamma_0 \tag{7.34}$$

where $\alpha_\perp$ is an $m \times (m - r)$ matrix such that $\alpha' \alpha_\perp = 0$.

Model III is the most commonly used specification in economics because in many long-run economic relationships, such as the relationship between consumption and income, trend components are normally not present. Tourism demand models tend to fall into this group of models as well (Kim and Song, 1998; Song and Witt, 2000).

*Model IV:* Both the time series in $Y_t$ and the cointegration models have linear trends:

$$\Phi Y_{t-p} + \Psi D_t = \alpha(\beta' Y_{t-p} + \rho_0 + \rho_1 t) + \alpha_\perp \gamma_0 \tag{7.35}$$

This type of model is normally associated with the demand for durable goods that involves habit persistence behaviour. For example, Romilly *et al.* (1998b) found a negative trend in their long-run car ownership model for Great Britain, and this negative trend reflects a change in consumers' attitudes towards not owning a car in the long run due to the increasing level of road congestion in the UK. However, there is not enough evidence to suggest that the long-run tourism demand model contains trend components.

*Model V:* The variables in levels form have quadratic trends, but the cointegration equations have linear trends:

$$\Phi Y_{t-p} + \Psi D_t = \alpha(\beta' Y_{t-p} + \rho_0 + \rho_1 t) + \alpha_\perp (\gamma_0 + \gamma_1 t) \tag{7.36}$$

This type of model is difficult to justify on economic grounds, especially when the variables enter the cointegration equations in log form, but it does imply that the long-run equilibrium relationship is evolving at an increasing or decreasing rate.

The critical values of the trace and maximal eigenvalue cointegration tests given by Equations (7.29) and (7.30) are not the same for each of these five models. Osterwald-Lenum (1992) provides simulated critical values for these models, and they are normally reported in computing packages (for example, Eviews 5.1 and Microfit 4.0).

A key question is, which of the above five specifications should be selected. There is no clear-cut answer; however, as a rule of thumb, a researcher should be guided by both economic interpretations of the estimated long-run cointegrating vectors (such as signs and magnitudes) and statistical criteria.

### 7.7.2    An Empirical Example

The aim of this example is to provide a step-by-step illustration of the Johansen cointegration methodology. We use the same data set on the demand for Korean tourism by UK and USA residents as used in the previous section. We are interested in testing for cointegration relationships among the following variables: $LTA_{it}$, $LGDP_{it}$, $LTV_{it}$ and $LRCPI_{it}$ where $i = 1,2$ and $1 = UK$ and $2 = USA$. Since the Engle-Granger two-stage approach identified a cointegration relationship between the demand variables for the UK but not for the USA, we will try to see whether the Johansen method confirms this or not. A comparison between the two procedures should be very useful.

*Step 1* Pretest the data and select the lag length of the VAR model. In this step, it is advisable to plot the data to see how the variables evolve over time. Although the variables with higher orders of integration might also be included in the VAR model, it is better to only include the variables which are integrated of order one plus some of the deterministic variables which are normally $I(0)$. According to the Dickey-Fuller and Phillips-Perron tests we already discovered in Chapter 6 that all the tourism demand variables in question are integrated or order one.

The Johansen cointegration tests can be very sensitive to the choice of the lag length of the VAR model, and therefore the number of lags chosen will directly affect the validity of the test results. The criteria used to determine the lag structure of the VAR model are those discussed in the previous section, that is, the AIC, SBC and the LR statistic. We already used these criteria in the determination of the order of the UK and USA VAR models in section 7.6, and the results suggest that the lag length of both the UK and USA VAR models should be equal to one.

*Step 2* Estimate the VECM and determine the rank of the parameter matrix $\Phi$. The VECM in our case can be formulated as

$$\Delta Y_t = \Phi_i \Delta Y_{t-1} + \Phi Y_{t-1} + U_t$$

or

$$
\begin{bmatrix} \Delta LTA_{it} \\ \Delta LGDP_{it} \\ \Delta LTV_{it} \\ \Delta LRCPI_{it} \end{bmatrix} = \begin{bmatrix} \phi^1_{11} & \phi^1_{12} & \phi^1_{13} & \phi^1_{14} \\ \phi^1_{21} & \phi^1_{22} & \phi^1_{23} & \phi^1_{24} \\ \phi^1_{31} & \phi^1_{32} & \phi^1_{33} & \phi^1_{34} \\ \phi^1_{41} & \phi^1_{42} & \phi^1_{43} & \phi^1_{44} \end{bmatrix} \begin{bmatrix} \Delta LTA_{it-1} \\ \Delta LGDP_{it-1} \\ \Delta LTV_{it-1} \\ \Delta LRCPI_{it-1} \end{bmatrix}
$$

$$
+ \begin{bmatrix} \phi_{11} & \phi_{12} & \phi_{13} & \phi_{14} \\ \phi_{21} & \phi_{22} & \phi_{23} & \phi_{24} \\ \phi_{31} & \phi_{32} & \phi_{33} & \phi_{34} \\ \phi_{41} & \phi_{42} & \phi_{43} & \phi_{44} \end{bmatrix} \begin{bmatrix} LTA_{it-1} \\ LGDP_{it-1} \\ LTV_{it-1} \\ LRCPI_{it-1} \end{bmatrix} + \begin{bmatrix} u_{1it} \\ u_{2it} \\ u_{3it} \\ u_{4it} \end{bmatrix}
$$

(7.37)

We see that OLS is not suitable for the estimation of the above VECM since we have to impose restrictions on the $\Phi$ matrix. Although we do not include an intercept vector in the formulation of the VECM for simplicity, when the model is estimated it is likely that intercept terms should be included since all of our series are trended.

Let us first look at the UK demand model. In the estimation of the UK VECM, an intercept vector is introduced into the long-run cointegrating equations. The estimation uses 32 observations from 1963 to 1994, since one data point is lost due to differencing. The results of the Johansen maximal eigenvalue and trace tests are reported in Tables 7.10 and 7.11 (printouts from Microfit 4.0).

The upper section of each table contains the information on the sample period, the names of the variables in the VECM and the calculated characteristic roots (eigenvalues). In the lower section of the tables, the calculated

*Table 7.10* Johansen Cointegration Test Based on $\lambda_{max}$ (UK)

32 observations from 1963 to 1994. Order of VAR = 1, chosen $r = 2$.

List of variables included in the cointegrating vector:

LTAUK   LGDPUK   LTVUK   LRCPIUK   Intercept

List of eigenvalues in descending order:

0.73681   0.49017   0.22565   0.16263   0.0000

| Null | Alternative | Statistic | 5% Critical Value | 10% Critical Value |
|------|-------------|-----------|-------------------|--------------------|
| $r = 0$ | $r = 1$ | 42.7166 | 28.27 | 25.80 |
| $r \leq 1$ | $r = 2$ | 21.5578 | 22.04 | 19.86 |
| $r \leq 2$ | $r = 3$ | 8.1832 | 15.87 | 13.81 |
| $r \leq 3$ | $r = 4$ | 5.6796 | 9.16 | 7.53 |

*Table 7.11* Johansen Cointegration Test Based on $\lambda_{trace}$ (UK)

32 observations from 1963 to 1994. Order of VAR = 1, chosen $r$ = 2.

List of variables included in the cointegrating vector:

LTAUK  LGDPUK  LTVUK  LRCPIUK  Intercept

List of eigenvalues in descending order:

0.73681  0.49017  0.22565  0.16263  0.0000

| Null | Alternative | Statistic | 5% Critical Value | 10% Critical Value |
|------|-------------|-----------|-------------------|--------------------|
| $r = 0$ | $r \geq 1$ | 78.1373 | 53.48 | 49.95 |
| $r \leq 1$ | $r \geq 2$ | 35.4206 | 34.87 | 31.93 |
| $r \leq 2$ | $r \geq 3$ | 13.8628 | 20.18 | 17.88 |
| $r \leq 3$ | $r = 4$ | 5.6796 | 9.16 | 7.53 |

maximal eigenvalue and trace statistics and the corresponding critical values of the two statistics are shown. The inference is that if the calculated statistics are greater than the corresponding critical values at specific significance levels, the null hypotheses which are presented in the first columns of the two tables should be rejected. For example, if we look at the maximal eigenvalue test in Table 7.10, we can see that the hypothesis that there is no cointegration relationship ($r = 0$) is rejected since the calculated $\lambda_{max}$ is 42.7166, which is greater than the critical values at both the 5% and 10 % significance levels. The $\lambda_{max}$ statistic suggests that there are two cointegration vectors at the 10% significance level, but not at the 5% level. The $\lambda_{trace}$ test in Table 7.11 suggests two cointegrating vectors at the 5% significance level. Therefore, it is safe to conclude that two cointegrating relationships exist among the variables in the UK tourism demand model.

Following the same procedure, we obtain the corresponding cointegration test statistics for the USA tourism demand model, and they are presented in Tables 7.12 and 7.13. The results also suggest that there are likely to be two cointegration vectors, which contradicts the results from the Engle-Granger two-stage approach, in which no cointegration relationship was found.

According to the $\lambda_{max}$ and $\lambda_{trace}$ tests we know that the variables in both the UK and USA demand models have two cointegrating relationships, and these are presented in Tables 7.14 and 7.15. The values in brackets are the normalised cointegrating vectors, that is, each value in the vector is divided by the first value in the same vector. As can be seen from the above equations, the income variable in the cointegration vector 1 in Table 7.14 and trade value variable in the cointegration vector 1 in Table 7.15 do not have the expected signs. Therefore, although two cointegrating vectors for each

*Table 7.12* Johansen Cointegration Test Based on $\lambda_{max}$ (USA)

32 observations from 1963 to 1994. Order of VAR = 1.

List of variables included in the cointegrating vector:

LTAUS   LGDPUS   LTVUS   LRCPIUS   Intercept

List of eigenvalues in descending order:

0.86810   0.51471   0.20891   0.089882   0.0000

| Null | Alternative | Statistic | 5% Critical Value | 10% Critical Value |
|------|-------------|-----------|-------------------|---------------------|
| $r = 0$ | $r = 1$ | 64.8231 | 28.27 | 25.80 |
| $r \leq 1$ | $r = 2$ | 23.1361 | 22.04 | 19.86 |
| $r \leq 2$ | $r = 3$ | 7.4991 | 15.87 | 13.81 |
| $r \leq 3$ | $r = 4$ | 3.0138 | 9.16 | 7.53 |

of the two countries have been identified, only one is economically meaningful for each country.

The two economically acceptable cointegration relationships, together with those obtained from the Engle-Granger (EG), Wickens-Breusch (WB) and ADLM methods (see Chapter 6), are presented in Table 7.16. The long-run cointegrating vectors actually represent the long-run demand elasticities. Table 7.16 shows that the estimated income elasticities for the UK and USA models based on the Johansen method are lower than those estimated by the

*Table 7.13* Johansen Cointegration Test Based on $\lambda_{trace}$ (USA)

32 observations from 1963 to 1994. Order of VAR = 1.

List of variables included in the cointegrating vector:

LTAUS   LGDPUS   LTVUS   LRCPIUS   Intercept

List of eigenvalues in descending order:

0.86810   0.51471   0.20891   0.089882   0.0000

| Null | Alternative | Statistic | 5% Critical Value | 10% Critical Value |
|------|-------------|-----------|-------------------|---------------------|
| $r = 0$ | $r \geq 1$ | 98.4721 | 53.48 | 49.95 |
| $r \leq 1$ | $r \geq 2$ | 33.6491 | 34.87 | 31.93 |
| $r \leq 2$ | $r \geq 3$ | 10.5129 | 20.18 | 17.88 |
| $r \leq 3$ | $r = 4$ | 3.0138 | 9.16 | 7.53 |

*Table 7.14* Estimated Cointegrated Vectors in Johansen Estimation (UK)

32 observations from 1963 to 1994. Order of VAR = 1, chosen $r = 2$.

List of variables included in the cointegrating vector:
LTAUK   LGDPUK   LTVUK   LRCPIUK   Intercept

|  | Vector 1 | Vector 2 |
|---|---|---|
| LTAUK | 0.0856 | −1.6713 |
|  | (−1.0000) | (−1.0000) |
| LGDPUK | 0.4128 | 3.1380 |
|  | (−4.8248) | (1.8776) |
| LTVUK | −0.0516 | 0.7826 |
|  | (0.6030) | (0.4683) |
| LRCPIUK | 0.1213 | −0.0569 |
|  | (−1.4181) | (−0.3406) |
| Intercept | −1.7031 | −6.6912 |
|  | (19.9052) | (−4.0035) |

other three approaches (with one exception in the UK model). In terms of the elasticities of trade volume in the UK models, the differences are relatively small no matter what methods are used (0.436–0.473), whilst for the USA the differences are much wider (from 0.277, based on the ADLM, to 2.456, based on the WB). A similar pattern is also observed for the price elasticities between the two countries. These results suggest that the structure of the long-run UK model is relatively stable in comparison with the structure of the long-run USA model. In Chapter 8, we shall discuss how to model unstable relationships using a time varying parameter (TVP) approach.

Another point is that we did not find any cointegration relationship using the Engle-Granger two-stage approach in the case of the USA model, but the Johansen method suggests two long-run cointegration relationships and in one of them the coefficients are correctly signed and have the expected orders of magnitude. Since two cointegrating vectors have been identified for both the UK and USA long-run tourism demand models, the estimates from the Johansen approach are likely to be more reliable. As mentioned earlier, the Engle-Granger method tends to 'average' multiple cointegration relationships, and therefore there is a possibility that the cointegration relationships

*Table 7.15* Estimated Cointegrated Vectors in Johansen Estimation (USA)

32 observations from 1963 to 1994. Order of VAR = 1, chosen $r$ = 2.

List of variables included in the cointegrating vector:

LTAUS   LGDPUS   LTVUS   LRCPIUS   Intercept

|  | *Vector 1* | *Vector 2* |
|---|---|---|
| LTAUS | –0.1484 | –0.8963 |
|  | (–1.0000) | (–1.0000) |
| LGDPUS | 0.4743 | 1.4388 |
|  | (3.1973) | (1.6053) |
| LTVUS | –0.0078 | 0.4585 |
|  | (–0.0529) | (0.5115) |
| LRCPIUS | –0.6857 | –0.5954 |
|  | (–4.6225) | (–0.6643) |
| Intercept | –4.6750 | –3.9957 |
|  | (–31.5136) | (–4.4582) |

among the USA tourism demand variables have been 'averaged' out by the Engle-Granger approach.

*Step 3* Generate forecasts with the VECM. Although we make our decisions about whether to accept a long-run cointegrating relationship based on the economic interpretations of the cointegration coefficients (demand elasticities, in our case), for forecasting purposes this restriction does not apply. We should utilise all possible cointegrating vectors when generating forecasts.

We now re-estimate the VECMs using the sample period 1962 to 1990 and then forecast the $\Delta \ln TA_{it}$s from 1991 to 1994 using both cointegrating vectors for each of the two generating countries. Table 7.17 presents the forecasting errors. These errors show that the cointegrating vectors (CV II for both countries), which make sense economically, do not necessarily produce better forecasts. Furthermore, comparing the results in Table 7.17 with those in Table 7.9, we can see that the Johansen method generates the most accurate forecasts for the USA no matter which CV is used, whilst for the UK the Johansen approach outperforms the VAR(1), EG and WB, but not the ADLM. In general, we conclude that the Johansen approach gives

*Table 7.16* Long-Run Cointegration Vectors Based on Different Estimation Methods

| | EG | | WB | | ADLM | | Johansen | |
|---|---|---|---|---|---|---|---|---|
| Variables | UK | US | UK | US | UK | US | UK | US |
| $\ln TA_{1t}$ | 1.000 | 1.000 | 1.000 | 1.000 | 1.000 | 1.000 | 1.000 | 1.000 |
| $\ln GDP_{it}$ | 2.097 | 1.655 | 1.363 | 1,557 | 1.702 | 2.380 | 1.878 | 1.605 |
| $\ln TV_{it}$ | 0.473 | 0.576 | 0.469 | 0.443 | 0.456 | 0.277 | 0.468 | 0.512 |
| $\ln RCPI_{it}$ | −0.213 | −0.861 | −0.402 | −1.313 | −0.322 | −1.871 | −0.341 | −0.664 |
| Intercept | −4.257 | −6.158 | −1.973 | −7.870 | −2.897 | −13.43 | −4.004 | −4.458 |

more reliable estimates of the long-run coefficients and generates more accurate forecasts if more than one cointegrating vector exists among a set of economic variables. Moreover, the methods of testing for a single cointegration relationship, such as the Engle-Granger approach, are likely to fail to identify the long-run equilibrium relationships, even when the variables are actually cointegrated. Therefore, our recommendation is to use the Johansen method whenever it is possible, especially in those cases where multiple cointegrating relationships are involved.

*Table 7.17* *Ex Post* Forecast Errors of the VECMs

| | UK | | US | |
|---|---|---|---|---|
| | CV I | CV II | CV I | CV II |
| MAE | 0.0366 | 0.0446 | 0.0401 | 0.0564 |
| RMSE | 0.0395 | 0.0528 | 0.0489 | 0.0618 |

# 8 Time Varying Parameter Modelling

## 8.1   INTRODUCTION

One of the recurrent features of causal tourism demand forecasting models, compared with simple time series models, such as the no change model, has been predictive failure (Witt and Witt, 1995). Predictive failure is normally associated with model structure instability, that is, the parameters of the demand model vary over time. There are two basic reasons why a causal model may suffer from structural instability. The first, and traditional view, is that our knowledge about the structure of the model is limited. Thus, when a failure occurs we add this information into our knowledge base and produce a better model encompassing both the new and earlier experiences. In this case structural change is regarded merely as a manifestation of an inadequate or inappropriate specification. The second view is that predictive failure and the apparent coefficient changes exhibited in a tourism demand model may well be a reflection of underlying structural change in the data generating process. This structural change is mainly related to important social, political and economic policy changes. Associated with these two views on the reasons for model instability there are two radically different approaches a modeller could adopt.

The first view requires re-specifying the unstable demand model to achieve a stable one encompassing the key characteristics of all existing models. This approach has many benefits, not least being the capacity to learn from the failures of the earlier models. In essence it is 'scientific' in the Poperian sense of establishing hypotheses which are subsequently modified in the light of experimental evidence. However, this methodology fails if the DGP is not constant. According to the second view of structural instability, the appropriate way of dealing with the problem is to choose an alternative approach, for example, the time varying parameter (TVP) regression, to model the structural change. Despite common recognition of these two causes of model instability, most people have adopted the former option of solving the problem of structural instability for two reasons. First, the traditional assumption of model parameter constancy, even if it is often unrealistic, has been accepted by most econometricians as doctrine. Second, the complexity of the TVP estimation approach and lack of readily available computer software has restricted its use. However, the number of studies that utilise the TVP approach to modelling and forecasting economic activities has been growing since the late 1980s. For example, the TVP method has been used successfully in modelling and forecasting rational expectations formation and inflation (Burmeister and Wall, 1982; Cuthbertson, 1988), demand for money (Swamy *et al.*, 1990), consumption (Song, 1995; Song *et al.*, 1998) and housing prices (Brown *et al.*, 1997). However, only limited efforts have been made to use the TVP approach in tourism demand forecasting; these studies include Song *et al.* (1999), Riddington (1999), Song and Wong (2003), Song *et al.* (2003a) and Li *et al.* (2006b).

The tourism industry has evolved from a supply-led industry to a demand-driven one since the 1970s. Political, economic and social shocks such as the two 'oil crises' in the 1970s, terrorism attacks in the 1980s and the Gulf War in the early 1990s have also had sustained impacts on the demand for international tourism. Although the dummy variable approach could be used to attempt to capture the structural change due to the above-mentioned shocks, the use of the TVP method is probably a more realistic alternative.

In section 8.2 the parameter stability of the tourism demand model is examined using recursive OLS. Section 8.3 discusses the specification and estimation of the TVP model. Section 8.4 presents some empirical results relating to TVP tourism demand models, and section 8.5 concludes the chapter.

## 8.2    ARE TOURISM DEMAND ELASTICITIES CONSTANT OVER TIME?

From Chapter 1, we know that the coefficients of the explanatory variables in the double-log demand model are the measures of the demand elasticities. According to OLS these demand elasticities are time invariant. Is this is a reasonable assumption? Are the demand elasticities or the structure of the demand model really constant over time? This section sets out to answer these questions with the help of some statistical evidence.

A number of statistics may be used to test for parameter constancy. These include recursive OLS and the two Chow structural instability tests (Chow, 1960). Recursive OLS initially involves estimating the demand model using OLS from a small sub-sample of data $t = 1,2, \ldots , n$, where $n \geq k$ and $k$ is the number of explanatory variables (including the constant term) in the demand model; the sample period is then extended by one observation to $t = 1,2, \ldots , n + 1$, and the model is re-estimated using OLS; this procedure continues until all the observations in the sample are used. Each time the regression is estimated, the estimated coefficients are plotted. Examination of the plotted coefficients should inform us whether the demand elasticities of the tourism demand model have changed over time or not. For example, from Equations (6.17) and (6.18) we can see that the long-run tourism demand models for the UK and USA are estimated as

UK:   $\ln TA_{1t} = -4.257 + 2.097 \ln GDP_{1t} + 0.473 \ln TV_{1t} - 0.213 \ln RCPI_{1t}$

USA:   $\ln TA_{2t} = -6.158 + 1.655 \ln GDP_{2t} + 0.536 \ln TV_{2t} - 0.861 \ln RCPI_{2t}$

These two models show that the long-run income elasticity is 2.097 for the UK and 1.655 for the USA; the trade volume elasticity is 0.473 for the UK and 0.536 for the USA; and the own price elasticity is –0.213 for the UK and –0.861 for the USA. These elasticities are estimated over the period 1964 to 1994 using OLS and they are assumed to be constant over the sample period.

However, if we re-estimate the above models using recursive OLS, we can see that the coefficient constancy assumption is too restrictive. Figures 8.1 and 8.2 present the recursive OLS estimates of the four elasticities in each of the two long-run models. The figures represent the estimated constant term, income elasticity, trade volume elasticity and own price elasticity, respectively. The estimation starts from 1970 as the observations from 1964 to 1969 are used for the initial estimation. It is clear from the recursive

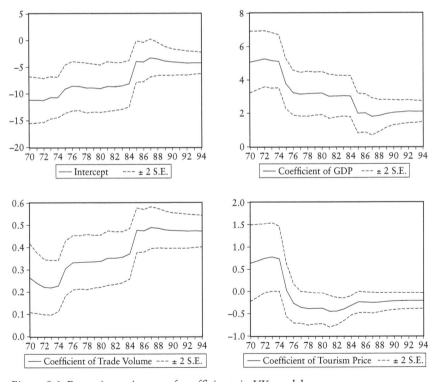

*Figure 8.1* Recursive estimates of coefficients in UK model.

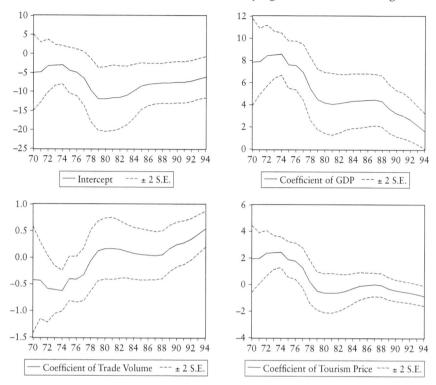

*Figure 8.2* Recursive estimates of coefficients in USA model.

estimates that some of the demand elasticities in the UK and USA models have changed significantly since the 1970s. For example, the income elasticity in the UK model changed from 5.0 in 1974 to 3.6 in 1976 and then dropped again to about 2.0 in 1985. The trade volume elasticity during the same period increased from 0.25 to 0.45. The change of income elasticity suggests that the demand for Korean tourism by UK residents was very sensitive to income changes in the 1970s, but the demand became relatively less sensitive to income changes in the 1980s and 1990s. The income and trade elasticities in the USA model experienced similar changes during the same period. Both models, however, show that the tourism price elasticity has been relative stable since a sharp fall in 1974 (the first oil crisis).

The two Chow tests for structural instability were given in Chapter 4 (Equations (4.14) and (4.15)). The first Chow test (the breakpoint test) is used here to see whether the elasticities are constant over time in the two demand models. In order to calculate the $F$-statistic based on Equation (4.14), we need to specify the point at which the structure of the model breaks. By looking at the recursive OLS estimates of the elasticities in Figures 8.1 and 8.2, we can see that there were two significant changes in demand elasticities, one was in 1974 and the other in 1984. Therefore, two values of the Chow breakpoint statistic can be calculated for each of the two models in relation to the two break points, and they are given below.

|  | 1974 | 1984 |
|---|---|---|
| UK Model: | $F_{Chow1}(4,24) = 7.56$ | $F_{Chow1}(4,24) = 2.64$ |
| USA Model: | $F_{Chow1}(4,24) = 46.07$ | $F_{Chow1}(4,24) = 3.58$ |

The critical value of $F_{Chow1}(4,24)$ at the 5% significance level is 2.54. From these figures we can see clearly that the demand elasticities have changed over the same period.

Recursive OLS is a useful tool to examine the structural stability of the regression model, especially to examine changes in the regression coefficients over the sample period due to persistent external shocks to the system. However, it suffers from the following problems in application. First, the validity of the recursive estimation depends on the length of the sample. If the sample is relatively small, the values of the parameters estimated by recursive OLS may exhibit structural change in the early part of the sample, but this does not necessarily mean that the structure of the model is unstable. The instability may simply be due to the small sample biases. Second, recursive OLS is not useful for forecasting if the structure of the model is indeed unstable due to external shocks, because when all observations are used in estimating the model the forecasts generated will be exactly the same as those obtained in the traditional constant parameter regression model, that is, the structural instability cannot be taken into account in the forecasting process. The TVP approach, however, allows for richer specifications that go far beyond the recursive OLS method. The TVP method is capable of simulating different types of shocks that may influence the relationship between the dependent and explanatory variables, and the model is also unique in incorporating structural changes into the forecasting process.

## 8.3   THE TVP MODEL AND KALMAN FILTER

The TVP model may be specified in state space (SS) form:

$$y_t = x_t \beta_t + u_t \tag{8.1}$$

$$\beta_t = \Phi \beta_{t-1} + R_t e_t \tag{8.2}$$

where $y_t$ is the dependent variable of tourism demand, $x_t$ is a row vector of $k$ explanatory variables, $\beta_t$ is a column vector of $k$ state variables known as the *state vector*, $\Phi$ is a $k \times k$ matrix, $R_t$ is a $k \times g$ matrix, $u_t$ is a residual with zero mean and constant covariance matrix $H_t$, and $e_t$ is a $g \times 1$ vector of serially uncorrelated residuals with zero mean and constant covariance matrix $Q_t$.

Equation (8.1) is called the measurement or system equation while Equation (8.2) is known as the transition equation. There are two additional assumptions related to Equations (8.1) and (8.2). The first is that the initial vector $\beta_0$ has a mean of $b_0$ and a covariance matrix $P_0$. The second assumption is that the residual terms $u_t$ and $e_t$ in the measurement and transition equations are not correlated. The matrices $x_t$, $H_t$, $R_t$ and $Q_t$ are also assumed to be non-stochastic.

If the components of the matrix $\Phi$ in Equation (8.2) equal unity, the transition equation becomes a *random walk*:

$$\beta_t = \beta_{t-1} + R_t e_t \tag{8.3}$$

If the transition equation is a random walk, the parameter vector $\beta_t$ is said to be non-stationary.

Another possible form of the transition equation is

$$\beta_t = \mu - \Phi(\beta_{t-1} - \mu) + R_t e_t \tag{8.4}$$

where $\mu$ is the mean of $\beta_t$. Equation (8.4) suggests a stationary process.

The specification of the transition equation is normally determined by experimentation. The criteria used to determine the structure of the transition equation are the goodness of fit and the predictive power of the model. Once the SS model is formulated, a convenience algorithm, known as the *Kalman filter* (KF), can be used to estimate the SS model (Kalman, 1960). The KF is a recursive procedure for calculating the optimal estimator of the state vector given all the information available at time $t$.

The derivation of the KF is now briefly demonstrated, but for a detailed exposition see Harvey (1987). Let $b_t$ and $P_t$ denote the optimal estimators of the state vector and the covariance of $\beta_t$ in Equation (8.2), respectively. Suppose the estimation starts at time $t-1$; then $b_{t/t-1}$ *and* $P_{t/t-1}$ can be calculated from

$$b_{t/t-1} = \Phi b_{t-1} \tag{8.5}$$

$$\text{and} \quad P_{t/t-1} = \Phi P_{t-1} \Phi' + R_t Q_t R_t' \tag{8.6}$$

Given Equations (8.5) and (8.6), we can estimate $y_t$ based on the information at $t-1$:

$$\hat{y}_{t/t-1} = x_t b_{t/t-1} \tag{8.7}$$

The prediction error of $y_t$ is

$$r_t = y_t - \hat{y}_{t/t-1} = \Phi(\beta_t - b_{t/t-1}) + u_t \tag{8.8}$$

and the mean squared error of $y_t$ is

$$F_t = \Phi P_{t/t-1} \Phi' + H_t \tag{8.9}$$

Once a new observation becomes available, the estimator of the state vector can be updated, and the updating process is written as

$$b_t = b_{t/t-1} + P_{t/t-1} x_t' F_t^{-1} (y_t - \Phi b_{t/t-1}) \qquad (8.10)$$

$$\text{and} \quad P_t = P_{t/t-1} - P_{t/t-1} \Phi' F_t^{-1} \Phi P_{t/t-1} \qquad (8.11)$$

Equations (8.5) through (8.11) are together called the KF. Given the initial values of $b_0$ and $P_0$, the Kalman filter produces the optimal estimator of the state vector as each observation becomes available. Therefore, one of the important steps in the KF estimation is to determine the initial values of $b_0$ and $P_0$, and we will return to this later. When all the $T$ observations are exhausted, $b_T$ should contain all the information needed for forecasting the future values of $b$, $P$ and $y$.

The $m$-period-ahead forecasts of $b$, $P$ and $y$ are based on Equations (8.12) through (8.14):

$$b_{T+m/T} = \Phi b_{T+m-1} \qquad (8.12)$$

$$P_{T+m/T} = \Phi P_{T+m-1/T} \Phi' + R_{T+m} Q_{T+m} R_{T+m}' \qquad (8.13)$$

$$\hat{y}_{T+m/T} = x_{T+m} b_{T+m/T} \qquad (8.14)$$

The mean square forecasting error is

$$F_{T/m} = x_{T+m} P_{T+m/T} x_{T+m}' + H_{T+m} \qquad (8.15)$$

The KF process estimates the state vector $\beta_t$, given information available up to time $t$. After the $\beta_t$ is estimated using the KF, the Kalman smoother (KS) is then applied to re-estimate $\beta_t$ using the information after time $t$; the KS estimator of $\beta_t$ is denoted $b_{t/T}$. Since the KS utilises more information than the KF, the estimated $b_{t/T}$ will always have a smaller covariance than the KF estimator.

To initialise the KF, the starting values of $b_0$ and $P_0$, known as the initial conditions of the KF, need to be determined first. There are a number of ways the initial values $b_0$ and $P_0$ may be determined (Harvey, 1993, pp. 88–89). The first way of determining $b_0$ and $P_0$ is to use a method called *diffuse priors*. This procedure assigns very large initial values to the covariance matrix $P$, while the initial values for the coefficients of the explanatory variables are chosen arbitrarily. If we assume that the coefficients follow a random walk process, an initial value of 1 should be assigned to those coefficients. The starting value of $P_0$ is then set to equal $\kappa I$, where $\kappa$ is a large but finite number and $I$ is a $k \times k$ identity matrix. After the values of $b_0$ and $P_0$ are determined, the KF can be used to estimate the TVPs. An alternative approach to choosing $b_0$ and $P_0$ is to estimate Equation (8.1) using OLS and then equate $b_0$ and $P_0$ to the corresponding OLS constant parameters. (Eviews uses this approach to initialise the Kalman filter estimation.)

Over the last decade, the cointegration, error correction and vector autoregressive models have been widely used, and sometimes even over-used, in the areas of modelling and forecasting virtually all macroeconomic and financial activities. Although these modelling methods are different in the ways in which the models are constructed, they are all derivatives of traditional OLS. According to Bomhoff (1994), if time series are stationary, their first and second moments are well defined and there is no conceptual problem in computing the unconditional means, variances and covariances based on the observations over the same period. However, when time series are non-stationary, as with most economic time series, OLS is invalid, since the properties of the time series depend on the length of the sample period. Therefore, unconditional means, variances and covariances cannot be calculated using OLS. To overcome this problem, the data need to be differenced. This often results in the loss of the long-run characteristics of the model. The TVP approach, on the other hand, estimates the parameters of the model sequentially using the forwards KF and backward KS, and produces conditional distributions for means and variances. It is therefore more useful in analysing non-stationary series. Moreover, the TVP approach does not require the data to be stationary before model estimation, and so the procedure of model specification and estimation is drastically simplified since one does not have to worry about unit root testing and data differencing.

In their comparative study of the forecasting performance of a number of econometric models of international tourism demand, Song *et al.* (2003a) found that the TVP model generated the most accurate short-run forecasts. This finding is consistent with previous studies on forecasting other macroeconomic activities (Brown *et al.*, 1997; Song, 1995; Song *et al.*, 1998).

## 8.4   A WORKED EXAMPLE

In this section we illustrate the process of specifying and estimating the tourism demand Equations (6.17) and (6.18) using the TVP approach. The specification of the demand model in SS form is given as

$$\ln TA_{it} = \alpha_{0t} + \alpha_{1t} \ln GDP_{it} + \alpha_{2t} \ln TV_{it} + \alpha_{3t} \ln RCPI_{it} + u_{it} \qquad (8.16)$$

$$\alpha_{jt} = \alpha_{jt-1} + \varepsilon_{jt} \qquad (8.17)$$

where $i = 1$ and 2, 1 refers to the UK and 2 to the USA, $j = 1,2,3$ and $4$ representing the number of TVPs in the system equation, and the variables are the same as those described in Chapter 6.

Equation (8.16) defines the relationship between the dependent and explanatory variables, while Equation (8.17) expresses the process according to which the parameters vary. In this example, we assume that the parameters follow a random walk process. Although the transition equation (8.17) can also be specified in other ways, the random walk process should always be tried first as this is the simplest process of parameter evolution. In fact, researchers have found that the random walk process can adequately capture the effects of parameter changes in many economic models (see, for example, Bohara and Sauer, 1992; Greenslade and Hall, 1996; Kim, 1993).

Equations (8.16) and (8.17) are estimated using the Kalman filter, which is available in the Eviews 5.1 program. The results are reported in Table 8.1. Since the transition equations all follow a random walk process, that is $\alpha_{jt} = \alpha_{jt-1}$, their estimates are not reported.

The results show that the two models fit the data very well, according to the very high $R^2$ values and the very low regression standard errors, compared with the OLS equivalents. However, the relative price variable in the UK model and the GDP variable in the USA model are insignificant at the 5% level[1]. It is also worth noting that the reported estimates of the demand elasticities are the final values from the whole sample. Researchers, however, may also wish to examine how the elasticities evolve over time. By looking at the patterns of the changes in model parameters over time, a researcher can gain useful insights into the behavioural changes of potential tourists in relation to policy and regime changes during the sample period. From basic economic theory we know that the magnitudes of the demand elasticities are unlikely to remain constant over time, since the nature of the product demanded and the tastes of consumers are time varying. One example may be that holiday travel to an overseas destination which was a luxury product for many UK residents in the 1970s (high income elasticity) had become a necessity for a considerable proportion of the UK population in the late 1980s and the 1990s (low income elasticity). The demand elasticities are also likely to vary with changes in market structure and the increasing competition within the tourism industry. To examine how the demand elasticities have evolved over time, it is therefore useful to plot the Kalman filter estimates of the elasticities during the sample period. Figures 8.3 and 8.4 give such plots.

*Table 8.1* Kalman Filter Estimates of the TVP Models (Dependent Variable: $\ln TA_{it}$)

| Variable | UK Model | USA Model |
|---|---|---|
| Intercept | 0.568 (0.159) | 2.047 (1.807) |
| $\ln GDP_{it}$ | 1.022* (0.418) | 0.146 (0.490) |
| $\ln TV_{it}$ | 0.549* (0.045) | 0.586* (0.094) |
| $\ln RCPI_{it}$ | −0.140 (0.170) | −0.573* (0.172) |
| $R^2$ | 0.999 | 0.998 |
| S.E. | 0.57E-5 | 0.91E-4 |

Notes: Values in parentheses are the standard errors; * denotes that the estimates are significant at the 5% level.

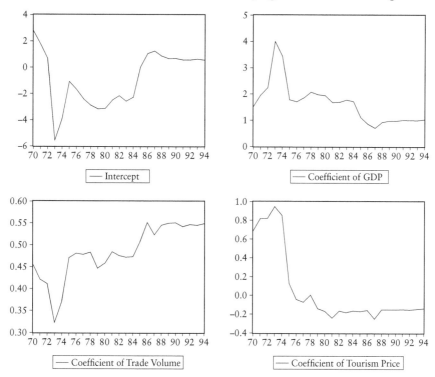

*Figure 8.3* Estimated coefficients in UK model based on Kalman filter approach.

If we ignore the first few years in the sample, we can see that the income elasticity in the UK model dropped from around 2 in the 1970s to about 1 in the 1990s, and this supports our discussion regarding the decline of income elasticity above. However, the change in income elasticity in the USA was much smaller. The tourism demand elasticities, with respect to trade volume, increased in both models by about 0.2 during the sample period. This suggests that business links have become more and more important in the determination of demand for Korean tourism by UK and USA residents. The Kalman filter estimates of the price elasticities in the two models appear to be stable over the last twenty years, and this is consistent with the estimates of the recursive OLS in section 8.2.

## 8.5    SUMMARY AND CONCLUSIONS

Demand elasticities in tourism demand models are likely to be time varying due to policy changes, evolution of consumers' tastes and economic regime shifts. The traditional econometric modelling approach that assumes parameter constancy is unable to take into account parameter instability, and

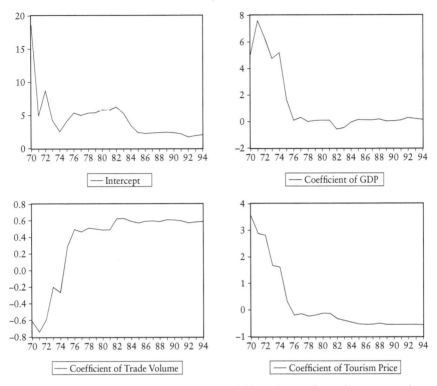

*Figure 8.4* Estimated coefficients in USA model based on Kalman filter approach.

therefore often generates poor forecasts. TVP is an alternative method that simulates structural changes in tourism demand models and therefore may well produce more accurate forecasts. The TVP model can be written in the SS form that includes a measurement/system equation and a transition equation. The specification of the transition equation is normally determined by experimentation, and the criteria used for the selection of the transition equation are the goodness of fit and the *ex post* forecasting accuracy. In most cases, the random walk process is adequate in capturing the instability in the parameters.

Once the TVP model is written in SS form, an algorithm known as the Kalman filter may be applied to estimate the parameters of the model. To start the KF estimation, initial values of the parameters and the corresponding covariances need to be determined. Once these initial values have been decided, based on either the *diffusion priors* or the OLS estimates, the estimation can proceed sequentially with a forward filter and the backward smoother.

The TVP model is likely to outperform the OLS regression model when the structure of the model is time dependent, and the forecasting performance of the TVP model will be evaluated in Chapter 11.

# 9 Panel Data Analysis

## 9.1 INTRODUCTION[1]

The increasing importance of international tourism in the balance of payments and in the creation of employment for both developed and developing economies has led to a large number of econometric studies on the determinants of international tourism demand over the past three decades. Witt and Witt (1995) provide a survey of the major studies. As noted by Lim (1997), however, although time series data are widely utilised in estimating tourism demand, few studies use cross-section or panel data. Exceptions are Carey (1991), Tremblay (1989), Witt (1980a, 1980b) and Yavas and Bilgin (1996), who pool their cross-section and time series data to estimate elasticities with respect to income, exchange rates, relative prices, transport costs and other explanatory variables for selected Caribbean countries, 18 European countries, UK, Germany and UK, and Turkey, respectively.

The purpose of this chapter is to quantify tourism demand relationships using the panel data approach and to ascertain whether variables of a social as well as an economic nature are important in the determination of international tourism demand. One of the advantages of panel data analysis over pure time series or pure cross-sectional modelling is the relatively large number of observations and the consequent increase in degrees of freedom. This reduces collinearity and improves the efficiency of the estimates. This is particularly important in tourism demand models where social variables, such as age structure, gender and education, are included in the models, as collinearity problems are likely to arise as a result of the lack of variation in the social variables over time. The use of panel data is not unproblematic, however, since the choice of an appropriate model depends *inter alia* on the degree of homogeneity of the intercept and slope coefficients and the extent to which any individual cross-section effects are correlated with the explanatory variables. These issues are discussed later in this chapter.

The remainder of this chapter is structured as follows. Section 9.2 provides an introduction to the panel data approach, section 9.3 presents an example of panel data analysis based on a data set of 138 countries over the period 1989 to 1995, and section 9.4 concludes the chapter.

## 9.2      MODEL SPECIFICATION AND ESTIMATION

### 9.2.1      Test for Poolability

Given observations on the tourism demand variable $y$ across $i = 1, \ldots, N$ regions over $t = 1, \ldots, T$ time periods and $k = 1, \ldots, K$ explanatory variables denoted by the $K \times 1$ vector $x$, the classical linear regression model is of the form:

$$y_{it} = a_i + b_i' x_{it} + \varepsilon_{it} \tag{9.1}$$

where the intercept and slope coefficients are allowed to vary across regions. The error term is identical and independently distributed or iid $(0, \sigma_\varepsilon^2)$ for all $i$ and $t$.

The first stage in the estimation procedure is to test for the poolability of the data. Although there are many examples of estimation using pooled data, poolability is by no means a foregone conclusion (see, for example, the results for tourism demand equations given in Tremblay (1989)). A starting point is to estimate a restricted model in which both the intercept and slope coefficients are assumed homogeneous across regions:

$$y_{it} = a + b' x_{it} + \varepsilon_{it} \tag{9.2}$$

and compare this with the unrestricted model above by means of an $F$ test. The first $F$ test is

$$F_1 = \frac{(RSS_{R1} - RSS_U) / [(N - 1)(K + 1)]}{RSS_U / [N(T - K - 1)]} \tag{9.3}$$

where $RSS_{R1}$ and $RSS_U$ are the residual sums of squares of the restricted and unrestricted models, respectively, and $(N - 1)(K + 1)$ and $N(T - K - 1)$ are the degrees of freedom.

If the calculated value of $F_1$ is smaller than the critical value, the null hypothesis of homogenous slopes and intercepts across the $N$ regions should be accepted. If the null hypothesis is accepted, this means that the data can be pooled and the panel data modelling approach is appropriate. However, if the null hypothesis is rejected, that is, either the intercept or the slope or both are heterogeneous, we then should proceed to test for homogeneous slopes and heterogeneous intercepts with the use of a second $F$ test:

$$F_2 = \frac{(RSS_{R2} - RSS_U) / [(N - 1)K]}{RSS_U / [N(T - K - 1)]} \tag{9.4}$$

where $RSS_{R2}$ is the residual sum of squares for the model in which the intercept terms are allowed to vary across regions but the slope coefficients are restricted to be equal.

If the calculated $F_2$ value is smaller than the critical value, we say that the intercepts of the models are heterogeneous but the slope coefficients are homogeneous. If this happens, we still can pool the data using the panel data approach.

If we accept this null hypothesis, it is also possible to test the null hypothesis of homogeneous intercepts conditional on homogeneous slopes by a third $F$ test:

$$F_3 = \frac{(RSS_{R1} - RSS_{R2})/(N-1)}{RSS_{R2}/[NT - N - K)]} \qquad (9.5)$$

To summarise, the decision rules based on the above statistics are given as follows:

a) If the null hypothesis of homogeneous intercepts and slopes is accepted based on $F_1$, this means that the cross-sectional and time series data may be pooled and further tests are not necessary.

b) However, if the null hypothesis in a) is rejected, we need to perform the $F_2$ test. This tests whether the slope coefficients are homogeneous across regions given heterogeneous intercepts. Acceptance of this null hypothesis indicates that we still can use the panel data approach to estimate the demand model. Rejection of this null hypothesis suggests that the data cannot be pooled, and therefore the panel data approach is not appropriate.

c) If the null hypothesis in b) is accepted, the $F_3$ statistics can be used to test for the null hypothesis of homogeneous intercepts conditional on homogenous slopes. Acceptance of the null hypothesis indicates that the intercepts are homogeneous if the slopes are restricted to be equal.

More detail concerning these procedures is given in Hsiao (1986).

## 9.2.2    Fixed and Random Effects

There are three ways in which the estimation of a pooled tourism demand model can take place, depending on the assumptions made about the intercept term. In the pooled ordinary least squares (POLS) model the intercept is treated as a constant across all cross-section units. Using appropriate dummy variables, the fixed effects (FE) model allows the intercept to vary between cross-section units, so that each unit has a fixed intercept specific to that unit. Differences in the intercepts reflect the unobserved differences between cross-section units. The random effects (RE) model also allows the intercept to vary between units, but treats the variation as randomly determined. The determination and estimation of the FE and RE models are described below.

Each model has its advantages and disadvantages. The POLS model is straightforward to estimate, but the assumption that the unit-specific effects do not differ is very restrictive and usually unrealistic. The FE model captures the unobserved differences between units, but the inclusion of dummy variables in the OLS estimation reduces the degrees of freedom and makes the estimates less efficient than those of the RE model. On the other hand, the RE model assumes that the unobserved unit-specific effects are uncorrelated with the regressors, since these effects are randomly determined. This assumption may not be appropriate, and its violation may cause the RE model to produce biased and inconsistent estimates.

In order to further explore the nature of the FE and RE models, we assume that the error term in Equation (9.1) can be re-specified as

$$w_{it} = u_i + \varepsilon_{it} \tag{9.6}$$

where $u_i$ denotes the unobservable cross-section-specific effects and $\varepsilon_{it}$ is the usual disturbance term, which varies across regions and time.

There are two assumptions which can be made about $u_i$. First, $u_i$ is correlated with $x_{it}$, in which case we have the FE model. Second, $u_i$ is uncorrelated with $x_{it}$, so that we have the RE model. Some care must be exercised in choosing between these models, since they can give widely differing coefficient estimates in panel data sets where, typically, the number of time series observations is small and the number of cross-section units is large (Hausman, 1978).

Because the FE model assumes that $u_i$ and $x_{it}$ are correlated, the model must be estimated *conditionally* on the presence of $u_i$, which is treated as a fixed parameter to be estimated:

$$y_{it} = u_i + b'x_{it} + \varepsilon_{it} \tag{9.7}$$

OLS estimation of this model will yield biased estimators because of the correlation between $u_i$ and $x_{it}$. Unbiased OLS estimates can be obtained by either first-differencing the variables or, alternatively, differencing them by cross-section-specific means. In both cases the fixed effect $u_i$ is eliminated and so is the correlation problem. A further implication is that the effect of any *observed* variable which is time-invariant is also eliminated. Thus the FE model is robust to the omission of any relevant time-invariant regressors.

A *priori* considerations suggest that the FE model is one from which inferences can be made conditional on the observed sample. If the focus of attention is on the sample itself, then the FE model is appropriate. If one wishes to make inferences about the population from which the sample is drawn, however, then it is more appropriate to view $u_i$ as randomly distributed across regions:

$$y_{it} = a + b'x_{it} + u_i + \varepsilon_{it} \tag{9.8}$$

where $u_i$ and $\varepsilon_{it}$ are independently and identically distributed (iid) as iid $(0, \sigma_u^2)$ and iid $(0, \sigma_\varepsilon^2)$, respectively.

Given that $u_i$ is assumed to be uncorrelated with $x_{it}$, OLS is asymptotically unbiased but inefficient compared with feasible generalised least squares (FGLS). A straightforward Lagrange multiplier test for the existence of random effects is based on the OLS residuals from the model in which both slope and intercept terms are assumed constant (Breusch and Pagan, 1980). The test is based on

$$H_o : \sigma_u^2 = 0 \quad (\text{or } \text{Corr}[w_{it}, w_{is}] = 0)$$
$$H_1 : \sigma_u^2 \neq 0$$

where the test statistic is

$$LM = \frac{nT}{2(T-1)} \left[ \frac{\sum_{i=1}^{n} [\sum_{t=1}^{T} e_{it}]^2}{\sum_{i=1}^{n} \sum_{t=1}^{T} e_{it}^2} - 1 \right]^2 \tag{9.9}$$

and $e_{it}$ is the residual from the pooled OLS regression. Under the null hypothesis $LM$ is distributed as chi-squared with one degree of freedom.

There are a number of alternatives to the Breusch-Pagan $LM$ test above, although it is not always clear which one should be used. Baltagi (1995) provides a detailed discussion of these tests. Alternatively, the RE model can be tested directly against the FE model. One of these tests is that devised by Hausman (1978). It is based on the idea that if $u_i$ is uncorrelated with $x_{it}$, there should be no systematic difference between the estimates from the FE and RE models, since both OLS in the FE model and FGLS in the RE model are consistent. The Hausman test is

$$H = (\hat{b}_{fe} - \hat{b}_{re})'(\hat{\Sigma}_{fe} - \hat{\Sigma}_{re})(\hat{b}_{fe} - \hat{b}_{re}) \tag{9.10}$$

where $\hat{\Sigma}_{fe}$ and $\hat{\Sigma}_{re}$ are the estimated slope covariance matrices for the FE and RE models, respectively.

Under the null hypothesis that $u_i$ is uncorrelated with $x_{it}$, the Hausman test statistic is distributed asymptotically as chi-squared with $K$ degrees of freedom. If the calculated value of $\chi^2(K)$ is greater than the critical value, this suggests that the RE model is relevant.

## 9.3  AN EMPIRICAL STUDY OF A TOURISM DEMAND MODEL BASED ON THE PANEL DATA APPROACH

Instead of investigating the role of traditional determinants in influencing international tourism demand from one or a few origin countries to one or a few destination countries, the current section focuses on the determinants of international tourism expenditure by 138 origin countries for the period 1989 to 1995.

## 9.3.1   The Data and the Model

The tourism expenditure variable is related to three economic explanatory variables and five 'social' variables, where the latter are included to control for changes in the demographic or socio-cultural structure of the country concerned. Specifically, we are interested in examining the following relationship:

$$TSP = f(GDP, EXC, EXV, AGE, GEN, HHS, LIT, URB) \qquad (9.11)$$
$$\quad\quad\quad + \quad ? \quad - \quad + \quad ? \quad - \quad + \quad +$$

where the variable definitions for country $i$ (the tourism-generating country) are: $TSP$ = real per capita international tourism spending (US\$) by country $i$, where the deflator is the price level index for country $i$; $GDP$ = real per capita gross domestic product (US\$) in country $i$, where the deflator is the price level index for country $i$; $EXC$ = real exchange rate = nominal exchange rate (units of country $i$'s currency per US\$) multiplied by the relative price level (world price level/country $i$ price level); $EXV$ = real exchange rate volatility = $\left|\dfrac{EXC_{it} - \mu_i}{\mu_i}\right|$ where $\mu_i$ = the arithmetic mean value of the real exchange rate for country $i$; $AGE$ = the proportion of 15 to 64-year-olds to the total population in country $i$ (%); $GEN$ = the proportion of males in the total population of country $i$ (%); $HHS$ = average household size of country $i$ (number of persons); $LIT$ = adult literacy rate in country $i$ (%); $URB$ = the proportion of urban population to total population in country $i$ (%)

Details of the variable sources are provided in the appendix. As in the traditional economic literature on the determination of international tourism, we include real income and real exchange rates as explanatory variables. Given the extreme fluctuations in some real exchange rates, however, we also include a measure of real exchange rate volatility as an explanatory variable. The relationship between $TSP$ and $GDP$ is expected to be positive, whilst that between $TSP$ and $EXV$ is expected to be negative because exchange rate volatility increases uncertainty and the transactions costs associated with holidays abroad. The real exchange rate variable $EXC$ captures two effects on the price of international tourism: first, the influence of the nominal exchange rate, which is defined as the number of units of country $i$'s currency per US dollar; and second, the influence of the relative price level between country $i$ and the world, where the USA price level is used as a proxy for the world price level[2]. The relationship between $TSP$ (which is measured in US dollars) and the nominal exchange rate as defined above is expected to be negative. An increase in the nominal exchange rate implies a fall in the value of the currency of country $i$, making overseas tourism more expensive for country $i$'s residents, and reducing the volume of outbound tourism trips from country $i$. Assuming the dollar price of an outbound tourist trip remains unchanged, $TSP$ will fall. On the other hand, the relationship between $TSP$ and the relative price level can be positive or negative, depending on the price elasticity of demand for outbound tourist trips. For a given nominal exchange rate and domestic price level, an increase in the relative price of outbound tourist trips will reduce the volume of outbound tourist trips. If demand is price-inelastic, *TSP* will increase and *vice versa*. Thus the relationship between *TSP* and *EXC* depends on whether the demand for outbound tourist trips is price-inelastic and, if so, whether this positive effect on *TSP* outweighs the negative effect associated with the nominal exchange rate. The estimation results in section 9.4 illustrate that this is indeed the case.

The age structure variable consists of those of working age who are likely to be income earners and more likely to consume international tourism services. The proportion of 15 to 64-year-olds to total population ranges from around 65% in developed countries to below 50% in some developing countries, so that it is necessary to control for the differences in demographic structure across countries in the sample. It is expected that there is a positive relationship between *TSP* and *AGE*.

The gender variable attempts to discover whether men or women have more influence on international tourism spending. In general it does not seem possible to determine *a priori* whether the sign of the coefficient of the gender variable should be negative or positive, although there is a tendency for men to travel more than women (particularly for business) and one might expect a weak positive association between *GEN* and *TSP*.

The household size variable enters the model because it may affect international tourism in the following ways. First, it may be inversely related to per capita income and thus inversely related to international tourist spending. Second, it may be positively associated with tourism demand if family holidays abroad are popular or negatively associated if singles or couples holidays abroad are popular. On balance, one would expect that the first effect is greater than the second, so that overall a negative relationship between *HHS* and *TSP* is likely.

The rate of literacy in a nation reflects its level of education. As education levels increase, so too does awareness of different countries and cultures. This is likely to promote greater interest in visiting other countries, so a positive relationship between *LIT* and *TSP* is expected.

Finally, the process of urbanisation of a nation is closely related to the process of industrialisation and civilisation. One basic feature of this process, apart from the associated rise in living standards, is the nation's closer contact with the outside world. Industrialisation both enables and provides an incentive for political, economic and cultural exchanges at an international level. Urbanisation not only confers advantages, but also creates social pressures. Living or working in cities can be an unpleasant experience, and international tourism is one way of providing an escape from the alienation and stress induced by urban living (Krippendorf, 1987, p. 17). For these reasons one would expect a positive relationship between *URB* and *TSP*.

The data set is based on editions one to four of the *World Economic Factbook* and covers 138 countries, from Afghanistan to Zimbabwe, over the period 1989 to 1995. Not all countries are included in the sample because of missing data. This problem is not confined to low-income countries, but also affects other income groups. Hong Kong and Brunei, for example, have no data on their international tourism spending. If there are significant gaps in the data for any of the variables used in this study, the country concerned is dropped from the sample. The countries remaining in the sample constitute two-thirds of all possible countries. The issue of whether these remaining countries can be regarded as a random sample from the population is an important question which is tested statistically later.

The explanatory variables are chosen both for their expected importance in determining *TSP* and their availability. This latter criterion is particularly relevant for low-income countries, where the availability of data for other potential explanatory variables, such as infant mortality, can vary considerably. Including these other variables would reduce the sample size for low-income countries in particular because of the missing data problem. For variables such as sales promotion there is almost no data available for low-income countries. There is also the problem that inclusion of more variables, even if this were feasible for all countries, would increase the possibility of multicollinearity in the estimation procedures and reduce the precision of the coefficient estimates. Finally, the inclusion of dummy variables to account for events such as currency restrictions, political disturbances, terrorism and so on, would be a daunting task for a sample of 138 countries. In any case, one of the advantages of panel data estimation is that such country-specific effects can be taken into account in the estimation procedures.

The countries in the sample range from the very rich to the very poor, so that there is considerable variation in per capita gross domestic product and international tourism spending across countries. Table 9.1 divides the sample into three groups of countries with low, medium and high incomes, where the division is based on the average real per capita GDP of each country. This average is derived as the average real per capita GDP for each country over the seven years of the sample. The division is based on the OECD classification where 'low-income' (or Group 1 countries) are those with a 1993 per capita income less than $650. In general, the results in Table 9.1 conform to expectations, although certain features of the economic variables are noteworthy. The variables *TSP* and *GDP* exhibit much greater sample variability, as measured by the standard deviation relative to the mean value, for Group 1 countries compared to Groups 2 and 3. For the real exchange rate variable *EXC* this situation is reversed, with Group 3 countries having the largest sample variability. Since these variables are measured in real terms, their variability arises not only from nominal changes but also from changes in the price level deflators. These changes are sometimes very large for countries with high inflation rates. In terms of exchange rate fluctuations

*Table 9.1* Low, Medium and High Income Country Groups: Descriptive Statistics

| Variables | Low Income (Group 1) GDP < $650 N = 63 | Medium Income (Group 2) $650 < GDP < $4258 N = 36 | High Income (Group 3) GDP > $4258 N = 39 | Overall N = 138 |
|---|---|---|---|---|
| TSP | 5.1 (9.4) | 34.0 (30.5) | 393.2 (351.5) | 122.3 (253.3) |
| GDP | 283.2 (285.0) | 1566.3 (910.8) | 13163.8 (7275.2) | 4258.1 (6835.3) |
| EXC | 172.8 (337.1) | 106.3 (281.6) | 73.8 (241.6) | 127.5 (301.3) |
| EXV | 0.29 | 0.15 | 0.10 | 0.20 |
| AGE | 54.37 (5.57) | 57.67 (6.28) | 64.19 (5.79) | 58.00 (7.13) |
| GEN | 49.76 (1.3) | 47.08 (10.8) | 49.73 (1.9) | 49.05 (5.8) |
| HHS | 4.78 (0.8) | 4.53 (0.9) | 3.36 (1.2) | 4.32 (1.1) |
| LIT | 61.87 (25.1) | 77.60 (18.2) | 91.56 (11.5) | 74.36 (23.8) |
| URB | 37.37 (21.1) | 47.17 (17.1) | 73.85 (18.4) | 50.24 (24.7) |

Note: The upper figure in each cell is the arithmetic mean value of the variable. The lower figure in parentheses is the standard deviation of the variable.

for a given group over time, however, real exchange rate volatility (*EXV*) is greatest in Group 1 countries.

The social variables have much less sample variability. They also exhibit a lack of variability within a given country over time. This is hardly surprising, since the social structure of a given country is unlikely to change significantly over a seven-year period. It does mean, however, that some estimation procedures are not possible because of matrix near-singularity caused by almost perfect collinearity between some of the variables. Nonetheless, there is still sufficient variability across countries within a given time period to estimate the fixed and random effects models, and it is these models which form the basis of our methodological approach, discussed in the next subsection.

Our aim is to construct a general model which explains international tourism spending in terms of both economic and social variables. The model is estimated in double-log form. Estimation results from the ordinary linear regression were unsatisfactory, and the double-log form enables direct comparisons to be made with many other studies in the area of tourism. The estimated slope coefficients also have the convenient property of representing constant elasticities. In the context of the panel data approach, given the stochastic multiplicative demand function:

$$TSP_{it} = \alpha_i GDP_{it}^{\beta_1} EXC_{it}^{\beta_2} EXV_{it}^{\beta_3} AGE_{it}^{\beta_4} GEN_{it}^{\beta_5} HHS_{it}^{\beta_6} LIT_{it}^{\beta_7} URB_{it}^{\beta_8} e_{it} \quad (9.12)$$

where $i$ and $t$ represent the cross-section and time series observations, respectively, $\alpha$ varies across countries but is constant over time, the $\beta$s are constant across countries and over time, and $e$ is a multiplicative error term which is iid $(1, \delta)$, then the double-log form is

$$\ln TSP_{it} = \ln \alpha_i + \beta_1 \ln GDP_{it} + \beta_2 \ln EXC_{it} + \beta_3 \ln EXV_{it} + \beta_4 \ln AGE_{it} \\ + \beta_5 \ln GEN_{it} + \beta_6 \ln HHS_{it} + \beta_7 \ln LIT_{it} + \beta_8 \ln URB_{it} + \varepsilon_{it} \quad (9.13)$$

where $\varepsilon_{it} = \ln e_{it}$ which is assumed iid $(0, \sigma^2)$. This assumption implies that the observations are serially uncorrelated for a given country, and that the errors have constant variance across countries and over time.

Imposing the restriction of intercept and slope coefficient homogeneity (either across countries, or over time, or both) is in effect 'pooling' or combining the time series and cross-section data. An increase in ln *GDP*, *ceteris paribus*, will have the same impact on ln *TSP* in every country and in every time period, where this impact is measured by $\beta_1$.

## 9.3.2   Estimating Income Elasticities in a Simple Model

Before proceeding to the full model, it may be of some value to consider the results of a simple double-log regression of *TSP* on *GDP* in order to determine the (constant) elasticity of *TSP* with respect to *GDP* for each of the three groups. The FE model is estimated with and without weights, where the weighted least squares procedure[3] allows for heteroscedasticity. The results are shown in Table 9.2.

In all cases $\beta_1$ is significant and positive. Apart from the pooled OLS case, it decreases as GDP increases across the three groups. This is consistent with economic theory and the empirical results on consumption spending functions generally, where the marginal propensity to spend tends to decrease at higher levels of income. The $\bar{R}^2$ from the POLS for Groups 2 and 3 is well below that for the other estimation procedures because POLS does not take into account country-specific effects. For the overall sample, all four methods yield an elasticity of around unity. But this latter result raises a very important question: can the sample observations be pooled in this way? The next section discusses this issue, as well as the estimation results.[4]

*Table 9.2* Simple Double-Log Regression of TSP on GDP

| | *Low Income (Group 1)* | *Medium Income (Group 2)* | *High Income (Group 3)* | *Overall* |
|---|---|---|---|---|
| Pooled OLS: | | | | |
| $\beta_1$ | 1.0100 | 1.3232 | 0.9178 | 1.1121 |
| $t$ | (40.5343) | (18.5775) | (10.4267) | (80.1614) |
| $\overline{R}^2$ | 0.7887 | 0.5782 | 0.2837 | 0.8694 |
| FE (no weights): | | | | |
| $\beta_1$ | 0.9229 | 0.8127 | 0.2486 | 0.9115 |
| $t$ | (42.6308) | (20.3703) | (2.5019) | (57.1259) |
| $\overline{R}^2$ | 0.9582 | 0.9559 | 0.9102 | 0.9778 |
| FE(weights): | | | | |
| $\beta_1$ | 0.9356 | 0.7715 | 0.4786 | 0.9155 |
| $t$ | (58.9573) | (20.3719) | (9.4065) | (68.0974) |
| $\overline{R}^2$ | 0.9958 | 0.9964 | 0.9082 | 0.9997 |
| RE(FGLS) | | | | |
| $\beta_1$ | 0.9331 | 0.8387 | 0.3620 | 0.9495 |
| $t$ | (45.0085) | (20.9136) | (3.9053) | (64.0295) |
| $\overline{R}^2$ | 0.9581 | 0.9539 | 0.9077 | 0.9770 |

Notes: $\beta_1$ is the (constant) elasticity of TSP with respect to GDP.
$t$ is the $t$ value.
$R^2$ is the adjusted $R^2$.

## 9.3.3   Testing for Poolability

In this section we present the test results from the $F_1$ and $F_2$ statistics only, since $F_3$ does not change the overall conclusion.

*The $F_1$ Test.* Due to computational constraints, a maximum of six explanatory variables can be used in this test, so it is necessary to drop a minimum of two of them from the model specification. A variety of model specifications are tested, and the variables which are consistently significant and of the expected sign are *GDP, EXC, AGE* and *URB*. Accordingly, these variables are used to derive the restricted residual sum of squares. Only *GDP* could be used to derive the unrestricted residual sum of squares, since inclusion of the other explanatory variables results in the problem of a near-singular matrix in the estimation process. The result is $F_{1_{(685,276)}} = 3.53$, which is greater than the critical $F$ value of $F_{1_c} = 1.4$ at the 1% significance level with $K = 4$. The null hypothesis of homogeneous slopes and intercepts is therefore rejected.

*The $F_2$ Test.* When the intercepts are allowed to vary across countries and the slope coefficients are restricted to be equal (unrestricted model), the $F_2$ statistic is calculated based on Equation (9.4), and the result is $F_{2_{(548,276)}}$, which is less than the corresponding critical $F$ value of $F_{2_c} = 1.33$ at the 1% significance level. This implies that we cannot reject the null hypothesis of homogeneous slopes and heterogeneous intercepts.

From the above statistics, we can see that the overall conclusion is that the data can be appropriately pooled in the form of a homogeneous slope and heterogeneous intercept model.

## 9.3.4    Testing for Fixed Effects and Random Effects Models

After establishing the fact that the cross-sectional and time series data can be pooled, we need to decide whether the fixed effect or random effect model should be used in modelling tourism expenditure. Based on Equation (9.9), a double-log regression of *TSP* on all eight explanatory variables gives *LM* = 1574.83, which is greater than the critical value of 6.64 at the 1% level of significance. The null hypothesis that the FE model is appropriate is clearly rejected, implying that REs are present. Based on Equation (9.10), the calculated Hausman statistic is $\chi^2_{(8)} = 64.60$, which is greater than the critical value of 15.51 at the 5% significance level. This result implies that the null hypothesis of no correlation should be rejected, that is, the demand model has FEs.

The result of the Breusch-Pagan test, which strongly indicates the existence of REs, is not supported by that from the Hausman test, which finds in favour of the FE model. The choice of model, however, must be guided by economic theory as well as statistical tests. Table 9.3 gives the estimation results for the FE (both with and without cross-sectional weights) and the RE model for two cases: case (i), in which all eight explanatory variables from Equation (9.3) are included; and case (ii), where only those explanatory variables from Equation (9.3) which tend to be significant and of the expected sign are included. These four variables are *GDP*, *EXC*, *AGE* and *URB*.

For the case (i) results, the *GDP*, *EXC*, *AGE* and *URB* variables are all significant and have the expected sign (assuming, in the case of *EXC*, that the demand for international tourism is price inelastic). The first three variables are all significant at the 1% level. In the FE models *LIT* is also highly significant but has the wrong sign. *EXV* and *HHS* are not significant at all; *EXV* is incorrectly signed in the FE models and correctly signed in the RE model, whilst the sign of *HHS* is negative and positive in the FE and RE models, respectively. *GEN* is also insignificant, although its sign is always negative, so there is a weak suggestion that the amount of international tourism spending is inversely related to the proportion of males in the country's population. Although the diagnostic statistics are somewhat better for the FE models, the RE model is more consistent with economic theory since it manages to give the expected sign for the *EXV* and *LIT* variables. All the models have extremely high $\bar{R}^2$ values.

The insignificant variables are dropped for case (ii) estimation and, as expected, the coefficient values and significance of the remaining variables do not change very much from the case (i) results. Concentrating on the case (ii) variables of *GDP*, *EXC*, *AGE* and *URB*, Table 9.3 shows that the income elasticities are all very similar in value. There is less agreement between the models for the other coefficient values. Taking the averages of the coefficient values for *GDP*, *EXC*, *AGE* and *URB* yields average elasticity values of $\beta_1$ = 0.86, $\beta_2$ = 0.09, $\beta_4$ = 1.17 and $\beta_8$ = 0.24, respectively.

The income elasticity value of 0.86 is lower than the value of around 1.8 reported in the study by Crouch and Shaw (1992), which was based on an average of 777 different estimates. It is also lower than the short- and long-run values of 2.22 and 2.37, respectively, found by Song *et al.* (2000). But the findings from these studies, in contrast to the present study, are based primarily on time series estimates. Naturally, there is no reason why one should necessarily expect to find similar values for time series and cross-section elasticities, since the two types of elasticity are conceptually different. This conceptual difference is underlined by the results from other panel data studies, where income elasticities of 1.09 (Carey, 1991), 1.18 (Tremblay, 1989), 0.52 (Witt, 1980a), 0.44 (Witt, 1980b) and 0.58 (Yavas and Bilgin, 1996) were obtained.[5]

Irrespective of the model specification used, the coefficient of *EXC* is always positive and significant. This implies that the positive effect on *TSP* arising from price inelasticity outweighs the negative effect from the nominal exchange rate. This hypothesis is easily verified by splitting *EXC* into its constituent parts (*NEXC* = the nominal exchange rate, and *RELP* = the relative price level) and including them as separate explanatory variables in the regression. Using the FE and RE models, the coefficient on *RELP* is always positive and highly significant, and the coefficient on *NEXC* is always negative (but not significant). These results imply that price levels in the origin and destination countries are more important than nominal exchange rates in determining international tourism spending. In terms of estimation, however, it is preferable to use the composite variable *EXC*; it is a more parsimonious specification, and use of the separate variables *NEXC* and *RELP* results in an unrealistically low income elasticity.

Own-price demand inelasticity for international tourist visits is consistent with a two-stage decision making process, where consumers choose a holiday on the basis of their income in the first instance and then subsequently on secondary factors such as price. Given this two-stage process,

*Table 9.3* Fixed and Random Effects Models: Estimation Results

| Coefficient | Fixed Effects (Weights) | | Fixed Effects (No Weights) | | Random Effects | |
|---|---|---|---|---|---|---|
| | (i) | (ii) | (i) | (ii) | (i) | (ii) |
| Constant | | | | | -11.500 (5.894)* | -10.979 (7.279)* |
| $\beta_1$ | 0.826 (43.193)* | 0.830 (42.949)* | 0.852 (57.235)* | 0.857 (59.206)* | 0.896 (50.616)* | 0.890 (51.028)* |
| $\beta_2$ | 0.115 (7.268)* | 0.113 (7.089)* | 0.075 (5.093)* | 0.068 (4.661)* | 0.073 (4.860)* | 0.077 (5.223)* |
| $\beta_3$ | 0.012 (0.820) | | 0.003 (1.056) | | -0.014 (0.904) | |
| $\beta_4$ | 1.250 (3.136)* | 1.268 (3.152)* | 0.792 (4.808)* | 0.842 (5.161)* | 1.401 (3.671)* | 1.401 (3.797)* |

| | | | | | | |
|---|---|---|---|---|---|---|
| $\beta_5$ | −0.099 (0.000) | | −1.058 (0.000) | | −0.150 (0.736) | |
| $\beta_6$ | −0.008 (0.024) | | −0.088 (0.956) | | 0.246 (0.948) | |
| $\beta_7$ | −1.866 (4.843)* | | −0.756 (3.143)* | | 0.138 (0.648) | |
| $\beta_8$ | 0.224 (1.747)** | 0.212 (1.671)** | 0.078 (1.374)*** | 0.088 (1.771)** | 0.444 (4.101)* | 0.419 (4.192)* |
| $\bar{R}^2$ | 0.983 | 0.982 | 0.999 | 0.999 | 0.978 | 0.978 |
| SSR | 183.1 | 188.4 | 172.4 | 182.5 | 236.6 | 229.1 |
| F | 6698.4 | 15259.2 | 297591.4 | 652708.3 | | |
| DW | 1.103 | 1.076 | 1.361 | 1.357 | 0.897 | 0.911 |

Notes: Figures in parentheses are *t* values.
*, ** and *** indicate significance at the 1%, 5% and 10% levels, respectively. The *t* tests for $\beta_2$ and $\beta_5$ are two-tailed; the remainder are one-tailed. SSR is the sum of the squared residuals.

consumer demand is likely to be less sensitive to changes in the secondary factors. It is also consistent with the empirical results of Song *et al.* (2000), where short- and long-run average own-price elasticities of –0.62 and –0.69, respectively, were obtained.

## 9.4    SUMMARY AND CONCLUSIONS

This chapter introduces the application of panel data techniques to tourism demand analysis. The advantages and limitations of this approach are also highlighted. Using the panel data modelling approach, an empirical tourism demand model is developed based on both economic and social variables for a total of 138 countries over seven years. A preliminary analysis is conducted by splitting the data set by income level into three groups and estimating the income elasticity of tourism for each group on the basis of a simple regression of real per capita tourism spending on real per capita GDP. Using the fixed and random effects models, the income elasticity diminishes as per capita GDP increases; the estimated income elasticities range from around 0.9 for the low income countries to 0.25 to 0.48 for the high income countries. Pooled OLS does not follow the same pattern, since the income elasticity for medium income countries is higher than that for low income countries.

A key question is whether the data for the three country groups can be pooled into a single group, thereby allowing the estimation of a general set of results. Analysis shows that the data is poolable in the form of a heterogeneous intercept, homogeneous slope coefficient model. Further analysis attempts to determine whether the fixed or random effects model is appropriate, although the results of these tests are inconclusive. The variables which are consistently significant (and of the expected sign) in determining international tourism spending are real per capita GDP, the real exchange rate, age structure and urbanisation. The variable which is by far the most significant is real per capita GDP, and the pooled income elasticity of international tourism spending is 0.86. This is lower than the values which are usually reported from pure time series analyses.

The use of panel data allows the influence of social variables to be investigated. In time series data these variables do not normally display sufficient variability for estimation purposes and are omitted from the model specification. This study includes five social variables in the model specification, and concludes that age structure and urbanisation are significant determinants of international tourism spending across countries. Although it is not necessarily the case that these variables will exert the same influence in a given country over time, it seems reasonable to assume that their temporal influence cannot be neglected.

The policy and methodological implications from this study follow accordingly. Demographic as well as economic changes affect international tourism spending, and national governments and tourism agencies, whether they are in an origin or destination country, should take these changes into account. This is particularly relevant in the area of forecasting international tourism demand, where a properly specified econometric forecasting model should control for the influence of social, as well as economic, variables. Indeed, the quantitative influence of social variables on international tourism spending needs to be analysed in greater detail. The present study is based on a relatively small number of social variables, and it is possible that other measures of social change could yield additional insights. The use of the adult literacy rate in this study, for example, gives unsatisfactory results, and it could be that the use of another measure, such as the proportion of the population enrolled in further and higher education institutions, would be more appropriate.

## APPENDIX 9.1 THE DATA SET AND VARIABLE DEFINITIONS

The data are compiled from the *World Economic Factbook* (WEF), editions one to four. This publication is updated regularly and provides a reasonably consistent set of observations over the sample period. Edition one (1993) is used for 1989 and 1990 data, edition two (1994/5) for 1991, edition three (1996) for 1992, 1993 and 1994, and edition four (1996/7) for 1995. The WEF collects data on international tourism spending directly from government agencies, national statistical bodies and customs and excise bodies. Where necessary, this is supplemented with data from the World Tourism Organization and the Organization for Economic Co-operation and Development. Data on gross domestic product and demographic characteristics are based mainly on national statistics, whilst data on inflation and exchange rates are derived mainly from International Monetary Fund statistics.

Not all countries are included in this study because of missing observations. In a number of cases, missing values are estimated where reliable estimates can be made and where the number of missing values is small. Over the sample period there were a number of changes to the status of certain countries, which prevented their inclusion in the sample. It was decided to retain the data for Germany and the Czech Republic in the sample, however. The West and East German data pre-1990 are combined, using per capita GDP weightings where necessary. The values for the *URB* variable, for example, cannot simply be added together and then averaged. This would imply that East German urbanisation has equal importance to that in West Germany in the determination of *TSP* in Germany, even though West German *TSP* and *GDP* is much higher than East German. Weighting by per capita GDP is one way, albeit somewhat crude, of allowing for the relative importance of East and West Germany in the combined data. Since East German *TSP* is small relative to West German *TSP*, any measurement error resulting from combining the data should also be small. The data for the Czech Republic pre-1991 are also adjusted by eliminating the data for Slovakia, where necessary, by appropriate per capita GDP weightings.

The measurement of the real exchange rate is problematic. The tourism spending data is for country $i$ to all overseas destinations, rather than for country $i$ tourism in country $j$, so a measure of the *general* cost of tourism is needed. The variable definition above measures the cost of international tourism from country $i$ as a function of the nominal exchange rate (defined in relation to US$) and the relative price level (defined in relation to the USA price level). An alternative measure of the nominal exchange rate which in theory might more accurately capture the general cost of international tourism is the effective exchange rate of country $i$, which would be based on a weighted average of all other countries' exchange rates. But this would only be an accurate measure of the general cost of international tourism if the weights used in the calculation of the effective exchange rate were similar to the weights of the tourist destinations in international tourism spending. For example, if the USA accounted for 20% of the effective exchange rate of Mexico, but 40% of Mexican tourist spending is in the USA, then this measure of general tourism cost would not be appropriate. Another problem is that the data for international tourism spending is for country $i$ on all other countries in the world, but the sample includes only two-thirds of total countries. Thus, even if weightings are computed, there is an inevitable disparity between the coverage of the tourism spending data and the weights used for the sample countries.

An alternative measure of the relative price level variable is a relative price index analogous to the effective exchange rate, that is, the weighted price level for the rest of the world relative to the price level in country $i$. This would be given by $P_r/P_i$ where $P_r$ and $P_i$ are the price levels in the rest of the world and country $i$, respectively. But this measure is open to the same objection as that for the effective exchange rate; the price level weightings for the rest of the world might not reflect the tourism spending weightings. For most countries in the sample, however, $P_r$ would be similar in value since each country would be small in relation to the rest of the world. Given that $P_r$ can be treated as a constant across countries (but obviously not over time), a reasonable proxy for $P_r$ is the USA price level. Differences in the levels of these two variables will be absorbed in the constant term, and will not affect the estimated slope coefficients.

# 10 Systems of Demand Equations

## 10.1    INTRODUCTION

This chapter introduces the system-of-equations approach in contrast to the single-equation approach such as ADLM models, and the predominant focus is on a particular model: the Almost Ideal Demand System (AIDS). Due to its rigorous grounding in economic theory, the AIDS model has gained great popularity for demand studies in various fields including tourism. This chapter aims to demonstrate the merits and usefulness of this approach to tourism demand analysis. Theoretical foundations, scientific merits and model specifications of the AIDS are covered in this chapter. The particular strengths of the AIDS model in demand elasticity analysis are also emphasised. A worked example of UK residents' demand for tourism in Western Europe is used to demonstrate the application of the AIDS model to tourism demand elasticity analysis. The latest developments of this model, such as the error correction and the time varying parameter versions of the AIDS model, are briefly introduced at the end of this chapter.

## 10.2    FEATURES OF AIDS MODELS

Most empirical studies on tourism demand modelling are based on single-equation methods, which suffer from specific limitations. Eadington and Redman (1991) note that these methods are incapable of analysing the interdependence of budget allocations to different consumer goods and services. For example, a tourism decision making process involves a choice among a group of alternative destinations. A change of price in one destination may affect tourists' decisions on travelling to a number of alternative destinations, and also influence their expenditures in those destinations. Clearly, the single-equation methods cannot adequately model the influence of a change in tourism price in a particular destination on the demand for travelling to other destinations. Another limitation of single-equation methods is that they cannot be used to test the symmetry and adding-up hypotheses which are associated with demand theory.

The system-of-equations approach initiated by Stone (1954) overcomes these limitations. By including a group of equations (one for each consumer product) in the system and estimating them simultaneously, this approach permits the examination of how consumers choose a bundle of goods and services in order to maximise their preference or utility given budget constraints. According to the system-of-equations approach, a consumer's decision on expenditure allocation is made by a 'stage budgeting process' (Sinclair and Stabler, 1997). The consumer allocates the total budget first to broad groups of goods and services such as food, clothing and tourism, and then further allocates the expenditure within each of these groups and subgroups, such as different destination regions and countries or different categories of tourism products within the broad tourism consumption group. So the decision making is a two- or three- (or even more) stage budgeting process. Tourism demand studies using the system-of-equations approach focus on the last stage of the budget allocation, that is, allocating the tourism consumption budget among different destinations or different tourism product categories.

Although there are a number of system-of-equations methods available, the AIDS introduced by Deaton and Muellbauer (1980b) has been the most popular one due to its favourable features. For example, it gives an arbitrary first-order approximation to any demand system; it has a functional form which complies with known household-budget data (Deaton and Muellbauer, 1980b); and it has a flexible functional form and does not impose any *a priori* restrictions on the elasticities, thus any good or service in the system can be either inferior or normal, and either a substitute or a complement to the others (Fujii *et al.*, 1985). Although other system-of-equations models also possess some of these features, none of them contain all the features that the AIDS has.

## 10.3    THE STATIC AIDS

The original AIDS introduced by Deaton and Muellbauer (1980b) has a purely static functional form. The implication is that only long-run consumer behaviour is of concern.

### 10.3.1    Model Specification

The static AIDS can be viewed as an extension of the Working-Leser model (Working, 1943; Leser, 1963) in which the budget share for good $i$ is related to the logarithms of prices and total real expenditure in the following manner:

$$w_i = a_i + \sum_j \gamma_{ij} \log p_j + b_i \log\left(\frac{x}{P}\right) + v_i \quad (i, j = 1, 2, ..., n) \tag{10.1}$$

where $w_i$ is the budget share of the $i$th good, $p_i$ is the price of the $i$th good, $x$ is total expenditure on all goods in the system, $P$ is the aggregate price index for the system, $v_i$ is the disturbance term, $v_i \sim N(0, \sigma_i^2)$, $n$ is the number of the products (or equations) in the system, and $a_i$, $b_i$ and $\gamma_{ij}$ are the parameters to be estimated.

The aggregate price index $P$ is defined as

$$\log P = a_0 + \sum_i \alpha_i \log p_i + \frac{1}{2} \sum_i \sum_j \gamma_{ij} \log p_i \log p_j \tag{10.2}$$

where $a_0$ is a parameter to be estimated.

Replacing $P$ with the Stone's (1954) price index ($P^*$) defined by Equation (10.3), the linearly approximated AIDS is derived and termed 'LAIDS'.

$$\log P^* = \sum_i w_i \log p_i \tag{10.3}$$

The LAIDS augmented with dummy variables can then be written as

$$w_i = a_i + \sum_j \gamma_{ij} \log p_j + b_i \log\left(\frac{x}{P^*}\right) + \sum_k \varphi_{ik} dum_k + v_i \quad (k = 1, 2, \ldots, m) \tag{10.4}$$

where $dum_k$ is a dummy variable, which handles the intervention of an exogenous shock; $m$ is the number of dummy variables included in the system; $\varphi_{ik}$ is a parameter to be estimated.

The LAIDS can be re-written more compactly in the vector-matrix notation:

$$w_t = \Pi z_t + \varphi dum_t + v_t \tag{10.5}$$

where $w_t$ is a $n$-vector of the dependent variables in the system, $z_t$ is a $q$-vector of intercept, prices and total real expenditure variables in logarithms ($q = n + 2$), $\Pi$ and $\varphi$ are $n \times q$ and $n \times m$ parameter matrices, respectively, and $\Pi = (\pi_1', \pi_2', \ldots, \pi_n')'$, where $\pi_i$ is a $q$-vector.

Since the LAIDS model has a simpler specification and is easier to estimate than its non-linear counterpart, it is often used in empirical studies. The following discussions of the AIDS approach are therefore based on its linear from.

## 10.3.2   Theoretical Restrictions

To comply with the properties of demand theory, that is, the budget constraint and utility maximisation, the following restrictions are imposed on the parameters in Equation (10.4):

*Adding up:* This follows from the budget constraint and the monotonicity assumption of preferences and implies that the budget is completely used

(Edgerton *et al.*, 1996). In the AIDS model, the adding up restriction requires $\sum_i a_i = 1$, $\sum_i \gamma_{ij} = 0$, $\sum_i b_i = 0$ and $\sum_i \varphi_{ik} = 0$, which allows for all budget shares to sum to unity, corresponding to the definition of a 'complete system'.

*Homogeneity:* This implies that consumers do not exhibit money illusion, that is, consumption decisions are made on the basis of relative prices and income alone. A proportional increase in all prices and expenditure has no effect on demand. Therefore the homogeneity restriction implies that prices are homogeneous of degree zero, that is, $\sum_j \gamma_{ij} = 0$ in Equation (10.4).

*Symmetry:* This property is known as 'Young's theorem' (Chiang, 1984). It requires $\gamma_{ij} = \gamma_{ji}$, which takes consistency of consumers' choices into account.

*Negativity:* This property is based on the law of demand, that is, a compensated demand function can never slope upwards. It implies that all compensated own-price elasticities must be negative.

The adding-up restrictions can be easily checked from Equation (10.4) to ensure $\sum w_i \equiv 1$. Negativity can be checked by examining the signs of the calculated own-price elasticities. The restrictions of homogeneity, symmetry and the joint hypothesis can be examined using the Wald test, likelihood ratio test and Lagrange multiplier test on the estimated coefficients. However, these standard tests have biases towards rejection of the null hypothesis, especially in large demand systems with relatively few observations (Balcombe and Davis, 1996). Hence sample-size corrected statistics are recommended, such as $T_B$ below suggested by Baldwin *et al.* (1983).

$$T_B = \frac{tr(\Omega^R)^{-1}(\Omega^R - \Omega^U)/d}{tr(\Omega^R)^{-1}\Omega^U/(n-1)(N-h)} \tag{10.6}$$

where $\Omega^R$ and $\Omega^U$ are the estimated residual covariance matrices with and without restrictions imposed, respectively, $N$ is the number of observations, $n$ is the number of equations in the system, $h$ is the number of estimated parameters in each equation, and $d$ denotes the number of restrictions. $T_B$ is approximately distributed as $F(d, N - h)$.

Subject to the satisfaction of the above restrictions, the unrestricted LAIDS in Equation (10.4) can be further written as two restricted versions: the homogeneous LAIDS and the homogeneous and symmetric LAIDS. The latter is the most theoretically sound, and further analysis and forecasting should be based on this version. However, the hypotheses of the above restrictions might be rejected by statistical tests in empirical studies. In this case, the unrestricted LAIDS or homogeneous LAIDS has to be considered.

## 10.3.3   Estimation Methods

Since the sum of all expenditure shares in the LAIDS model is equal to unity, the residual variance-covariance matrix $\Omega$ is singular. The usual solution is to delete an equation from the system and estimate the remaining equations, and then calculate the parameters in the deleted equation in accordance with the adding-up restrictions. The LAIDS model can be estimated using three methods: ordinary least square (OLS), maximum likelihood (ML) and Zellner's (1962) iterative approach to seemingly unrelated regression (SUR) estimation. If the disturbances are serially independent, all of the three methods provide similar estimates of the parameters, which are invariant to the choice of the equation deleted (Barten, 1969; Johnston, 1986). However, in the system with the symmetry restriction, the SUR estimation performs more efficiently than OLS, and the efficiency varies according to the degree of correlation between the disturbances in the system (Syriopoulos, 1995). Furthermore, the SUR estimation iterates over $\Omega$ and converges to the ML estimator, provided that the residuals are distributed normally (Rickertsen, 1998).

## 10.3.4   Demand Elasticities

Due to the flexible functional form of the LAIDS model, elasticity analysis can be easily carried out. The demand elasticities are calculated as functions of the estimated parameters, and they have standard implications.

*Expenditure Elasticity:* The expenditure elasticity ($\varepsilon_{ix}$) measures the sensitivity of demand in response to changes in expenditure. It is calculated as

$$\varepsilon_{ix} = 1 + \frac{b_i}{w_i} \tag{10.7}$$

*Uncompensated Price Elasticities:* The uncompensated own-price elasticity ($\varepsilon_{ii}$) and cross-price elasticity ($\varepsilon_{ij}$) measure how a change in the price of one product affects the demand for this product and for other products, with the total expenditure and other prices held constant. They are given by

$$\varepsilon_{ii} = \frac{\lambda_{ii}}{w_i} - b_i - 1 \tag{10.8}$$

and

$$\varepsilon_{ij} = \frac{\lambda_{ij}}{w_i} - b_i \frac{w_j}{w_i} \tag{10.9}$$

*Compensated Price Elasticities:* In the same way, the compensated price elasticities ($\varepsilon_{ii}^*$ and $\varepsilon_{ij}^*$), which measure the price effects on the demand assuming the *real* expenditure ($x/P$) is constant (Pyo *et al.*, 1991), are calculated as

$$\varepsilon_{ii}^{*} = \frac{\gamma_{ii}}{w_i} + w_i - 1 \tag{10.10}$$

and

$$\varepsilon_{ij}^{*} = \frac{\gamma_{ij}}{w_i} + w_j \tag{10.11}$$

In particular, the sign of the calculated $\varepsilon_{ij}^{*}$ indicates the substitutability or complementarity between the alternative products in the demand system under consideration, such as different destinations in the tourism context (Edgerton *et al.*, 1996).

## 10.4    ERROR CORRECTION LAIDS MODELS

As can be seen from Equation (10.4), the static LAIDS focuses on the long-run solutions to the model, ignoring the short-run dynamics of the demand system. In other words, it is implicitly assumed that the consumers' behaviour is always 'in equilibrium'. However, in reality, habit persistence, adjustment costs, imperfect information, incorrect expectations and misinterpreted real price changes often prevent consumers from adjusting their expenditure instantly to price and income changes (Anderson and Blundell, 1983). Therefore, until full adjustment takes place consumers are 'out of equilibrium'. This is one of the reasons why most static LAIDS models cannot always satisfy the theoretical restrictions (Duffy, 2002). Thus it is necessary to introduce the error correction mechanism into the static LAIDS in order to overcome the above problems. As discussed in Chapter 6, an ECM augments the long-run equilibrium relationship with a short-run adjustment mechanism, which takes account of the short-run correction process. Hence an error correction LAIDS (that is, EC-LAIDS) embodies the properties of both long-run equilibrium and the short-run dynamics of a demand system.

Following Engle and Granger's two-stage approach to CI and ECM analysis, the EC-LAIDS can be written in the following form (Edgerton *et al.*, 1996; Chambers and Nowman, 1997; Duffy, 2002):

$$A(L)\Delta w_t = B(L)\Delta z_t + \phi(L)\Delta dum_t + \Gamma(w_{t-1} - \Pi z_{t-1} - \varphi dum_{t-1}) + v_t \tag{10.12}$$

where $A(L) = I + \sum_{i=1}^{l} A_i L^i$, $B(L) = \sum_{i=0}^{g} B_i L^i$ and $\phi(L) = \sum_{i=0}^{s} \phi_i L^i$ are matrix polynomials in the lag operator L; $l$, $g$ and $s$ can be determined by using order selection techniques; $(w_{t-1} - \Pi z_{t-1} - \varphi dum_{t-1})$ is the error correction term.

In the short run, changes in shares depend on the changes in prices, real expenditure, dummies, and the disequilibrium error in the previous period. However, in the long run when all differenced terms become zero, Equation

(10.12) is reduced to Equation (10.5), that is, the system achieves its steady state. $A_i$, $B_i$, $\phi_i$ and $\Gamma$ are parameter matrices to be estimated. It should be noted that due to different cointegration approaches in use, alternative specifications of EC-LAIDS are available. Due to space constraints, they are neglected here.

Given that annual data are used, most tourism demand studies employing error correction models have shown that it is appropriate to set the lag length of differenced variables equal to zero. Therefore, Equation (10.12) can be reduced to the following form:

$$\Delta w_t = B \Delta z_t + \phi \Delta dum_t + \Gamma(w_{t-1} - \Pi z_{t-1} - \varphi dum_{t-1}) + v_t \tag{10.13}$$

Considering the degrees of freedom and statistical significance of the estimates of the error correction terms, some empirical studies, such as Ray (1985) and Blanciforti *et al.* (1986), use a more restrictive formulation, involving only the disequilibrium in the own budget share in each equation. In other words, $\Gamma$ becomes diagonal, and the off-diagonal terms, the estimates of which are normally insignificant, are restricted to zero. The theoretical restrictions imposed on the AIDS model imply that the $\Gamma_{ii}$s are equal in such a diagonal form of $\Gamma$.

## 10.5  A WORKED EXAMPLE

The following worked example is based on a study by Li *et al.* (2004) focusing on UK tourism demand in Western Europe. In this study, a three-stage budgeting process is followed. It is assumed that UK residents first allocate their consumption expenditure between total tourism consumption and consumption of other goods and services. In the second stage, UK residents further allocate their expenditure between tourism in Western Europe and in other regions. In the last stage, the budget of tourism expenditure in Western Europe is allocated among the alternative destinations in this region. The LAIDS models are applied to the last stage of tourism expenditure allocation. Among twenty-two countries in this region, France, Spain, Italy, Greece and Portugal are the major destinations, and tourist spending in these five countries accounts for more than 50% of the total. Therefore, this study focuses on these five key destinations, with the other seventeen aggregated to a sixth group: *Others*.

### 10.5.1  Variables and Data Description

The long-run static LAIDS model in this study takes the following form:

$$w_i = a_i + \sum_{j=1}^{6} \gamma_{ij} \log p_j + b_i \log\left(\frac{x}{P^*}\right) + \sum_{k=1}^{3} \varphi_{ik} dum_k + v_i \tag{10.14}$$

where $w_i$ is the share of UK tourists' expenditure in destination $i$ ($i$ = 1,2,...,6, representing France, Greece, Italy, Portugal, Spain and *Others*, respectively), and $p_j$ is the tourism price in destination $j$ relative to that of the UK, following the definition of Equation (4.24) in Chapter 4. With regard to the aggregate price for the *Others* group, it takes the form of Stone's price index. $x$ is the per capita expenditure. $P^*$ is Stone's price index defined in Equation (10.3). Three dummy variables are included in the model to account for the effects of the first oil crisis (1974 to 1975), the second oil crisis (1979) and the first Gulf War (1990 to 1991), respectively. The values are set as 1 during the periods these events occurred and 0 at other times. Annual data are used in this study and the data set covers the period 1972 to 2000.

Subject to satisfaction of the CI test, the above long-run AIDS model can be written as an EC-LAIDS model following Engle and Granger's two-stage approach. The EC-LAIDS is given by

$$\Delta w_i = \sum_{j=1}^{6} \gamma_{ij} \Delta \log p_j + b_i \Delta \log\left(\frac{x}{P^*}\right) + \sum_{k=1}^{3} \varphi_{ik} \Delta dum_k + \lambda \mu_{it-1} + v_i \qquad (10.15)$$

where $\mu_{jt-1}$ is the error correction term, which is derived from the estimated long-run AIDS in Equation (10.14).

Slightly different from the EC-LAIDS in Li *et al.* (2004), Equation (10.15) is a more restrictive specification with respect to the parameter of the error terms, that is, $\lambda$ becomes a negative scalar. Thus the degrees of freedom are increased in the estimated model.

## 10.5.2   Model Estimation

The ADF test for unit roots suggests that all the variables (excluding dummies) in Equation (10.14) are $I(1)$, and the CI relationship cannot be rejected by the Engle-Granger approach at the 5% significance level in any case. Thus both the long-run and dynamic LAIDS models can be estimated. Tables 10.1 and 10.2 present the estimates of the unrestricted static LAIDS and EC-LAIDS using the iterative SUR method. To carry out model estimation, the last equation concerning the demand for *Others* is deleted from the system. The coefficients in this equation can be calculated in accordance with the adding-up restrictions. Since they are not of interest in this study, the results are not reported here. EViews 5.1 is employed to estimate all LAIDS models.

With theoretical restrictions imposed on the parameters of unrestricted LAIDS models, homogeneity-restricted and homogeneity-and-symmetry-restricted static LAIDS and EC-LAIDS are estimated (the results are omitted due to space constraints). With the homogeneity restriction imposed on Equation (10.14), the following model is estimated to test the hypotheses:

*Table 10.1* Estimates of Unrestricted Static LAIDS

|  | France | Greece | Italy | Portugal | Spain |
|---|---|---|---|---|---|
| $a_i$ | 0.172*** | 0.048*** | 0.116*** | 0.011 | 0.132*** |
|  | (0.016) | (0.015) | (0.009) | (0.008) | (0.026) |
| $\gamma_{i1}$ | 0.023 | −0.031 | 0.049 | −0.054 | 0.055 |
|  | (0.066) | (0.060) | (0.037) | (0.030) | (0.103) |
| $\gamma_{i2}$ | −0.044 | −0.133*** | 0.064** | 0.003 | −0.020 |
|  | (0.047) | (0.042) | (0.026) | (0.021) | (0.073) |
| $\gamma_{i3}$ | −0.157*** | −0.053** | −0.014 | 0.047*** | 0.114*** |
|  | (0.025) | (0.023) | (0.014) | (0.011) | (0.039) |
| $\gamma_{i4}$ | 0.079 | −0.019 | −0.030 | −0.022 | −0.068 |
|  | (0.041) | (0.037) | (0.023) | (0.019) | (0.065) |
| $\gamma_{i5}$ | 0.163*** | 0.108*** | −0.051*** | 0.039*** | −0.245*** |
|  | (0.032) | (0.056) | (0.018) | (0.015) | (0.050) |
| $\gamma_{i6}$ | −0.167*** | 0.099 | −0.065 | 0.009 | 0.293*** |
|  | (0.062) | (0.056) | (0.035) | (0.028) | (0.096) |
| $b_i$ | 0.008** | 0.005 | −0.009*** | 0.006*** | 0.028*** |
|  | (0.003) | (0.003) | (0.002) | (0.002) | (0.005) |
| $\varphi_1$ | −0.007 | −0.015 | −0.007 | −0.007 | 0.023 |
|  | (0.009) | (0.008) | (0.005) | (0.004) | (0.013) |
| $\varphi_2$ | −0.015 | −0.017 | 0.012** | −0.008 | 0.021 |
|  | (0.011) | (0.010) | (0.006) | (0.005) | (0.017) |
| $\varphi_3$ | 0.030 | −0.013 | 0.009 | −0.008 | −0.039*** |
|  | (0.0009) | (0.008) | (0.005) | (0.004) | (0.014) |
| $\overline{R}^2$ | 0.898 | 0.747 | 0.800 | 0.815 | 0.570 |
| DW | 2.568 | 1.480 | 2.367 | 2.046 | 2.487 |

Notes: *** and ** indicate the 1% and 5% significance levels, respectively. Values in parentheses are standard errors. DW refers to the Durbin-Watson statistic.

$$w_i = a_i + \sum_{j=1}^{5} \gamma_{ij}(\log p_j - \log p_6) + b_i \log\left(\frac{x}{P^*}\right) + \sum_{k=1}^{3} \varphi_{ik} dum_k + v_i \qquad (10.16)$$

Restriction tests (using $T_B$ of Equation (10.6)) suggest that, lacking dynamics, neither symmetry nor the joint hypothesis of homogeneity and symmetry can be accepted at the 5% significance level in the static AIDS, although the latter is accepted at a lower significance level (see Table 10.3). On the contrary, all of these restrictions are accepted at the 5% significance

*Table 10.2* Estimates of Unrestricted EC-LAIDS

|  | France | Greece | Italy | Portugal | Spain |
|---|---|---|---|---|---|
| $\gamma_{i1}$ | 0.097*** (0.032) | 0.061 (0.034) | 0.054** (0.024) | −0.024 (0.021) | −0.083 (0.071) |
| $\gamma_{i2}$ | −0.022 (0.027) | −0.021 (0.032) | 0.014 (0.021) | 0.032 (0.019) | −0.024 (0.061) |
| $\gamma_{i3}$ | −0.095*** (0.020) | −0.045 (0.029) | −0.003 (0.016) | 0.056*** (0.015) | 0.141*** (0.044) |
| $\gamma_{i4}$ | 0.062 (0.028) | −0.033 (0.045) | −0.034 (0.021) | −0.022 (0.020) | −0.032 (0.060) |
| $\gamma_{i5}$ | 0.020 (0.026) | 0.056 (0.040) | −0.035 (0.020) | 0.018 (0.018) | −0.162*** (0.056) |
| $\gamma_{i6}$ | −0.142*** (0.040) | 0.0001 (0.012) | −0.065** (0.029) | −0.019 (0.025) | 0.319*** (0.087) |
| $b_i$ | 0.021*** (0.007) | 0.011 (0.011) | −0.012** (0.005) | 0.009 (0.005) | 0.026 (0.015) |
| $\lambda$ | −1.344*** (0.066) | −1.344*** (0.066) | −1.344*** (0.066) | −1.344*** (0.066) | −1.344*** (0.066) |
| $\varphi_1$ | −0.004 (0.005) | −0.007 (0.006) | −0.005 (0.003) | −0.002 (0.003) | −0.001 (0.010) |
| $\varphi_2$ | −0.006 (0.004) | −0.017*** (0.006) | 0.008** (0.003) | −0.008*** (0.003) | 0.026*** (0.010) |
| $\varphi_3$ | 0.030*** (0.005) | −0.012** (0.005) | 0.008** (0.003) | −0.009*** (0.003) | −0.050*** (0.010) |
| $\overline{R}^2$ | 0.854 | 0.259 | 0.590 | 0.430 | 0.720 |
| DW | 1.821 | 1.516 | 1.887 | 2.131 | 1.938 |

Notes: *** and ** indicate the 1% and 5% significance levels, respectively. Values in parentheses are standard errors. DW refers to the Durbin-Watson statistic.

level when the EC-LAIDS models are concerned. Therefore, the LAIDS specifications with both long-run and short-run effects being taken into account are more appropriate for this study.

### 10.5.3   Demand Elasticities

The long-run and short-run expenditure and price elasticities are calculated in terms of the homogeneity and symmetry restricted systems (the model

*Table 10.3* Restriction Tests for Homogeneity and Symmetry

|  | Homogeneity | Symmetry | Homogeneity and Symmetry |
|---|---|---|---|
| Static LAIDS | 2.259** | 3.461 | 3.066* |
| EC-LAIDS | 2.042** | 1.973** | 2.004** |

Note: * and ** denote acceptance at the 1% and 5% significance
levels, respectively.

estimates are omitted due to space constraints), with $w_i$ and $w_j$ being replaced by the average budget shares $\overline{w}_i$ and $\overline{w}_j$, respectively. The calculated elasticities are given in Tables 10.4 and 10.5.

With respect to expenditure elasticities, the values are all greater than or close to unity as far as both long-run and short-run elasticities are concerned. This suggests that travelling to the major Western European countries is generally regarded as a luxury by UK tourists, although the demand for such short-haul travel is not as sensitive as its long-haul counterpart to the tourists' budget variations.

With regard to the own-price elasticities, all of the values are negative, in line with demand theory. Since there is no significant difference between the uncompensated and compensated price elasticities, only the compensated elasticities are reported. With regard to the demand for France, Greece and Italy, Table 10.4 shows that the long-run own-price elasticities are greater than their short-run counterparts in terms of the absolute magnitude, while there is no significant difference in the cases of Portugal and Spain. This implies that in the long run tourists are more flexible in response to price changes. Comparing the magnitude of elasticities across destinations, UK tourists seem to be the most sensitive to price variations in Greece, while the demand for tourism to Italy appears to be the least price elastic.

With respect to cross-price elasticities, significant substitution effects are identified between France and Spain in both the long run and the short run,

*Table 10.4* Long-Run and Short-Run Expenditure and Own-Price Elasticities

|  | Long-Run $\varepsilon_{ix}$ | Short-Run $\varepsilon_{ix}$ | Long-Run $\varepsilon_{ii}^*$ | Short-Run $\varepsilon_{ii}^*$ |
|---|---|---|---|---|
| France | 1.093 | 1.176 | −0.885 | −0.406 |
| Greece | 1.165 | 1.138 | −3.202 | −1.742 |
| Italy | 0.871 | 0.960 | −0.529 | −0.187 |
| Portugal | 1.218 | 1.069 | −1.649 | −1.666 |
| Spain | 1.060 | 1.021 | −1.467 | −1.513 |

*Table 10.5* Long-Run and Short-Run Compensated Cross-Price Elasticities

|  | France | Greece | Italy | Portugal | Spain |
|---|---|---|---|---|---|
| France |  |  |  |  |  |
| Long-Run |  | 0.001 | –0.325 | 0.114 | **1.042** |
| Short-Run |  | 0.147 | –0.110 | 0.121 | **0.604** |
| Greece |  |  |  |  |  |
| Long-Run | 0.002 |  | 0.061 | –0.028 | 0.347 |
| Short-Run | 0.366 |  | –0.286 | 0.368 | 0.178 |
| Italy |  |  |  |  |  |
| Long-Run | **–0.723** | 0.054 |  | **0.372** | –0.137 |
| Short-Run | –0.245 | –0.255 |  | 0.217 | 0.139 |
| Portugal |  |  |  |  |  |
| Long-Run | 0.527 | –0.051 | **0.770** |  | 0.241 |
| Short-Run | 0.558 | 0.681 | 0.449 |  | 0.110 |
| Spain |  |  |  |  |  |
| Long-Run | **0.695** | 0.093 | –0.041 | 0.035 |  |
| Short-Run | **0.403** | 0.048 | 0.042 | 0.016 |  |

Note: Figures in the bold type are significant at the 5% level.

and between Italy and Portugal in the long run. Meanwhile, a certain degree of complementarity is identified between France and Italy in the long run. The lower values of the cross-price elasticities in comparison to the own-price elasticities suggest that the demand for a destination in this region is less sensitive to price changes in alternative destinations than the price of the destination concerned.

## 10.6  FURTHER DEVELOPMENTS OF THE AIDS MODEL

As has been seen in Chapter 8, the TVP model has a number of advantages over its fixed-parameter counterparts. Meanwhile, the necessity of estimating the dynamic LAIDS, that is, EC-LAIDS, has been illustrated above. Therefore, further integrations of the TVP technique with the static LAIDS model and with the EC-LAIDS model are both preferable. These new models, that is, TVP-LAIDS and TVP-EC-LAIDS, feature the latest developments of the AIDS approach.

## 10.6.1 TVP-LAIDS

Relaxing the fixed-parameter restriction, the unrestricted LAIDS in Equation (10.4) can be re-written as a TVP system. It should be noted that dummy variables as exogenous variables have fixed parameters instead of time-varying parameters (Ramajo, 2001). Each equation of the system can be written in the following one-dimension state space form:

$$w_{it} = z_t' \pi_{it} + \vartheta_i dum_t + u_{it} \quad u_{it} \sim N(0, H_t), \quad t = 1, \dots, T \quad (10.17)$$

$$\pi_{it+1} = \pi_{it} + \xi_{it} \quad \pi_1 \sim N(c_1, P_1), \xi_{it} \sim N(0, Q_t) \quad (10.18)$$

where $w_{it}$ and $u_{it}$ are the $i$th elements of $w_t$ and $u_t$ respectively, $\vartheta_i$ is the $i$th row of $\vartheta$, $\xi_{it}$ is a $q$-vector of disturbance terms, $\pi_{it}$ is an unobserved state vector and follows a multivariate random walk, and the matrices $H_t$ and $Q_t$ are initially assumed to be known.

Correspondingly, the whole system can be specified as

$$w_t = z_t^* \Pi_t^* + \vartheta \, dum_t + u_t \quad (10.19)$$

$$\Pi_{t+1}^* = \Pi_t^* + \xi_t^* \quad (10.20)$$

where $z_t^* = I_n \otimes z_t'$, $\Pi_t^* = (\pi_{1t}, \pi_{2t}, \dots, \pi_{nt})'$ and $\xi_t^* = (\xi_{1t}, \xi_{2t}, \dots, \xi_{nt})'$.

In a homogeneity or symmetry restricted LAIDS model, the restrictions $(M)$, which are linear, can be written as

$$M = G\Pi_t^* \quad (10.21)$$

where $G$ is the coefficient matrix of the restriction.

Combining linear restrictions Equation (10.21) with Equation (10.19) gives a new augmented measurement equation in the form:

$$W_t = Z_t^* \Pi_t^* + D_t + U_t \quad (10.22)$$

where $W_t = \begin{bmatrix} w_t \\ M \end{bmatrix}$, $Z_t^* = \begin{bmatrix} z_t^* \\ G \end{bmatrix}$, $D_t = \begin{bmatrix} \vartheta \, dum_t \\ 0 \end{bmatrix}$, and $U_t = \begin{bmatrix} u_t \\ 0 \end{bmatrix}$.

## 10.6.2 TVP-EC-LAIDS

As with Equations (10.17) and (10.18), each equation of the unrestricted TVP-EC-LAIDS can be described as the following SSF:

$$\Delta w_{it} = (z_t^\Delta)' \pi_{it}^\Delta + \phi_i \Delta dum_t + u_{it}^\Delta \quad (10.23)$$

$$\pi_{t+1}^\Delta = \pi_t^\Delta + \xi_{it}^\Delta \quad (10.24)$$

where $z_t^\Delta = (\Delta z_t, w_{t-1} - \Pi z_{t-1} - \varphi dum_{t-1})'$, $\pi_{it}^\Delta$ is the corresponding parameter vector, $\phi_i$ is the $i$th row of $\phi$, $u_{it}^\Delta$ is the $i$th item of $u_t^\Delta$—the disturbance vector of the measurement equation, and $\xi_{it}^{\Delta}$ is the disturbance vector of the state equation.

Accordingly, the whole unrestricted TVP-EC-LAIDS is written as

$$\Delta w_t = (z_t^{\Delta^*})\Pi_t^{\Delta} + \phi\Delta dum_t + u_t^{\Delta} \tag{10.25}$$

$$\Pi_{t+1}^{\Delta} = \Pi_t^{\Delta} + \xi_t^{\Delta^*} \tag{10.26}$$

where $z_t^{\Delta^*} = I_{q+1} \otimes (z_t^{\Delta})'$, $\Pi_t^{\Delta} = (\pi_{1t}^{\Delta}, \pi_{2t}^{\Delta}, \ldots, \pi_{mt}^{\Delta})'$ and $\xi_t^{\Delta^*} = (\xi_{1t}^{\Delta}, \xi_{2t}^{\Delta}, \ldots, \xi_{mt}^{\Delta})'$.

The empirical application of the TVP-LAIDS and TVP-EC-LAIDS models is beyond the content of this chapter due to space constraints. Readers who are interested in these methods can refer to Li *et al.* (2006b).

## 10.7   SUMMARY

Following the simple-to-advanced order, this chapter introduces a number of variations of the AIDS approach. In particular, the EC-LAIDS embodies both long-run equilibrium and short-run disequilibrium adjustment of a demand system. Therefore, it is useful for analysing the dynamic nature of international tourism demand. With a strong theoretical foundation, the AIDS approach is more appropriate for demand elasticity analysis. To examine the evolution of demand elasticities, the TVP version of LAIDS and TVP-EC-LAIDS are favourable. The superiority of TVP models in terms of forecast accuracy enables TVP-LAIDS and TVP-EC-LAIDS to improve the forecasting performance of the static LAIDS. This will be discussed in detail in the next chapter.

# 11 Evaluation of Forecasting Performance

## 11.1    INTRODUCTION

So far we have explained the construction and estimation of various econometric models and their applications to tourism demand analysis. The advantages and disadvantages associated with each of these models have also been discussed. Table 11.1 summarises the applicability of the various models under different conditions.

This chapter aims to evaluate the forecasting performance of the alternative models which have been introduced in the previous chapters, except the panel data technique, due to lack of empirical results. This chapter incorporates seventeen recent studies on tourism forecasting as empirical evidence to illustrate the forecasting performance of the various econometric models.

The organisation of this chapter is as follows. It starts with the fundamentals of forecasting evaluation, including definitions of *ex post* and *ex ante* forecasting and different measures of forecasting accuracy. Then, a particular focus is given to the factors that influence the forecasting performance of different models. Five key factors are identified: measures of forecasting error magnitudes, time horizons of forecasting, data frequency, forecasting competitors, and geographic regions being forecast. A comprehensive comparison among a number of empirical studies is conducted to illustrate the effects of the five factors on forecasting performance. As concluding remarks of the book, the key features and general forecasting performance of the alternative econometric methods introduced in the book are summarised and future trends in tourism demand studies using econometric approaches are presented.

## 11.2    MEASURES OF FORECASTING ACCURACY

### 11.2.1    Ex Post and Ex Ante Forecasting

Before explaining the different measures of forecasting accuracy, two concepts related to forecasting need to be explained, *ex post* forecasting and *ex ante* forecasting. These two concepts are illustrated by Figure 11.1.

*Table 11.1* Summary of Model Selection Criteria

| Model | When to Use |
|---|---|
| Engle-Granger ECM | 1. When the sample size is large (minimum 40 annual or 80 quarterly observations for each of the variables in the model); |
| | 2. When there are a maximum of two explanatory variables in the cointegration regression or, if more than two, only one cointegration relationship is identified; |
| | 3. When it is necessary to examine both the long-run equilibrium relationship and short-run dynamics of the tourism demand model; |
| | 4. When both policy evaluation and forecasting are of interest. |
| Wickens-Breusch ECM | 1. When the sample size is small (less than 40 annual or 80 quarterly observations for each of the variables in the model); |
| | 2–4. Same as above. |
| Johansen Method | 1. Ideally, the sample size should be a minimum of 40 annual or 80 quarterly observations for each of the variables in the model; |
| | 2. When there are more than two explanatory variables in the model; |
| | 3–4. Same as above. |
| VAR Model | 1. When the distinction between endogenous and exogenous variables is not clear; |
| | 2. When the effects of policy 'shocks' on forecasting are of interest (impulse response analysis); |
| | 3. When the direction of causality of tourism demand variables is of interest (Granger block causality test). |

*(Continued)*

In Figure 11.1, $t$ and $Y$ represent the time-span and the time-series data, respectively. The figure shows that the data are available from period 1 to $N$ (the historical data). If a tourism demand model is estimated based on the data from $t_1$ to $t_n$ (the sample data) and the forecasts from $t_n$ to $t_N$ are generated, these forecasts are called *ex post* forecasts. In this case, we know the values of the explanatory and dependent variables over the forecasting period, and the comparison of *ex post* forecasts between different models allows us to decide which model produces the best forecasts. In practice, practitioners and managers are more interested in the forecasts beyond time $t_N$, and the forecasts beyond $t_N$ are termed *ex ante* forecasts. In this case, the values of the explanatory variables are not known and have to be

*Table 11.1* (*Continued*)

| Model | | When to Use |
|---|---|---|
| TVP Model | 1. | When the structure of the model is unstable (based on the two Chow structural instability tests and recursive OLS); |
| | 2. | When the effects of policy changes on demand elasticities are of interest; |
| | 3. | When only short-term forecasts are of interest. |
| Panel Data Method | 1. | When both time-series and cross-sectional data are available; |
| | 2. | When only the relationship between the tourism demand variable and its determinants is of interest, but not forecasts. |
| AIDS Method | 1. | When a complete demand system (either a group of tourist destinations or different types of tourism consumption) is concerned; |
| | 2. | When interdependence of budget allocations to different goods and services (for example, different destinations) is of interest; |
| | 3. | When tourist expenditure data are available and the prediction of the market shares is of interest. |
| Non-Causal Models | 1. | When it is difficult to obtain data on the explanatory variables in the demand model; |
| | 2. | When only forecasting, but not the casual relationship, is of interest; |
| | 3. | When the forecasting performance of various models is compared (non-causal time-series models are normally used as benchmarks). |

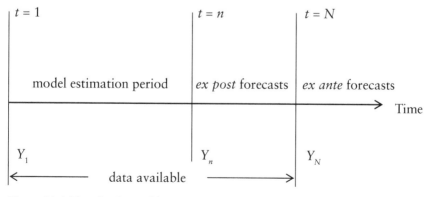

*Figure 11.1* Time horizon of forecasts.

determined (forecast) before the forecasts of the tourism demand variable can be obtained. Since there is no information available on the time-series variables after $t_N$, it is impossible to evaluate the forecasting accuracy of the models. The purpose of this chapter is to examine the forecasting performance of the different models under consideration. It is possible to generate *ex ante* forecasts over the period $t_n$ to $t_N$ by not utilising any information which becomes available after period n, and then to evaluate these forecasts using the known values of the dependent variable. However, this is much more complicated than using known values of the explanatory variables, and so we generate *ex post* forecasts in this chapter.

### 11.2.2   Forecasting Errors

The accuracy of a forecasting model depends on how close the forecast values of Y ($\hat{Y}$) are to the actual values of Y. The differences between the actual and forecast values are known as the forecasting errors, which are defined by

$$e_t = Y_t - \hat{Y}_t \tag{11.1}$$

In theory, if the model is correctly specified, the forecasting errors are expected to be a random series with a mean of zero. Therefore, when the forecasting accuracy of a model over a certain forecasting horizon is evaluated, the sum of the forecasting errors is likely to be zero. Models which generate very poor forecasts can give very small forecasting errors simply because the positive and negative forecasting errors cancel out. To overcome this problem, the forecasting errors of Equation (11.1) are transformed either to $|e_t|$ or $e_t^2$. As a general rule, the smaller the $\sum_{t=1}^{m}|e_t|$ or $\sum_{t=1}^{m} e_t^2$ (where $m$ is the length of the forecasting horizon), the better the forecasts.

Although there are a number of error measures that can be used in model evaluation (Martin and Witt, 1989; Witt and Witt, 1992), in this chapter we only use the following two measures to evaluate the forecasting performance of the tourism demand models.

*The mean absolute percentage error* (MAPE):

$$MAPE = \frac{\sum_{t=1}^{m} \frac{|e_t|}{Y_t}}{m} \tag{11.2}$$

*The root mean square percentage error* (RMSPE):

$$RMSPE = \sqrt{\frac{1}{m}\sum_{t=1}^{m}(\frac{e_t}{Y_t})^2} \tag{11.3}$$

where $m$ is the length of forecasting horizon, and $e_t$ and $Y_t$ are the forecasting error and actual value of the dependent variable, respectively.

The reasons why the MAPE and RMSPE are good measures to use in evaluating the forecasting performance of tourism demand models are explained in Witt and Witt (1992). One of the reasons is that these measures do not depend on the magnitudes of the demand variables being predicted. In practice, we are normally interested in forecasting either outbound demand for tourism from a given origin to a number of destinations or inbound tourism demand to a given destination from several tourist-generating countries, and the magnitudes of the demand variables are likely to vary from country to country (unit to unit). The use of unit independent measures allows us to compare forecasting accuracy not only between different models but also across countries (units).

## 11.3 EVALUATION OF DIFFERENT MODELS' FORECASTING PERFORMANCE

Seventeen post-1990 studies on international tourism demand are identified that focus on forecasting performance comparisons among various econometric models or between econometric and time-series forecasting approaches, based on various error magnitude measures. The rankings of compared models in each of the seventeen studies, in terms of forecast accuracy, are tabulated for detailed analysis (Table 11.2). The rankings of individual forecasting models are based on the MAPE except for two studies in which only the MAE or RMSE is available. Due to space limitations, the results of other measures are omitted from this table. The rankings of competing models at each forecasting horizon and the overall ranks are presented. Where the aggregate performance was not reported in the original papers, it is calculated based on the individual MAPEs reported.

### 11.3.1 Overall Performance of Forecasting Models

In a forecasting performance comparison, the naïve model, which is also known as 'no change' model, is often used as a benchmark. Various ECMs, especially the JML-ECM, are considered most often in the econometric forecasting of tourism demand. The static regression model frequently appeared in the comparison as either a benchmark for econometric models or a competitor for time-series models. The TVP model and its combination with ECM, that is, TVP-ECM, and their further integration with the LAIDS model, that is, TVP-LAIDS and TVP-EC-LAIDS, feature the latest developments of econometric methods for tourism demand forecasting. They did not appear in the tourism demand forecasting literature until recently. Within the time-series forecasting group of models, autoregressive (integrated) moving average (AR(I)MA) models and the seasonal version, SAR(I)MA, have been the most popular methods. They often appear in the comparison of forecasting performance between econometric and time-series approaches. In

Table 11.2 Rankings of Forecasting Accuracy Comparison

| Study | Data Frequency | Naïve | ES | MA | ARI | ARI2 | AR(I)MA | SARIMA | LCM | TFM | BSM | STSM | Static Regression | ADLM | ADL-ECM | WB-ECM | EG-ECM | JML-ECM | VAR | TYP | TYP-ECM | Static LAIDS | EC-LAIDS | TVP-LAIDS | TVP-EC-LAIDS | Error Measure | Best Model |
|---|---|---|---|---|---|---|---|---|---|---|---|---|---|---|---|---|---|---|---|---|---|---|---|---|---|---|---|
| González and Moral (1995) | M | | | | | | | | | | | | | | | | | | | | | | | | | RMSE | TFM |
| 1 step ahead | | | | | | | | 3 | | 1 | | 2 | | | | | 4 | | | | | | | | | | |
| Kim and Song (1998) | A | | | | | | | | | | | | | | | | | | | | | | | | | MAE | |
| 3 steps ahead | | 6 | 4 | 5 | 3 | | 1 | | | | | | | | | | | 2 | 7 | | | | | | | | |
| 5 steps ahead | | 7 | 5 | 6 | 4 | | 1 | | | | | | | | | | | 3 | 2 | | | | | | | | |
| 7 steps ahead | | 7 | 5 | 6 | 3 | | 2 | | | | | | | | | | | 1 | 4 | | | | | | | | |
| 10 steps ahead | | 6 | 4 | 5 | 3 | | 1 | | | | | | | | | | | 2 | 7 | | | | | | | | |
| Overall | | 7 | 4 | 5 | 3 | | 1 | | | | | | | | | | | 2 | 6 | | | | | | | | |
| Kulendran and King (1997) | Q | | | | | | | | | | | | | | | | | | | | | | | | | MAPE | ARMA |
| 1 step ahead | | 3 | 5 | 3 | | | 1 | | | | | 2 | | | | | | 6 | | | | | | | | | |
| 2 steps ahead | | 3 | 6 | 3 | | | 1 | | | | | 2 | | | | | | 3 | | | | | | | | | |

| Forecast horizon | | | (Q) | | | | | Best (MAPE) |
|---|---|---|---|---|---|---|---|---|
| 4 steps ahead | 1 | 6 | 3 | 2 | 5 | 3 | | |
| 8 steps ahead | 1 | 6 | 2 | 4 | 5 | 3 | | |
| Overall | 2 | 6 | 3 | 1 | 4 | 5 | | SARIMA |
| **Kulendran and Wilson (2000)** Q | | | | | | | | |
| 1 step ahead | 2 | | 3 | | | | 1 | EG-ECM |
| **Kulendran and Witt (2001)** Q | | | | | | | | |
| 1 step ahead | 3 | 5 | 1 | 2 | 4 | | | |
| 2 steps ahead | 1 | 5 | 3 | 2 | 4 | | | |
| 4 steps ahead | 1 | 5 | 3 | 2 | 4 | | | |
| 8 steps ahead | 1 | 2 | 5 | 4 | 3 | | | |
| Overall | 1 | 5 | 4 | 2 | 3 | | | Naïve |
| **Kulendran and Witt (2003a)** Q | | | | | | | | |
| 1 step ahead | 6 | 5 | 1 | 7 | 2 | 4 | 3 | |
| 4 steps ahead | 1 | 5 | 4 | 7 | 3 | 6 | 2 | |
| 6 steps ahead | 1 | 4 | 3 | 7 | 2 | 6 | 5 | |
| Overall | 1 | 4 | 3 | 7 | 2 | 6 | 5 | Naïve |

(Continued)

Table 11.2 Rankings of Forecasting Accuracy Comparison (*Continued*)

| Study | Data Frequency | Naïve | ES | MA | ARI | ARI2 | AR(1)MA | SARIMA | LCM | TFM | BSM | STSM | Static Regression | ADLM | ADL-ECM | WB-ECM | EG-ECM | JML-ECM | VAR | TVP | TVP-ECM | Static LAIDS | EC-LAIDS | TVP-LAIDS | TVP-EC-LAIDS | Error Measure | Best Model |
|---|---|---|---|---|---|---|---|---|---|---|---|---|---|---|---|---|---|---|---|---|---|---|---|---|---|---|---|
| Kulendran and Witt (2003b) | Q | | | | | | | | | | | | | | | | | | | | | | | | | MAPE | |
| 1 step ahead | | | | | | | | 1 | | 2 | | | | | | | | 3 | | | | | | | | | |
| 2 steps ahead | | | | | | | | 2 | | 1 | | | | | | | | 3 | | | | | | | | | |
| 4 steps ahead | | | | | | | | 1 | | 3 | | | | | | | | 2 | | | | | | | | | |
| 8 steps ahead | | | | | | | | 2 | | 3 | | | | | | | | 1 | | | | | | | | | |
| Overall | | | | | | | | 2 | | 3 | | | | | | | | 1 | | | | | | | | | JML-ECM |
| Li et al. (2006a) | A | | | | | | | | | | | | | | | | | | | | | | | | | MAPE | |
| 1 step ahead | | 6 | | | | | 5 | | | | | | 9 | 7 | 8 | 4 | | 1 | 3 | 2 | | | | | | | |
| 2 steps ahead | | 5 | | | | | 7 | | | | | | 9 | 4 | 8 | 3 | | 2 | 6 | 1 | | | | | | | |
| 3 steps ahead | | 6 | | | | | 2 | | | | | | 3 | 4 | 8 | 5 | | 7 | 8 | 1 | | | | | | | |
| 4 steps ahead | | 6 | | | | | 2 | | | | | | 5 | 3 | 9 | 4 | | 7 | 9 | 1 | | | | | | | |
| 5 steps ahead | | 7 | | | | | 5 | | | | | | 6 | 2 | 4 | 3 | | 8 | 9 | 1 | | | | | | | |

| Study / Horizon | Criterion | Model | Rankings |
|---|---|---|---|
| Overall | | TVP | 5  4  8  3  7  2  6  9  1 |
| Li *et al.* (2004) | MAPE | EC-LAIDS | A |
| 1 step ahead | | | 2  1 |
| Li *et al.* (2006b) | MAPE | | A |
| 1 step ahead | | | 4  2  3  1 |
| 2 steps ahead | | | 4  3  1  2 |
| 3 steps ahead | | | 3  4  1  2 |
| 4 steps ahead | | | 4  1  2  3 |
| Overall | | TVP-LAIDS | 4  3  1  2 |
| Li *et al.* (2006c) | MAPE | | A |
| 1 step ahead | | | 8  9  10  4  7  3  5  6  1  2 |
| 2 steps ahead | | | 9  8  10  4  7  6  3  5  1  2 |
| 3 steps ahead | | | 10  8  9  3  5  4  6  7  2  1 |
| 4 steps ahead | | | 10  7  9  3  6  5  4  8  2  1 |
| Overall | | TVP-ECM | 9  8  10  3  6  5  4  7  2  1 |
| Riddington (1999) | MAPE | | |
| 1 step ahead | | TVP | 2  3  1 |

(*Continued*)

Table 11.2 Rankings of Forecasting Accuracy Comparison (Continued)

| Study | Data Frequency | Naïve | ES | MA | ARI | ARI2 | AR(1)MA | SARIMA | LCM | TFM | BSM | STSM | Static Regression | ADLM | ADL-ECM | WB-ECM | EG-ECM | JML-ECM | VAR | TVP | TVP-ECM | Static LAIDS | EC-LAIDS | TVP-LAIDS | TVP-EC-LAIDS | Error Measure | Best Model |
|---|---|---|---|---|---|---|---|---|---|---|---|---|---|---|---|---|---|---|---|---|---|---|---|---|---|---|---|
| Song et al. (2000) | A | | | | | | | | | | | | | | | | | | | | | | | | | MAE | EG-ECM |
| 1 step ahead | | 5 | | | 3 | | 4 | | | | | | | | | | 1 | | 2 | | | | | | | | |
| Song et al. (2003b) | A | | | | | | | | | | | | | | | | | | | | | | | | | MAPE | |
| 1 step ahead | | 4 | | | | | 6 | | | | | | 2 | 3 | | 5 | | 8 | 7 | 1 | | | | | | | |
| 2 steps ahead | | 3 | | | | | 7 | | | | | | 1 | 4 | | 5 | | 8 | 6 | 2 | | | | | | | |
| 3 steps ahead | | 4 | | | | | 7 | | | | | | 1 | 6 | | 5 | | 8 | 3 | 2 | | | | | | | |
| 4 steps ahead | | 3 | | | | | 7 | | | | | | 1 | 6 | | 5 | | 8 | 2 | 4 | | | | | | | |
| Overall | | 3 | | | | | 7 | | | | | | 1 | 6 | | 5 | | 8 | 4 | 2 | | | | | | | SR |
| Song and Witt (2000) | A | | | | | | | | | | | | | | | | | | | | | | | | | MAPE | |
| 1 step ahead | | 3 | | | | | | | | | | | | 4 | | 5 | 5 | 2 | 7 | 1 | | | | | | | |
| 2 steps ahead | | 1 | | | | | | | | | | | | 6 | | 4 | 5 | 2 | 7 | 3 | | | | | | | |
| Overall (1 to 4 steps ahead) | | 2 | | | | | | | | | | | | 3 | | 4 | 6 | 5 | 7 | 1 | | | | | | | TVP |

| Veloce (2004) | Q | | | | | | EG-ECM |
| --- | --- | --- | --- | --- | --- | --- | --- |
| | | | | | | | MAPE |
| 1 step ahead | 7 | 2 | 4 | 8 | 5 | 6 | 1 |
| 4 steps ahead | 4 | 6 | 7 | 8 | 1 | 5 | 2 |
| 8 steps ahead | 3 | 5 | 8 | 6 | 1 | 7 | 4 |
| Overall | 6 | 5 | 7 | 8 | 1 | 4 | 2 |

| Witt *et al.* (2003) | A | | | | | | | ADLM |
| --- | --- | --- | --- | --- | --- | --- | --- | --- |
| | | | | | | | | MAPE |
| 1 step ahead | 3 | 4 | 5 | 1 | 6 | 8 | 7 | 2 |
| 2 steps ahead | 3 | 4 | 7 | 2 | 5 | 8 | 1 | 6 |
| 3 steps ahead | 3 | 4 | 5 | 2 | 7 | 8 | 1 | 6 |
| Overall | 3 | 4 | 6 | 1 | 7 | 8 | 2 | 5 |

Legend:
Naïve: no change model
ES: exponential smoothing
MA: moving average
AR: autoregressive process
AR(I)MA: autoregressive (integrated) moving average
SARIMA: seasonal ARIMA
LCM: learning curve model
TFM: transfer function model
BSM: basic structural model
STSM: structural time-series model with causal variables

addition to the above forecasting methods, a few other econometric models (for example, structural time-series models with causal variables and transfer function models) and time-series models (for example, basic structural time-series models without causal variables, exponential smoothing models) are included in forecasting performance comparisons, but relatively less frequently.

As can be seen from Table 11.2, there is no single forecasting model that can outperform all the others in all situations. Overall, the TVP model performs most consistently and satisfactorily, especially as far as short-run (that is, one-step-ahead) forecasting is concerned. On the other hand, the VAR model performs the least consistently, and its rankings vary from the top to the bottom. The forecasting performance of a model varies according to forecast error measurement, the forecasting horizon, data frequency, destination or origin country being concerned, and the competitors in a comparison.

### 11.3.2   Measures of Forecasting Error Magnitudes

Different measures of forecasting error magnitudes are available for tourism demand forecasting evaluations. The predominant measure is MAPE, commonly used in most forecasting studies. It is followed by RMSE and RMSPE, and very often MAPE and RMSE (or RMSPE) are used in pairs. Comparing different measures of the relative forecasting performance of the estimated models, the MAPE and RMSE (or RMSPE) do not always provide the same ranking results. For example, in the study by Li *et al.* (2006a), MAPE and RMSPE suggest different rankings in 60% of all forecasting comparisons. In particular, JML-ECM generates the most accurate one-step-ahead forecasts measured by MAPE, while it is ranked sixth among nine models based on RMSPE. The inconsistency between the rankings given by two groups of measures is due to different assumptions regarding the forms of the loss functions. The MAPE is associated with a linear loss function, while the RMSE and RMSPE are consistent with the notion of a quadratic form (Theil, 1966). The discrepancy between the two sets of measures is evident, especially when large variations appear among individual forecast errors. The RMSE and RMSPE are more sensitive to one extremely poor forecast. It should be noted that the above measures such as MAPE and RMSPE do not have a statistical underpinning. Statistical tests of equal forecast accuracy should be given more attention in future forecasting performance comparisons.

### 11.3.3   Time-Horizons of Forecasting

The forecasting power varies over different forecasting horizons. In general, due to increasing uncertainty, the longer the forecasting horizon, the less accurate the predictions. With regard to the relative performance of a model in comparison to its competitors, fluctuations can be observed across different forecasting horizons. For example, the VAR model is ranked second in five-step-ahead forecasting but bottom for three- and ten-step-ahead forecasting horizons in the study by Kim and Song (1998). The TVP model and TVP-ECM generally outperform their competitors in the short run, especially for one-step-ahead forecasting (Li *et al.*, 2006c; Song *et al.*, 2003b). The JML-ECM forecasts more accurately in the medium to long run than in the short run except in the studies by Song *et al.* (2003b) and Witt *et al.* (2003). As far as other econometric models are concerned, mixed performances have been observed and it is impossible to generalise the conclusions.

## 11.3.4   Data Frequency

Annual data are used most frequently in the above forecasting exercises, followed by quarterly data and then monthly data. Monthly and quarterly data possess different properties compared to annual data, because tourism demand exhibits strong seasonality. Some forecasting models may perform differently as far as seasonal (that is, monthly and quarterly) and non-seasonal (that is, annual) data are concerned. For example, the reduced ADLM forecasts more accurately when annual data are used than when quarterly data are used. On the other hand, the JML-ECM performs better when dealing with seasonal data rather than annual data. The differences in their forecast performance are likely to be associated with the ways in which seasonality is treated. In a reduced ADLM, seasonality is regarded as deterministic and seasonal dummies are used to deal with seasonal variations of tourism demand. In a JML-ECM seasonality is regarded as stochastic and seasonal differencing is used. Where statistical evidence of stochastic seasonality is shown, seasonal dummies are not efficient in dealing with seasonality. The applications of econometric models are most often related to annual data except the JML-ECM, and the accuracy of forecasting seasonal tourism demand is somewhat unknown. In the future it will be worth testing the forecasting abilities of other advanced econometric models in dealing with seasonality in tourism demand.

## 11.3.5   Origins/Destinations under Study

Within a single study where the same models are applied for different origin-destination pairs, their performance may vary from case to case. An extreme example can be seen in the results of Li *et al.* (2006a), in which tourism demand in Thailand by a number of source markets is concerned. The ARIMA model generates the most accurate forecasts in the cases of Japan and Singapore, while the second poorest for Australia and the USA. Furthermore, the WB-ECM outperforms all the other candidates in Australia's case, but it is ranked second from last in the case of the UK. Similar phenomena are observed in Kim and Song (1998), Kulendran and King (1997) and Kulendran and Wilson (2000). Such discrepancies in the performance of models across different countries may well result from different data properties relating to these destinations or origins, especially in the cases where destination- or origin-specific one-off events take place.

### 11.3.6   Forecasting Competitors

The relative forecasting performance, in terms of the rank of an evaluated model, depends to a certain extent on which competitors take part in the comparison. For example, in the comparisons where the static regression model was the only causal model (Law, 2000; Law and Au, 1999; Witt and Witt, 1991 and 1992), it was always outperformed by time-series models. In particular, all the results of the one-year-ahead forecasting of Witt and Witt (1992) showed that the naïve model was superior to all the other non-causal and causal candidates. However, in the forecasting comparisons involving more advanced causal models, non-causal models did not show outstanding performance, especially when annual data were used. Non-causal models outperformed causal models and were ranked top in only six out of sixteen studies in terms of the overall ranking, four being associated with quarterly data. In particular, the naïve model generated the best forecasts only in three out of twelve overall evaluations and six out of thirty-two comparisons at individual forecast horizons. These results suggest that applying advanced econometric techniques to tourism demand forecasting should be encouraged, especially in the cases where annual data are to be used.

### 11.3.7   Forecasting Performance of Emerging Models

The forecasting performances of the AR(I)MA model augmented with the explanatory variables, termed the AR(I)MAX model, and the dynamic LAIDS models, including EC-LAIDS, TVP-LAIDS and TVP-EC-LAIDS, have been examined in the tourism context recently. Cho (2001) compares the forecasting accuracy of the ARIMAX model with the ARIMA and two exponential smoothing models. The results show that the ARIMAX model is always ranked in the top two, and is ranked first in two out of six cases. Akal (2004) finds that the ARMA model outperforms the static regression model in his study. However, none of the advanced econometric models entered the competitions in these two studies, and it should be of interest to fill this gap in further research. The study by Li *et al.* (2004) appears to be the first study that compares forecast accuracy among demand system models. Forecasts of tourism demand measured by market shares have particular importance for destination competitiveness analysis. Li *et al.* (2004) show that by incorporating the ECM into the LAIDS specification, its short-run (one-year-ahead) forecast accuracy of market shares can improve remarkably. Li *et al.* (2006b) demonstrate that TVP-LAIDS and TVP-EC-LAIDS (without restriction) outperform their fixed-parameter counterparts in the overall evaluation of demand level forecasts. In addition, TVP-EC-LAIDS also shows very good performance (ranked second) as far as demand growth forecasts are concerned. It should be noted that, due to the complexity of model estimation, the restricted TVP-LAIDS and restricted TVP-EC-LAIDS have not been included in the above study. Their forecasting performances in comparison to the other variations of the LAIDS models will be of interest in future studies.

## 11.4    CONCLUDING REMARKS

As the review of the post-1990 studies has identified, the measure of forecast accuracy, forecasting horizon, data frequency, origins/destinations under study and competing models included in the forecasting comparison all influence a model's relative forecasting performance. Although there has not been clear-cut evidence that shows any model can consistently outperform all others on all occasions, recent studies suggest that the newer and more advanced forecasting techniques tend to result in improved forecast accuracy under certain circumstances. Therefore, the advanced forecasting models are recommended for future forecasting exercises. Moreover, attention should be paid to further developments of these advanced forecasting techniques. Alternative approaches to improving forecast accuracy should be explored. For example, the emerging literature has shown that to combine the forecasts generated by individual forecasting methods is likely to contribute to forecast accuracy improvement (Oh and Morzuch, 2005; Wong *et al.* 2007). However, the research on forecast combination has been exceptionally limited in the tourism context. Further exploration in this direction is recommended.

# Notes

NOTE TO CHAPTER 4

1. In contrast to the $F$ and $LR$ tests, in which the statistics are calculated using the information from both the restricted and unrestricted models, the Wald test does not require estimation of the restricted model, and this is particularly useful if the restricted model is difficult to estimate, as in the case of the $COMFAC$ model. (For a detailed explanation of the Wald test see Stewart and Gill, 1998, pp. 129–33.)

NOTE TO CHAPTER 5

1. The corresponding Phillips-Perron test statistic is –2.954.

NOTES TO CHAPTER 6

1. When quarterly or monthly data are used, the lag structure will be changed accordingly—4 lags for quarterly data and 12 for monthly data.
2. The estimation of the cointegration and error correction models based on the ADLM approach is carried out using Microfit 4.0. Therefore, some diagnostic statistics reported may differ from those given by the Eviews programme.
3. The heteroscedasticity test reported here is based on the regression of the squared residuals on the squared fitted values.

NOTE TO CHAPTER 8

1. It is possible to improve the significance of these two variables by using other specifications for the transition equations, such as allowing the transition equations to follow AR or ARMA processes. However, for the purpose of simplicity, we only report the estimates based on the random walk specification for the transition equations.

NOTES TO CHAPTER 9

1. This chapter is written jointly with Peter Romilly of the University of Abertay Dundee and Xiaming Liu of the University of London.

2. The appropriate measurement of $EXC$ is discussed further in the appendix.
3. This procedure weights the regression variables by $w$, where $w$ is a series which is proportional to the reciprocals of the standard deviations of the error terms obtained from the unweighted regression.
4. A number of other tests were conducted as part of a pre-modelling data analysis, including a test of whether the model specification should be in nominal rather than real terms (or, alternatively, whether money illusion is a significant factor in the determination of tourism spending). Specifying the model in nominal terms gave poor estimation results.
5. Each of the cited studies reports more than one estimated income elasticity value. The values given above are the unweighted averages of the values reported.

# References

Aguiló, E., Riera, A. and Rosselló, J. (2005). The Short-term Price Effect of a Tourist Tax Through a Dynamic Demand Model: The Case of the Balearic Islands. *Tourism Management*, 26, 359–365.

Akaike, H. (1974). A New Look at the Statistical Model Identification. *IEEE Transactions on Automatic Control*, AC-19, 716–723.

Akal, M. (2004). Forecasting Turkey's Tourism Revenues by ARMAX Model. *Tourism Management*, 25, 565–580.

Akis, S. (1998). A Compact Econometric Model of Tourism Demand for Turkey. *Tourism Management*, 19, 99–102.

Algieri, B. (2006). An Econometric Estimation of the Demand for Tourism: The Case of Russia. *Tourism Economics*, 12, 5–20.

Alleyne, D. (2006). Can Seasonal Unit Root Testing Improve the Forecasting Accuracy of Tourist Arrivals? *Tourism Economics*, 12, 45–64.

Anderson, G. and Blundell, R. (1983). Testing Restrictions in a Flexible Dynamic Demand System: An Application to Consumers' Expenditure in Canada. *Review of Economic Studies*, 50, 397–410.

Armstrong, J. S. (2001). Combining Forecasts, in J. S. Armstrong (ed), *Principles of Forecasting: A Handbook for Researchers and Practitioners*, 417–439. Kluwer Academic Publisher, Amsterdam.

Artus, J. R. (1972). An Econometric Analysis of International Travel. *IMF Staff Papers*, 19, 579–614.

Ashworth, J. and Johnson, P. (1990). Holiday Tourism Expenditure: Some Preliminary Econometric Results. *The Tourist Review*, 3, 12–19.

Au, N. and Law, R. (2000). The Application of Rough Sets to Sightseeing Expenditures. *Journal of Travel Research*, 39, 70–77.

Au, N. and Law, R. (2002). Categorical Classification of Tourism Dining. *Annals of Tourism Research*, 29, 819–833.

Bakkal, I. (1991). Characteristics of West German Demand for International Tourism in the Northern Mediterranean Region. *Applied Economics*, 23, 295–304.

Balcombe, K. G. and Davis, J. R. (1996). An Application of Cointegration Theory in the Estimation of the Almost Ideal Demand System for Food Consumption in Bulgaria. *Agricultural Economics*, 15, 47–60.

Baldwin, M. A., Hadid, M. and Phillips, G. D. A. (1983). The Estimation and Testing of A System of Demand Equations for the UK. *Applied Economics*, 15, 81–90.

Baltagi, B. H. (1995). *Econometric Analysis of Panel Data*. Wiley, Chichester.

Bar-On, R. (1989). *Travel and Tourism Data*. Euromonitor Publications Ltd, Cambridge.

Barten, A. P. (1969). Maximum Likelihood Estimation of a Complete System of Demand Equations. *European Economic Review*, 1, 7–73.

Bewley, R. (1979). The Direct Estimation of the Equilibrium Response in a Linear Dynamic Model. *Economics Letters*, 55, 251–276.

Bicak, H. A., Altinay, M. and Jenkins, H. (2005). Forcasting Tourism Demand of North Cyprus. *Journal of Hospitality and Leisure Marketing*, 12, 87–99.

Blackwell, J. (1970). Tourist Traffic and the Demand for Accommodation: Some Projections. *Economic and Social Review*, 1, 323–343.

Blake, A., Durbarry, R., Eugenio–Martin, J. L., Gooroochurn, N., Hay, B., Lennon, J., Thea Sinclair, M., Sugiyarto, G. and Yeoman, I. (2006). Integrating Forecasting and CGE Models: The Case of Tourism in Scotland. *Tourism Management*, 27, 292–305.

Blanciforti, L., Green, R. and King, G. (1986). U.S. Consumer Behaviour over the Post-War Period: An Almost Ideal Demand System Analysis. Monograph Number 40, Giannini Foundation of Agricultural Economics, University of California.

Bohara, A. K. and Sauer, C. (1992). Competing Macro-Hypotheses in the United States: A Kalman Filter Approach. *Applied Economics*, 24, 389–399.

Bomhoff, E. J. (1994). *Financial Forecasting for Business and Economics*. Dryden Press, London.

Box, G. and Jenkins, G. M. (1976). *Time Series Analysis: Forecasting and Control*. Holden-Day, San Francisco.

Breusch, T. (1978). Testing for Autocorrelation in Dynamic Linear Models. *Journal of Australian Economic Papers*, 17, 334–355.

Breusch, T. and Pagan, A. (1980). The LM Test and Its Applications to Model Specification in Econometrics. *Review of Economic Studies*, 47, 239–254.

Brown, J., Song, H. and McGillivray, A. (1997). Forecasting UK House Prices: A Time Varying Coefficient Approach. *Economic Modelling*, 14, 529–548.

Burger, C. J. S. C., Dohnal, M., Kathrada, M. and Law, R. (2001). A Practitioner's Guide to Time-Series Methods for Tourism Demand Forecasting—A Case Study of Durban, South Africa. *Tourism Management*, 22, 403–409.

Burmeister, E. and Wall, K. D. (1982). Kalman Filtering Estimation of Unobserved Rational Expectations with an Application to the German Hyperinflation. *Journal of Econometrics*, 20, 255–284.

Carey, K. (1991). Estimation of Caribbean Tourism Demand: Issues in Measurement and Methodology. *Atlantic Economic Journal*, 19, 32–40.

Chambers, M. J. and Nowman, K. B. (1997). Forecasting with the Almost Ideal Demand System: Evidence from Some Alternative Dynamic Specifications. *Applied Economics*, 29, 935–943.

Chen, K. Y. and Wang, C. H. (2007). Support Vector Regression with Genetic Algorithms in Forecasting Tourism Demand. *Tourism Management*, 28, 215–226.

Chiang, A. C. (1984). *Fundamental Methods of Mathematical Economics*, 3rd ed. McGraw-Hill, New York.

Cho, V. (2001). Tourism Forecasting and Its Relationship with Leading Economic Indicators. *Journal of Hospitality and Tourism Research*, 25, 399–420.

Cho, V. (2003). A Comparison of Three Different Approaches to Tourist Arrival Forecasting. *Tourism Management*, 24, 323–330.

Chow, G. (1960). Test of Equality Between Sets of Coefficients in Two Linear Regressions. *Econometrica*, 28, 591–605.

Chu, F. L. (2004). Forecasting Tourism Demand: A Cubic Polynomial Approach. *Tourism Management*, 25, 209–218.

Clements, M. P. and Hendry, D. F. (1997). An Empirical Study of Seasonal Unit Roots in Forecasting. *International Journal of Forecasting*, 13, 341–355.

Clements, M. P. and Hendry, D. F. (1998). *Forecasting Economic Time Series*. Cambridge University Press, Cambridge.

Cochrane, E. and Orcutt, G. H. (1949). Application of Least Squares Regression to Relationships Containing Autocorrelation Error Terms. *Journal of the American Statistical Association*, 44, 32–61.

Croes, R. R. and Vanegas Sr., M. (2005). An Econometric Study of Tourist Arrivals in Aruba and Its Implications. *Tourism Management*, 26, 879–890.

Crouch, G. I. (1994). Demand Elasticities for Short-haul versus Long-haul Tourism. *Journal of Travel Research*, 33, 2–7.

Crouch, G. I. (1996). Demand Elasticities in International Marketing: A Meta-analytical Application to Tourism. *Journal of Business Research*, 36, 117–136.

Crouch, G. I. and Shaw, R. N. (1992). International Tourism Demand: A Meta-analytical Integration of Research Findings, in P. Johnson and B. Thomas (eds), *Choice and Demand in Tourism*, 175–207. Mansell, London.

Crouch, G. I., Schultz, L. and Valerio, P. (1992). Marketing International Tourism to Australia: A Regression Analysis. *Tourism Management*, 13, 196–208.

Cuthbertson, K. (1988). Expectations, Learning and the Kalman Filter. *The Manchester School*, vol. 56, 223–246.

Daniel, A. C. M. and Ramos, F. F. R. (2002). Modelling Inbound International Tourism Demand to Portugal. *International Journal of Tourism Research*, 4, 193–209.

Davidson, J., Hendry, D. F., Saba, F. and Yeo, S. (1978). Econometric Modelling of the Aggregate Time Series Relationships between Consumers' Expenditure and Income in the United Kingdom. *Economic Journal*, 88, 661–692.

Davidson, R. and MacKinnon, J. G. (1981). Several Tests for Model Specification in the Presence of Alternative Hypotheses. *Econometrica*, 49, 781–793.

De Mello, M. M. and Fortuna, N. (2005). Testing Alternative Dynamic Systems for Modelling Tourism Demand. *Tourism Economics*, 11, 517–537.

De Mello, M. M. and Nell, K. S. (2005). The Forecasting Ability of a Cointegrated VAR System of the UK Tourism Demand for France, Spain and Portugal. *Empirical Economics*, 30, 277–308.

De Mello, M. M., Pack, A. and Sinclair, M. T. (2002). A System of Equations Model of UK Tourism Demand in Neighbouring Countries. *Applied Economics*, 34, 509–521.

Deaton, A. S. and Muellbauer, J. (1980a). *Econometric and Consumer Behaviour*. Cambridge University Press, Cambridge.

Deaton, A. S. and Muellbauer, J. (1980b). An Almost Ideal Demand System. *American Economic Review*, 70, 312–326.

Di Matteo, L. (1999). Using Alternative Methods to Estimate the Determinants of Cross-Border Trips. *Applied Economics*, 31, 77–88.

Di Matteo, L. and Di Matteo, R. (1993). The Determinants of Expenditures by Canadian Visitors to the United States. *Journal of Travel Research*, 31, 34–42.

Dickey, D. A. and Fuller, W. A. (1979). Distribution of the Estimates for Autoregressive Time Series with Unit Roots. *Journal of the American Statistical Association*, 74, 427–431.

Dickey, D. A. and Fuller, W. A. (1981). Likelihood Ratio Statistics for Autoregressive Time Series with a Unit Root. *Econometrica*, 49, 1057–1072.

Dickey, D. A., Hasza, D. P. and Fuller, W.A. (1984). Testing for Unit Roots in Seasonal Time Series. *Journal of American Statistical Association*, 79, 355–367.

Divisekera, S. (2003). A Model of Demand for International Tourism. *Annals of Tourism Research*, 30, 31–49.

Doan, T., Littleman, R. B. and Sims, C. A. (1984). Forecasting and Conditional Projection Using Realistic Prior Distributions. *Econometric Review*, 3, 1–100.

Dritsakis, N. (2004). Cointegration Analysis of German and British Tourism Demand for Greece. *Tourism Management*, 25, 111–119.

Dritsakis, N. and Athanasiadis, S. (2000). An Econometric Model of Tourist Demand: The Case of Greece. *Journal of Hospitality and Leisure Marketing*, 7, 39–49.

Dritsakis, N. and Papanastasiou, J. (1998). An Econometric Investigation of Greek Tourism: A Note. *Journal for Studies in Economics and Econometrics*, 22, 115–122.

Duffy, M. (2003). Advertising and Food, Drink and Tobacco Consumption in the United Kingdom: A Dynamic Demand System. *Agricultural Economics*, 28, 51–70.

Durbarry, R. and Sinclair, M. T. (2003). Market Shares Analysis: The Case of French Tourism Demand. *Annals of Tourism Research*, 30, 927–941.

Eadington, W. R. and M. Redman (1991). Economics and Tourism, *Annals of Tourism Research*, 18, 41–56.

Edgerton, D. L., Assarsson, B., Hummelmose, A., Laurila, I. P., Rickertsen, K. and Vale, P. H. (1996). *The Econometrics of Demand Systems with Applications to Food Demand in the Nordic Countries*. Kluwer Academic Publishers, London.

Edwards, A. (1985). *International Tourism Forecasts to 1995: EIU Special Report No. 188*. Economist Publication, London.

Engle, R. F. (1982). Autoregressive Conditional Heteroscedasticity with Estimates of the Variance of UK Inflation. *Econometrica*, 50, 987–1007.

Engle, R. F. and Granger, C. W. J. (1987). Cointegration and Error Correction: Representation, Estimation and Testing. *Econometrica*, 55, 251–276.

Eugenio-Martin, J., Sinclair, M. T. and Yeoman, I. (2005). Quantifying the Effects of Tourism Crises: An Application to Scotland. *Journal of Travel & Tourism Marketing*, 19, 21–34.

Friedman, M. (1957). *A Theory of the Consumption Function*. Princeton University Press, Princeton, New Jersey.

Fuller, W. A. (1976). *Introduction to Statistical Time Series*. John Wiley, New York.

Fujii, E., Khaled, M. and Mark, J. (1985). An Almost Ideal Demand System for Visitor Expenditures. *Journal of Transport Economics and Policy*, 19, 161–171.

Gallet, C. A. and Braun, B. M. (2001). Gradual Switching Regression Estimates of Tourism Demand. *Annals of Tourism Research*, 28, 503–507.

García-Ferrer, A. and Queralt, R. (1997). A Note on Forecasting International Tourism Demand in Spain. *International Journal of Forecasting*, 13, 539–549.

Garín-Muñoz, T. and Amaral, T. P. (2000). An Econometric Model for International Tourism Flows to Spain. *Applied Economics Letters*, 7, 525–529.

Gerakis, A. S. (1965). Effects of Exchange-rate Devaluations and Revaluations on Receipts from Tourism. *International Monetary Fund Staff Papers*, 12, 365–384.

Geweke, J. (1984). Inference and Causality in Economic Time Series Models, in Z. Griliches and M. D. Intriligator (eds), *Handbook of Econometrics*, vol. 2, 1101–1144. North Holland, Amsterdam.

Godfrey, L. G. (1978). Testing for Higher Order Serial Correlation in Regression Equations when the Regressors Contain Lagged Dependent Variables. *Econometrica*, 46, 1303–1310.

Goh, C. and Law, R. (2002). Modeling and Forecasting Tourism Demand for Arrivals with Stochastic Nonstationary Seasonality and Intervention. *Tourism Management*, 23, 499–510.

Goh, C. and Law, R. (2003). Incorporating the Rough Sets Theory into Travel Demand Analysis. *Tourism Management*, 24, 511–517.

Goldfeld, S. M. and Quandt, R. E. (1965). Some Tests for Homoskedasticity. *Journal of the American Statistical Association*, 60, 539–547.

González, P. and Moral, P. (1995). An Analysis of the International Tourism Demand in Spain. *International Journal of Forecasting*, 11, 233–251.

González, P. and Moral, P. (1996). Analysis of Tourism Trends in Spain. *Annals of Tourism Research*, 23, 739–754.

Gouveia, P. M. D. C. B. and Rodrigues, P. M. M. (2005). Dating and synchronizing tourism growth cycles. *Tourism Economics*, 11, 501–515.

Granger, C. W. J. (1969). Investigating Causal Relationships by Econometric Models and Cross Spectral Methods. *Econometrica*, 37, 424–438.

Gray, H. P. (1966). The Demand for International Travel by the United States and Canada. *International Economic Review*, 7, 83–92.

Greenidge, K. (2001). Forecasting Tourism Demand: An STM Approach. *Annals of Tourism Research*, 28, 98–112.

Greenslade, J. V. and Hall, S. G. (1996), Modelling Economies Subject to Structural Change: The Case of Germany. *Economic Modelling*, 13, 545–559.

Guthrie, H. W. (1961). Demand for Tourists' Goods and Services in a World Market. *Papers and Proceedings of the Regional Science Association*, 7, 159–175.

Hall, R. E. (1978). Stochastic Implications of the Life Cycle-Permanent Income Hypothesis: Evidence. *Journal of Political Economy*, 86, 971–987.

Hamilton, J. D. (1994). *Time Series Analysis*. Princeton University Press, Princeton, New Jersey.

Han, Z., Durbarry, R. and Sinclair, M. T. (2006). Modelling US Tourism Demand for European Destinations. *Tourism Management*, 27, 1–10.

Harris, R. and Sollis, R. (2003). *Applied Time Series Modeling and Forecasting*. Wiley, Chichester.

Harvey, A. C. (1987). Applications of the Kalman Filter in Econometrics, in T. F. Bewley (ed), *Advances in Econometrics—Fifth World Congress*, vol. 1, 85–313. Cambridge University Press, Cambridge.

Harvey, A. C. (1993). *Time Series Models*, 2nd ed. Harvester Wheatsheaf, London.

Hausman, J. A. (1978). Specification Tests in Econometrics. *Econometrica*, 46, 251–272.

Hendry, D. F. (1995). *Dynamic Econometrics: Advanced Text in Econometrics*. Oxford University Press, Oxford.

Hendry, D. F. and von Ungern-Sternberg, T. (1981). Liquidity and Inflation Effects on Consumers Expenditure, in Deaton A. S. (ed), *Essays in the Theory and Measurement of Consumer Behaviour*, 237–261. Cambridge University Press, Cambridge.

Holmes, R. A. and Shamsuddin, A. F. M. (1997). Short- and Long-Term Effects of World Exposition 1986 on US Demand for British Columbia Tourism. *Tourism Economics*, 3, 137–160.

Hsiao, C. (1986). *Analysis of Panel Data*. Cambridge University Press, Cambridge.

Hu, C., Chen, M. and McCain, S. C. (2004). Forecasting in Short-Term Planning and Management for a Casino Buffet Restaurant. *Journal of Travel & Tourism Marketing*, 16, 79–98.

Hylleberg, S., Engle, R. F., Granger, C. W. J. and Yoo, B. S. (1990). Seasonal Integration and Cointegration. *Journal of Econometrics*, 44, 215–218.

Icoz, O., Var, T. and Kozaka, M. (1998). Tourism Demand in Turkey. *Annals of Tourism Research*, 25, 236–240.

Ismail, J. A., Iverson, T. J. and Cai, L. A. (2000). Forecasting Japanese Arrivals to Guam: An Empirical Model. *Journal of Hospitality and Leisure Marketing*, 7, 51–63.

Jarque, C. M and Bera, A. K. (1980). Efficient Tests for Normality, Homoskedastcity and Serial Independence of Regression Residuals. *Economic Letters*, 6, 255–259.

Jensen, T. C. (1998). Income and Price Elasticities by Nationality for Tourists in Denmark. *Tourism Economics*, 4, 101–130.

Johansen, S. (1988). A Statistical Analysis of Cointegration Vectors. *Journal of Economic Dynamics and Control*, 12, 231–254.

Johansen S. (1995). *Likelihood Based Inference on Cointegration in the Vector Autoregressive Model*. Oxford University Press, Oxford.

Johansen, S. and Juselius, K. (1990). Maximum Likelihood Estimation and Inference on Cointegration with Application to Demand for Money. *Oxford Bulletin of Economics and Statistics*, 52, 169–210.

Johnston, J. (1986). *Econometric Methods*, 3rd ed. McGraw-Hill, New York.

Jørgensen, F. and, Solvoll, G. (1996). Demand Models for Inclusive Tour Charter: The Norwegian Case. *Tourism Management*, 17, 17–24.

Kalman, R. E. (1960). A New Approach to Linear Filtering and Prediction Problems. *Transactions ASME Journal of Basic Engineering*, D82, 35–45.

Kim, C. J. (1993). Sources of Monetary Growth, Uncertainty and Economic Activity: The Time Varying Parameter Model with Heteroskedastic Disturbances. *The Review of Economics and Statistics*, 74, 483–492.

Kim, J. H. and Moosa, I. A. (2001). Seasonal Behaviour of Monthly International Tourist Flows: Specification and Implications for Forecasting Models. *Tourism Economics*, 7, 381–396.

Kim, J. H. and Moosa, I. A. (2005). Forecasting International Tourist Flows to Australia: A Comparison Between the Direct and Indirect Methods. *Tourism Management*, 26, 69–78.

Kim, J. H. and Ngo, M. T. (2001). Modelling and Forecasting Monthly Airline Passenger Flows Among Three Major Australian Cities. *Tourism Economics*, 7, 397–412.

Kim, S. and Song, H. (1998). An Empirical Analysis of Demand for Korean Tourism: A Cointegration and Error Correction Approach. *Tourism Analysis*, 3, 25–41.

Kim, Y. and Uysal, M. (1998). Time-Dependent Analysis for International Hotel Demand in Seoul. *Tourism Economics*, 4, 253–263.

Kliman, M. L. (1981). A Quantitative Analysis of Canadian Overseas Tourism. *Transportation Research*, 15, 487–497.

Krippendorf, J. (1987). *The Holiday Makers: Understanding the Impact of Leisure and Travel*. Butterworth-Heinemann, Oxford.

Kulendran, N. (1996). Modelling Quarterly Tourism Flows to Australia Using Cointegration Analysis. *Tourism Economics*, 2, 203–222.

Kulendran, N. and King, M. L. (1997). Forecasting International Quarterly Tourist Flows Using Error Correction and Time Series Models. *International Journal of Forecasting*, 13, 319–327.

Kulendran, N. and Shan, J. (2002). Forecasting China's Monthly Inbound Travel Demand. *Journal of Travel & Tourism Marketing*, 13, 5–19.

Kulendran, N. and Wilson, K. (2000). Modelling Business Travel. *Tourism Economics*, 6, 47–59.

Kulendran, N. and Witt, S. F. (1997). Modelling UK Outbound Tourism Demand. Paper presented at the *17th International Symposium on Forecasting*. Bridgetown, Barbados.

Kulendran, N. and Witt, S. F. (2001). Cointegration versus Least Squares Regression. *Annals of Tourism Research*, 28, 291–311.

Kulendran, N. and Witt, S. F. (2003a). Forecasting the Demand for International Business Tourism. *Journal of Travel Research*, 41, 265–271.

Kulendran, N. and Witt, S. F. (2003b). Leading Indicator Tourism Forecasts. *Tourism Management*, 24, 503–510.

Kulendran, N. and Wong K. K. F. (2005). Modeling Seasonality in Tourism Forecasting. *Journal of Travel Research*, 44, 163–170.

Kwack, S. Y. (1972). Effects of Income and Prices on Travel Spending Abroad 1960III–1967IV. *International Economic Review*, 13, 245–256.

Lanza, A., Temple, P. and Urga, G. (2003). The Implications of Tourism Specialization in the Long Run: An Econometric Analysis for 13 OECD Economies. *Tourism Management*, 24, 315–321.

Lathiras, P. and Siriopoulos, C. (1998). The Demand for Tourism to Greece: A Cointegration Approach. *Tourism Economics*, 4, 171–185.

Law, R. (2000). Back-propagation Learning in Improving the Accuracy of Neural Network-based Tourism Demand Forecasting. *Tourism Management*, 21, 331–340.

Law, R. (2001). The Impact of the Asian Financial Crisis on Japanese Demand for Travel to Hong Kong: A Study of Various Forecasting Techniques. *Journal of Travel & Tourism Marketing*, 10, 47–66.

Law, R. (2004). Initially Testing an Improved Extrapolative Hotel Room Occupancy Rate Forecasting Technique. *Journal of Travel & Tourism Marketing*, 16, 71–77.

Law, R. and Au, N. (1999). A Neural Network Model to Forecast Japanese Demand for Travel to Hong Kong. *Tourism Management*, 20, 89–97.

Law, R. and Au, N. (2000). Relationship Modeling in Tourism Shopping: A Decision Rules Induction Approach. *Tourism Management*, 21, 241–249.

Law, R., Goh, C. and Pine, R. (2004). Modeling Tourism Demand: A Decision Rules Based Approach. *Journal of Travel & Tourism Marketing*, 16, 61–69.

Ledesma-Rodríguez, F. J., Navarro-Ibáñez, M. and Pérez-Rodríguez, J. V. (2001). Panel Data and Tourism: A Case Study of Tenerife. *Tourism Economics*, 7, 75–88.

Lee, C. K., Var, T. and Blaine, T. W. (1996). Determinants of Inbound Tourism Expenditure. *Annals of Tourism Research*, 23, 527–542.

Leser, C. E. V. (1963). Forms of Engel Functions. *Econometrica*, 31, 694–703.

Li, G., Song, H. and Witt, S. F. (2004). Modeling Tourism Demand: A Dynamic Linear AIDS Approach. *Journal of Travel Research*, 43, 141–150.

Li, G., Song, H. and Witt, S. F. (2005). Recent Developments in Econometric Modeling and Forecasting. *Journal of Travel Research*, 44, 82–99.

Li, G., Song, H. and Witt, S. F. (2006a). Forecasting Tourism Demand Using Econometric Models, in D. Buhalis and C. Costa (eds.) *Tourism Management Dynamics: Trends, Management and Tools*, 219–228. Elsevier, Oxford.

Li, G., Song, H. and Witt, S. F. (2006b). Time Varying Parameter and Fixed Parameter Linear AIDS: An Application to Tourism Demand Forecasting. *International Journal of Forecasting*, 22, 57–71.

Li, G., Wong, K. F., Song, H. and Witt, S. F. (2006c). Tourism Demand Forecasting: A Time Varying Parameter Error Correction Model. *Journal of Travel Research*, 45, 175–185.

Lim, C. (1997a). An Econometric Classification and Review of International Tourism Demand Models. *Tourism Economics*, 3, 69–81.

Lim, C. (1997b). Review of International Tourism Demand Models. *Annals of Tourism Research*, 24, 835–849.

Lim, C. (1999). A Meta Analysis Review of International Tourism Demand. *Journal of Travel Research*, 37, 273–284.

Lim, C. (2004). The Major Determinants of Korean Outbound Travel to Australia. *Mathematics and Computers in Simulation*, 64, 477–485.

Lim, C. and McAleer, M. (2000). A Seasonal Analysis of Asian Tourist Arrivals to Australia. *Applied Economics*, 32, 499–509.

Lim, C. and McAleer, M. (2001a). Cointegration Analysis of Quarterly Tourism Demand by Hong Kong and Singapore for Australia. *Applied Economics*, 33, 1599–1619.

Lim, C. and McAleer, M. (2001b). Monthly Seasonal Variations: Asian Tourism to Australia. *Annals of Tourism Research*, 28, 68–82.

Lim, C. and McAleer, M. (2002). Time Series Forecasts of International Travel Demand for Australia. *Tourism Management*, 23, 389–396.

Little, J. S. (1980). International Travel in the US Balance of Payments. *New England Economic Review*, (May/June) 42–55.

Loeb, P. (1982). International Travel to the United States: An Economic Evaluation. *Annals of Tourism Research*, 9, 5–20.

Louvieris, P. (2002). Forecasting International Tourism Demand for Greece: A Contingency Approach. *Journal of Travel & Tourism Marketing*, 13, 21–40.

Lyssiotou, P. (2000). Dynamic Analysis of British Demand for Tourism Abroad. *Empirical Economics*, 15, 421–436.

MacKinnon, J. G. (1991). Critical Values for Cointegration Tests, in R. F. Engle and C. W. Granger (eds), *Long-Run Equilibrium Relationships*, 266–276. Oxford University Press, Oxford.

Mak, J., Moncur, J. and Yonamine, D. (1977). Determinants of Visitor Expenditures and Visitor Lengths of Stay: A Cross-section analysis of U.S. Visitors to Hawaii. *Journal of Travel Research*, 15, 5–8.

Mangion, M. L., Durbarry, R., and Sinclair, M. T. (2005). Tourism Competitiveness: Price and Quality Tourism Competitiveness: Price and Quality. *Tourism Economics*, 11, 45–68.

Martin, C. A. and Witt, S. F. (1987). Tourism Demand Forecasting Models: Choice of Appropriate Variable to Represent Tourists' Cost of Living. *Tourism Management*, 8, 233–246.

Martin, C. A. and Witt, S. F. (1988). Substitute Prices in Models of Tourism Demand. *Annals of Tourism Demand*, 15, 255–268.

Martin, C. A. and Witt, S. F. (1989). Forecasting Tourism Demand: A Comparison of the Accuracy of Several Quantitative Methods. *International Journal of Forecasting*, 5, 7–19.

Min, J. C. H. (2005). The Effect of the SARS Illness on Tourism in Taiwan: An Empirical Study. *International Journal of Management*, 22, 497–506.

Mizon, G. E. and Richard, J. F. (1986). The Encompassing Principle and Its Application to Testing Non-Nested Hypotheses. *Econometrica*, 54, 657–678.

Morley, C. L. (1996). A Comparison of Three Methods for Estimating Tourism Demand Models. *Tourism Economics*, 2, 223–234.

Morley, C. L. (1997). An Evaluation of the Use of Ordinary Least Squares for Estimating Tourism Demand Model. *Journal of Travel Research*, 35, 69–73.

Morley, C. L. (1998). A Dynamic International Demand Model. *Annals of Tourism Research*, 25, 70–84.

Morris, A., Wilson, K. and Bakalis, S. (1995). Modelling Tourism Flows from Europe to Australia. *Tourism Economics*, 1, 147–167.

Narayan, P. K. (2004). Fiji's Tourism Demand: The ARDL Approach to Cointegration. *Tourism Economics*, 10, 193–206.

Naudé, W. A. and Saayman, A. (2005). Determinants of Tourist Arrivals in Africa: A Panel Data Regression Analysis. *Tourism Economics*, 11, 365–391.

Oh, C.O. (2005). The Contribution of Tourism Development to Economic Growth in the Korean Economy. *Tourism Management*, 26, 39–44.

Oh, C. O. and Morzuch, B. J. (2005). Evaluating Time-series Models to Forecast the Demand for Tourism in Singapore: Comparing Within-sample and Postsample Results. *Journal of Travel Research*, 43, 404–413.

O'Hagan, J. W. and Harrison, M. J. (1984). Market Shares of US Tourist Expenditure in Ireland: Some Econometric Findings. *Applied Economics*, 16, 919–931.

Osborn, D. R., Chui, A. P. L., Smith, J. P. and Birchenhall, C. R. (1988). Seasonality and the Order of Integration for Consumption. *Oxford Bulletin of Economics and Statistics*, 50, 361–377.

Osterwald-Lenum, M. (1992). A Note with Quantiles of the Asymptotic Distribution of the ML Cointegration Rank Test Statistics. *Oxford Bulletin of Economics and Statistics*, 54, 461–472.

Papatheodorou, A. (1999). The Demand for International Tourism in the Mediterranean Region. *Applied Economics*, 31, 619–630.

Papatheodorou, A. and Song, H. (2005). International Tourism Forecasts: Time-series Analysis of World Regional Data. *Tourism Economics*, 11, 11–23.

Patsouratis, V., Frangouli, Z. and Anastasopoulos, G. (2005). Competition In Tourism Among the Mediterranean Countries. *Applied Economics*, 37, 1865–1870.

Payne, J. E. and Mervar, A. (2002). A Note on Modelling Tourism Revenues in Croatia. *Tourism Economics*, 8, 103–109.

Pesaran, M. H. and Shin, Y. (1995). An Autoregressive Distributed Lag Modelling Approach to Cointegration Analysis, DAE working paper no. 1054, Department of Applied Economics, University of Cambridge.

Petropoulos, C., Nikolopoulos, K., Patelis, A. and Assimakopoulos, V. (2005). A Technical Analysis Approach to Tourism Demand Forecasting. *Applied Economics Letters*, 12, 327–333.

Petropoulos, C., Patelis, A., Metaxiotis, K., Nikolopoulos, K. and Assimakopoulos, V. (2003). SFTIS: A Decision Support System for Tourism Demand Analysis and Forecasting. *The Journal of Computer Information Systems*, 44, 21–32.

Phillips, P. C. B. and Perron, P. (1988). Testing for a Unit Root in Time Series Regression. *Biometrica*, 75, 335–346.

Pyo, S., Uysal, M. and McLellan, R. (1991). A Linear Expenditure Model for Tourism Demand. *Annals of Tourism Research*, 31, 619–630.

Qiu, H. and Zhang, J. (1995). Determinants of Tourist Arrivals and Expenditures in Canada. *Journal of Travel Research*, 34, 43–49.

Qu, H. and Lam, S. (1997). A Travel Demand Model for Mainland Chinese Tourists to Hong Kong. *Tourism Management*, 18, 593–597.

Quandt, R. E. and Young, K. H. (1969). Cross-sectional Travel Demand Models: Estimation and Tests. *Journal of Regional Science*, 9, 201–214.

Ramajo, J. (2001). Time-Varying Parameter Error Correction Models: The Demand for Money in Venezuela, 1983.I–1994.IV. *Applied Economics*, 33, 771–782.

Ramsey, J. B. (1969). Test for Specification Errors in Classical Linear Least-Squares Regression Analysis. *Journal of the Royal Statistical Society*, Series B, 31, 350–371.

Ray, R. (1985). Specification and Time Series Estimation of Dynamic Gorman Polar Form Demand Systems. *European Economic Review*, 27, 357–374.

Rickertsen, K. (1998). The Demand for Food and Beverages in Norway. *Agricultural Economics*, 18, 89–100.

Riddington, G. L. (1999). Forecasting Ski Demand: Comparing Learning Curve and Varying Parameter Coefficient Approaches. *Journal of Forecasting*, 18, 205–214.

Riddington, G. L. (2002) Learning and Ability to Pay: Developing a Model to Forecast Ski Tourism. *Journal of Travel & Tourism Marketing*, 13, 109–124.

Rodrigues, P. M. M. and Gouveia, P. M. D. C. B. (2004). An Application of PAR Models for Tourism Forecasting. *Tourism Economics*, 10, 281–303.

Roget, F. M. and González, X. A. R. (2006). Rural Tourism Demand in Galicia, Spain. *Tourism Economics*, 12, 21–31.

Romilly, P., Liu, X. and Song, H. (1998a). Economic and Social Determinants of International Tourism Spending: A Panel Data Analysis. *Tourism Analysis*, 3, 3–15.

Romilly, P., Song, H. and Liu, X. (1998b). Modelling and Forecasting Car Ownership in Britain: Cointegration and General to Specific Approach. *Journal of Transport Economics and Policy*, 32, 165–185.

Rosselló, J. (2001). Forecasting Turning Points in International Visitor Arrivals in the Balearic Islands. *Tourism Economics*, 7, 365–380.

Rosselló, J., Aguiló, E. and Riera, A. (2005). Modeling Tourism Demand Dynamics. *Journal of Travel Research*, 44, 111–116.

Rosselló, J., Font, A. R. and Rosselló, A. S. (2004). The Economic Determinants of Seasonal Patterns. *Annals of Tourism Research*, 31, 697–711.

Sakai, M., Brown, J. and Mak, J. (2000). Population Aging and Japanese International Travel in the 21st Century. *Journal of Travel Research*, 38, 212–220.

Salman, A. K. (2003). Estimating Tourist Demand through Cointegration Analysis: Swedish Data. *Current Issues in Tourism*, 6, 323–339.

Sargan, J. D. (1964). Wages and Prices in the United Kingdom: A Study of Econometric Methodology, in P. E. Hart and J. K. Whittaker (eds), *Econometric Analysis for National Economic Planning*, Colston Papers, vol. 16, 25–63. Butterworth, London.

Schwarz, G. (1978). Estimating the Dimension of a Model. *Annals of Statistics*, 6, 461–464.

Schwartz, Z. and Cohen, E. (2004). Subjective Estimates of Occupancy Forecast Uncertainty by Hotel Revenue Managers. *Journal of Travel & Tourism Marketing*, 16, 59–66.

Shan, J. and Wilson, K. (2001). Causality between Trade and Tourism: Empirical Evidence from China. *Applied Economics Letters*, 8, 279–283.

Sheldon, P. J. (1993). Forecasting Tourism: Expenditure versus Arrivals. *Journal of Travel Research*, 32, 13–20.

Sheldon, P. J. and Var, T. (1985). Tourism Forecasting: A Review of Empirical Research. *Journal of Forecasting*, 4, 183–195.

Sims, C. (1972). Money, Income and Causality. *American Economic Review*, 62, 540–552.

Sims, C. (1980). Macroeconomics and Reality. *Econometrica*, 48, 1–48.

Sinclair, M. T. and Stabler, M. (1997). *The Economics of Tourism*. Routledge, London.

Smeral, E. (2004). Long-term Forecasts for International Tourism. *Tourism Economics*, 10, 145–166.

Smeral, E. and Weber, A. (2000). Forecasting International Tourism Trends to 2010. *Annals of Tourism Research*, 27, 982–1006.

Smeral, E. and Witt, S. F. (1996). Econometric Forecasts of Tourism Demand to 2005. *Annals of Tourism Research*, 23, 891–907.

Smeral, E., Witt, S. F. and Witt, C. A. (1992). Econometric Forecasts: Tourism Trends to 2000. *Annals of Tourism Research*, 19, 450–466.

Smeral, E. and Wüger, M. (2005). Does Complexity Matter? Methods for Improving Forecasting Accuracy in Tourism: The Case of Australia. *Journal of Travel Research*, 44, 100–110.

Song, H. (1995). A Time Varying Parameter Consumption Model for the UK. *Applied Economics Letters*, 2, 339–342.

Song, H., Romilly, P. and Liu, X. (1997). A Time Varying Parameter Approach to the Chinese Aggregate Consumption Function. *Economics of Planning*, 29, 185–203.

Song, H., Romilly, P. and Liu, X. (1998). The UK Consumption Function and Structural Instability: Improving Forecasting Performance Using a Time Varying Parameter Approach. *Applied Economics*, 30, 975–983.

Song, H., Romilly, P. and Liu, X. (2000). An Empirical Study of Outbound Tourism Demand in the UK. *Applied Economics*, 32, 611–624.

Song, H. and Turner, L. (2006). Tourism Demand Forecasting, in L. Dwyer and P. Forsyth (eds), *International Handbook on the Economics of Tourism*, 89–114. Edward Elgar, Cheltenham.

Song, H. and Witt, S. F. (2000). *Tourism Demand Modelling and Forecasting: Modern Econometric Approaches*. Pergamon, Oxford.

Song, H. and Witt, S. F. (2003). Tourism Forecasting: The General-to-Specific Approach. *Journal of Travel Research*, 42, 65–74.

Song, H. and Witt, S. F. (2006). Forecasting International Tourist Flows to Macau. *Tourism Management*, 27, 214–224.

Song, H., Witt, S. F. and Jensen, T. C. (2003a). Tourism Forecasting: Accuracy of Alternative Econometric Models. *International Journal of Forecasting*, 19, 123–141.

Song, H., Witt, S. F. and Li, G. (2003b). Modelling and Forecasting the Demand for Thai Tourism. *Tourism Economics*, 9, 363–387.

Song, H. and Wong, K. K. F. (2003). Tourism Demand Modeling: A Time-Varying Parameter Approach. *Journal of Travel Research*, 42, 57–64.

Song, H., Wong, K. K. F. and Chon, K. K. S. (2003c). Modelling and Forecasting the Demand for Hong Kong Tourism. *International Journal of Hospitality Management*, 22, 435–451.

Stewart, J. and Gill, L. (1998). *Econometrics*, 2nd ed. Prentice-Hall, London.

Stock, J. H. (1987). Asymptotic Properties of Least Squares Estimators of Cointegrating Vectors. *Econometrica*, 55, 1035–1056.

Stock and Watson (1988). Testing for Common Trends. *Journal of the American Statistical Association*, 83, 1097–1107.

Stone, J. R. N. (1954). Linear Expenditure Systems and Demand Analysis—An Application to the Pattern of British Demand. *Economic Journal*, 64, 511–527.

Swamy, P. A. V. B., Kennickell, A. B. and von zur Muechien, P. (1990). Comparing Forecasts from Fixed and Variable Coefficient Models: The Case of Money Demand. *International Journal of Forecasting*, 6, 469–477.

Syriopoulos, T. C. (1995). A Dynamic Model of Demand for Mediterranean Tourism. *International Review of Applied Economics*, 9, 318–336.

Syriopoulos, T. C. and Sinclair, M. T. (1993). An Econometric Study of Tourism Demand: The AIDS Model of US and European Tourism in Mediterranean Countries. *Applied Economics*, 25, 1541–1552.

Tan, A. Y. F., McCahon, C. and Miller, J. (2002). Modelling Tourist Flows to Indonesia and Malaysia. *Journal of Travel and Tourism Marketing*, 13, 61–82.

Theil, H. (1965). The Information Approach to Demand Analysis. *Econometrica*, 33, 67–87.

Theil, H. (1966). *Applied Economic Forecasting*. North-Holland, Amsterdam.

Thomas, R. L. (1993). *Introductory Econometrics: Theory and Applications*. Longman, London.

Thomas, R. L. (1997). *Modern Econometrics: An Introduction*. Addison-Wesley, Hallow.

Toshinori, M. (1998). *Fundamentals of the New Artificial Intelligence*, New York: Springer.

Tremblay, P. (1989). Polling International Tourism in Western Europe. *Annals of Tourism Research*, 16, 677–691.

Turner, L. W., Kulendran, N. and Fernando, H. (1997). The Use of Composite National Indicators for Tourism Forecasting. *Tourism Economics*, 3, 309–317.

Turner, L. W., Reisinger, Y. and Witt, S. F. (1998). Tourism Demand Analysis Using Structural Equation Modelling. *Tourism Economics*, 4, 301–323.

Turner, L. W. and Witt, S. F. (2001a). Factors Influencing the Demand for International Tourism: Tourism Demand Analysis Using Structural Equation Modelling, Revisited. *Tourism Economics*, 7, 21–38.

Turner, L. W. and Witt, S. F. (2001b). Forecasting Tourism Using Univariate and Multivariate Structural Time Series Models. *Tourism Economics*, 7, 135–147.

Uysal, M. and Crompton, J. L. (1985). An Overview of Approaches Used to Forecast Tourism Demand. *Journal of Travel Research*, 24, 7–15.

Uysal, M. and Roubi, M. (1999). Artificial Neural Networks versus Multiple Regression in Tourism Demand Analysis. *Journal of Travel Research*, 38, 111–118.

Vanegas Sr., M. and Croes, R. R. (2000). Evaluation of Demand: US Tourists to Aruba. *Annals of Tourism Research*, 27, 946–963.

Var, T., Mohammad, G. and Icoz, O. (1990). Factors Affecting International Tourism Demand for Turkey. *Annals of Tourism Research*, 17, 606–610.

Veloce, W. (2004). Forecasting Inbound Canadian Tourism: An Evaluation of Error Corrections Model Forecasts. *Tourism Economics*, 10, 263–280.

Vogt, M. G. and Wittayakorn, C. (1998). Determinants of the Demand for Thailand's Exports of Tourism. *Applied Economics*, 30, 711–715.

Vu, C. J. and Turner, L. W. (2005). Data Disaggregation in Demand Forecasting. *Tourism and Hospitality Research*, 6, 38–52.

Webber, A. G. (2001). Exchange Rate Volatility and Cointegration in Tourism Demand. *Journal of Travel Research*, 39, 398–405.

White, H. (1980). A Heteroskedasticity-Consistent Covariance Matrix Estimator and a Direct Test of Heteroskedasticity. *Econometrica*, 48, 817–838.

White, K. J. (1985). An International Travel Demand Model: US Travel to Western Europe. *Annals of Tourism Research*, 12, 529–545.

Wickens, M. R. and Breusch, T. S. (1988). Dynamic Specification, the Long-Run and the Estimation of Transformed Regression Models. *Economic Journal*, 98 (Conference),189–205.

Witt, S. F. (1980a). An Abstract Mode-Abstract (Destination) Node Model of Foreign Holiday Demand. *Applied Economics*, 12, 163–180.

Witt, S. F. (1980b). An Econometric Comparision of UK and German Foreign Holiday Behaviour. *Managerial and Decision Economics*, 1, 123–131.

Witt, S. F. and Martin, C. A. (1987a). International Tourism Demand Models: Inclusion of Marketing Variables. *Tourism Management*, 8, 33–40.

Witt, S. F. and Martin, C. A. (1987b). Measuring the Impacts of Mega-Events on Tourism Flows, the Role and Impact of Mega-Events and Attractions on Regional and National Tourism Development. *Proceedings of International Association of Scientific Experts in Tourism (AIEST)*, 37th Congress (AIEST), St. Gallen, Switzerland, 213–221.

Witt, S. F. and Song, H. (2000). Forecasting Future Tourism Flows, in S. Medlik and A. Lockwood (eds), *Tourism and Hospitality in the 21st Century*, 106–118. Butterworth-Heinemann, Oxford.

Witt, S. F., Song, H. and Louvieris, P. (2003). Statistical Testing in Forecasting Model Selection. *Journal of Travel Research*, 42, 151–158.

Witt, S. F., Song, H. and Wanhill, S. P. (2004). Forecasting Tourism-Generated Employment: The Case of Denmark. *Tourism Economics*, 10, 167–176.

Witt, S. F. and Turner, L. W. (2002). Trends and Forecasts for Inbound Tourism to China. *Journal of Travel & Tourism Marketing*, 13, 97–107.

Witt, C. A. and Witt, S. F. (1990). Appraising an Econometric Forecasting Model. *Journal of Travel Research*, 28, 30–34.

Witt, S. F. and Witt, C. A. (1991). Tourism Forecasting: Error Magnitude, Direction of Change Error and Trend Change Error. *Journal of Travel Research*, 30, 26–33.

Witt, S. F. and Witt, C. A. (1992). *Modeling and Forecasting Demand in Tourism*. Academic Press, London.

Witt, S. F. and Witt, C. A. (1995). Forecasting Tourism Demand: A Review of Empirical Research. *International Journal of Forecasting*, 11, 447–475.

Woking, H. (1943). Statistical Laws of Family Expenditure. *Journal of the American Statistical Association*, 38, 43–56.

Wong, K. K. F., Song, H. and Chon, K. S. (2006). Bayesian Models for Tourism Demand Forecasting. *Tourism Management*, 27, 773–780.

Wong, K. K. F., Song, H., Witt, S. F. and Wu, D. C. (2007). Tourism Forecasting: To Combine or Not to Combine? *Tourism Management*, 28, 1068–1078.

World Economic Factbook (editions one to four), Euromonitor Publishing Ltd., Cambridge.

Wu, D. M. (1973). Alternative Tests of Independence between Stochastic Regressors and Disturbances. *Econometrica*, 41, 733–750.

Yavas, B. F. and Bilgin, Z. (1996). Estimation of Tourism Demand in Turkey: A Pooled Cross-Section and Time Series Analysis. *Tourism Analysis*, 1, 19–27.

Zellner, A. C. (1962). An Efficient Method of Estimating Seemingly Unrelated Regressions and Tests for Aggregation Bias. *Journal of the American Statistical Association*, 57, 348–368.

# Author Index

**A**
Aguiló, E. 14
Akal, M. 14, 194
Akis, S. 14
Algieri, B. 14
Amaral, T.P. 16, 32
Anderson, G. 172
Artus, J.R. 48
Ashworth, J. 14, 28
Athanasiadis, S. 15
Au, N. 18, 194

**B**
Bakkal, I. 14
Balcombe, K.G. 170
Baldwin, M.A. 170
Baltagi, B.H. 153
Barten, A.P. 171
Bera, A.K. 55
Bewley, R. 93
Bicak, H.A. 14
Bilgin, Z. 38, 149, 161
Blake, A. 14
Blanciforti, L. 173
Blundell, R. 172
Bohara, A.K. 145
Bomhoff, E.J. 145
Box, G. 48–49
Braun, B.M. 16
Breusch, T. 53, 153
Breusch, T.S. 91–92
Brown, J. 139, 145
Burmeister, E. 139

**C**
Carey, K. 38, 161
Chambers, M.J. 172
Chiang, A.C. 170
Cho, V. 14, 194

Chow, G. 139
Croes, R.R. 15, 24, 30
Crouch, G.I. 6, 15, 29, 30, 33, 34, 161
Cuthbertson, K. 139

**D**
Daniel, A.C.M. 15
Davidson, J. 47, 59
Davis, J.R. 170
De Mello, M.M. 15
Deaton, A.S. 32, 168
Di Matteo, L. 15, 29
Di Matteo, R. 15, 29
Dickey, D.A. 76, 79, 80
Divisekera, S. 15
Doan, T. 114
Dritsakis, N. 15, 16, 29
Duffy, M. 172
Durbarry, R. 16, 32

**E**
Eadington, W.R. 167
Edgerton, D.L. 172
Edwards, A. 8
Engle, R.F. 55, 72, 80, 84, 86, 88
Eugenio-Martin, J. 16, 30

**F**
Fortuna, N. 15
Friedman, M. 34
Fujii, E. 16, 32, 168
Fuller, W.A. 76, 79

**G**
Gallet, C.A. 16
García-Ferrer, A. 16
Garín-Muñoz, T. 16, 32
Geweke, J. 114
Godfrey, L.G. 53

Goldfeld, S.M. 54
González, P. 16, 28
González, X.A.R. 21
Granger, C.W.J. 72, 80, 84, 86, 88
Gray, H.P. 48
Greenidge, K. 17
Greenslade, J.V. 145

**H**
Hall, R.E. 50
Hall, S.G. 145
Hamilton, J.D. 127
Han, Z. 17, 30
Harrison, M.J. 20
Harvey, A.C. 143, 144
Hausman, J.A. 58, 153
Hendry, D.F. 47, 50
Holmes, R.A. 17, 32
Hsaio, C. 151
Hyllberg, S. 80

**I**
Icoz, O. 17
Ismail, J.A. 17

**J**
Jarque, C.M. 55
Jenkins, G.M. 48–49
Jensen, T.C. 17
Johansen, S. 105, 129
Johnson, P. 14, 28
Johnston, J. 171
Jørgensen, F. 17
Juselius, K. 129

**K**
Kalman, R.E. 143
Kim, C.J. 145
Kim, S. 17, 28, 30, 51, 126, 130, 193
Kim, Y. 17
King, M.L. 17, 29, 49, 51, 105, 193
Kliman, M.L. 4, 50
Kulendran, N. 17, 18, 28, 29, 32, 49,
    51, 105, 193
Kwack, S.Y. 48

**L**
Lam, S. 21
Lanza, A. 18
Lathiras, P. 18
Law, R. 18, 194
Ledesma-Rodríguez, F.J. 19, 29, 30
Lee, C.K. 8, 19, 50, 95
Leser, C.E.V. 168

Li, G. 19, 29, 32, 33, 34, 139, 173, 192,
    193, 194
Lim, C. 19, 29, 30, 39, 149
Little, J.S. 48
Loeb, P. 48
Lyssiotou, P. 19, 33

**M**
MacKinnon, J.G. 59, 85
Mak, J. 38
Mangion, M.L. 19, 32
Martin, C.A. 4, 6, 8, 30, 50, 184
McAleer, M. 19, 29
Mervar, A. 21
Mizon, G.E. 47, 58
Moral, P. 16, 28
Morley, C.L. 19, 20
Morris, A. 20
Morzuch, B.J. 195
Muellbauer, J. 32, 168

**N**
Narayan, P.K. 20
Naudé, W.A. 20
Nell, K.S. 15
Nowman, K.B. 172

**O**
O'Hagan, J.W. 20
Oh, C.O. 20, 195
Osborn, D.R. 80
Osterwald-Lenum, M. 131

**P**
Pagan, A. 153
Papanastasiou, J. 16
Papatheodorou, A. 20
Patsouratis, V. 20
Payne, J.E. 21
Perron, P. 78
Pesaran, M.H. 31, 92, 93
Phillips, P.C.B. 78
Pyo, S. 21, 171

**Q**
Qiu, H. 21, 29, 30
Qu, H. 21
Quandt, R.E. 38, 54
Queralt, R. 16

**R**
Ramajo, J. 179
Ramos, F.F.R. 15
Ramsey, J.B. 55

Ray, R. 173
Redman, M. 167
Richard, J.F. 47, 58
Rickertsen, K. 171
Riddington, G.L. 21, 31, 139
Roget, F.M. 21
Romilly, P. 38, 130
Roselló, J. 21
Roubi, M. 24

S
Saayman, A. 20
Sakai, M. 21
Salman, A.K. 22
Sargan, J.D. 47
Sauer, C. 145
Shamsuddin, A.F.M. 17
Shan, J. 22
Shaw, R.N. 161
Sheldon, P.J. 22
Shin, Y. 31, 92, 93
Sims, C. 105, 113, 114
Sinclair, M.T. 16, 23, 32, 168
Siriopoulos, C. 18
Smeral, E. 8, 22
Solvoll, G. 17
Song, H. 17, 22, 23, 28, 30, 33, 34, 51,
        105, 126, 130, 139, 145, 161,
        164, 193
Stabler, M. 168
Stock, J.H. 91
Stone, J.R.N. 168, 169
Swamy, P.A.V.B. 139
Syriopoulos, T.C. 23, 28, 29, 34, 171

T
Tan, A.Y.F. 23
Theil, H. 192
Thomas, R.L. 52, 58, 60

Tremblay, P. 38, 149, 150, 161
Turner, L.W. 23, 24, 32, 49

U
Uysal, M. 17, 24

V
Vanegas Sr., M. 15, 24, 30
Var, T. 24
Veloce, W. 24
Vogt, M.G. 24
von Ungern-Sternberg, T. 47

W
Wall, K.D. 139
Webber, A.G. 24, 29
Weber, A. 22
White, H. 54
White, K.J. 24
Wickens, M.R. 91–92
Wilson, K. 18, 22, 28, 194
Witt, C.A. 8, 25, 29, 194
Witt, S.F. 4, 6, 8, 18, 22, 23, 24, 25, 28,
        29, 30, 32, 38, 50, 51, 105,
        149, 161, 184, 194
Wittayakorn, C. 24
Wong, K.K.F. 23, 25, 30, 32, 34, 139,
        195
Wu, D.M. 58

Y
Yavas, B.F. 38, 149, 161
Yoo, B.S. 80
Young, K.H. 38

Z
Zellner, A.C. 171
Zhang, J. 21, 29, 30

# Subject Index

## A

ADF (augmented Dickey-Fuller) test 77–78

ADLM *see* autoregressive distributed lag model (ADLM)

AIDS *see* almost ideal demand system (AIDS)

Akaike information criterion (AIC) 42, 78, 81–83, 92, 100, 108,114–17, 131

almost ideal demand system (AIDS) 27, 32, 167–68, 180; demand elasticities 171–72, 176–78; EC-LAIDS 32, 172–73, 194; estimation methods 171; LAIDS 169–72; selection criteria 183; static model 168–72; theoretical restrictions 169–70; TVP-EC-LAIDS 32, 179–80, 194–95; TVP-LAIDS 32, 179, 194–95; worked example 173–78

AR (autoregressive) model 48, 49

ARCH test 55

ARIMA model 49, 185, 193, 194

ARIMAX model 194

augmented Dickey-Fuller (ADF) test 77–78

autocorrelation tests 53–54

autoregressive (AR) model 48, 49; testing for 55

autoregressive conditional heteroscedasticity (ARCH) test 55

autoregressive distributed lag model (ADLM) 31, 47–51, 88–90, 92–93, 100–102; autocorrelation tests 53–54; diagnostic checking 52–59; encompassing test 58–59; exogeneity test 57–58; heteroscedasticity tests 54–55; mis-specification test 55–56; model selection 59–60; normality test 55; restriction tests 51–52; structure instability tests 56–57; worked example 61–69

autoregressive integrated moving average (ARIMA) model 49, 185, 193, 194

## B

block Granger causality test (block exogeneity test) 113, 117–18

breakpoint test 56–57, 141–42

Breusch-Godfrey test 53–54

Breusch-Pagan test 153

## C

Chow parameter constancy test 56–57, 139, 141–42

Chow predictive failure test 57

CIDW statistic 86–87

coefficient of determination 41–42

cointegration 31, 72–73; Dickey-Fuller (DF) tests 76–79, 85; and error correction mechanism 88–90; integration order, test for 73–84; non-stationary series and unit roots 74–76; Phillips-Perron tests 78; seasonal unit roots 79–81; stationary and non-stationary series 73–75; test for 84–87; unit root testing 78–79, 81–84; and VAR modelling 126–37

Cointegration Durbin-Watson (CIDW) statistic 86–87

common factor (COMFAC) model 48,
50; testing for 65
compensated price elasticities 171–72
consumer price index (CPI) 29, 39, 70,
71, 94
consumer tastes 2
cost of living 4, 5, 97
cost of travel 4
cross-sectional data 38

**D**
data collection 38–39
data generation process (DGP) 47, 107,
138
data frequency 27, 193
dead start model 48, 50–51; testing for
65
demand elasticities 8–12, 33–34,
139–42, 146, 147; evolution
of 34; LAIDS model 171–72,
176–78; long-run and short-
run 33–34
demand function for tourism product 2
dependent variable 2–3
DF (Dickey-Fuller) tests 76–78, 85
diagnostic checking 52–59; autocorrelation 53–54; encompassing
test 58–59; exogeneity 57–58;
heteroscedasticity 54–55; mis-
specification 55–56; normality 55; structural instability
56–57
Dickey-Fuller (DF) tests 76–78, 85
diffuse priors 144
disaggregate demand analysis 28
disequilibrium error 72
double-log model 37
dummy variables 7–8, 30, 151–52, 156
Durbin-Watson (DW) statistic 53, 86

**E**
EC-LAIDS model 32, 172–73; forecasting performance 194
ECM *see* error correction model (ECM)
econometric studies 13–26, 34; data frequency 27; demand elasticities
33–34; explanatory variables
28–30; functional form 30;
measures of demand 27–28;
models 31–32; study origins/
destinations 14–26, 27
effective exchange rate 166
encompassing tests 58–59
Engel curve 36

Engle-Granger two-stage approach 31,
48–49, 90–91, 96–97, 99–100,
126–27, 135–36, 137; selection criteria 182
Engle test for autoregressive conditional
heteroscedasticity 62
error correction LAIDS (EC-LAIDS)
model 32, 172–73; forecasting
performance 194
error correction model (ECM) 28,
31, 33, 48, 51, 52; ADLM
approach 92–93, 100–102;
cointegration and error correction 88–90; cointegration
testing 94–95; Engle-Granger
two-stage approach 90–91,
96–97; estimation procedures
90–93; forecasting performance 102; Wickens-Breusch
one-stage approach 91–92,
97–100; worked examples
93–104
error variance decomposition 110–11
*ex ante* forecasting 181
exchange rate 4–5, 29, 61
exchange rate volatility (EXV) 154
exogeneity test 57–58, 112–13
expectations and habit persistence variable 6–7, 50
expenditure elasticity 171
explanatory variables 3–8, 28–30
*ex post* forecasting 181
*ex post* forecasting performance 57,
102, 125

**F**
*F* statistic 44, 48, 51–52, 54–55, 57, 59,
63–64, 78–82
*F* test 44, 51–52, 62, 64, 150–51
feasible generalised least squares
(FGLS) 153
finite distributed lag model 48, 50; testing for 65
fixed effects (FE) model 151–53
forecasting performance 44, 181, 195;
accuracy comparison 186–91;
accuracy measures 181–85;
data frequency 193; emerging
models 194–95; evaluation
of different models 185–95;
forecasting competitors 194;
forecasting errors 184–85,
192; origins/destinations
193–94; overall performance

comparison 185–92; time-horizons 192–93
forecasting variance decomposition 120–25
functional form 8–12, 30, 37

**G**
general-to-specific modelling 47–51; autocorrelation tests 53–54; autoregressive (AR) model 48, 49; common factor (COM-FAC) model 48, 50; dead start model 48, 50–51; diagnostic checking 52–59; encompassing test 58–59; error correction model (ECM) 48, 51; exogeneity test 57–58; finite distributed lag model 48, 50; growth rate model 48, 49; heteroscedasticity tests 54–55; leading indicator model 48, 49; misspecification test 55–56; model selection 59–60; normality test 55; partial adjustment model 48, 50; restriction tests 51–52; static model 48–49; structure instability tests 56–57; model selection 59–61; worked example 61–69
Goldfeld-Quandt test 54
Granger causality 112–14
Granger Representation Theorem 88
growth rate model 48, 49; testing for 63

**H**
habit persistence 6, 50, 130, 172
Hannan-Quinn criterion (HQC) 100
Hausman statistic 160
HEGY seasonal unit root test 80–81
heteroscedasticity tests 54–55
hypothesis formulation 36–37
hypothesis testing 43–44

**I**
IMF (International Monetary Fund) 39
impulse response analysis 108–10
income variable 3–4, 28
income elasticities 9, 11–12, 95, 134, 140–41, 158, 161
independent variables 8, 10, 30
inflation 4, 70
instrumental variables 58
integration order, test for 73–84; Dickey-Fuller (DF) tests

76–78; non-stationary series and unit roots 74–76; Phillips-Perron tests 78; seasonal unit roots 79–81; stationary and non-stationary time series 73–75; unit root testing 78–79, 81–84
*International Financial Statistics* 39
International Monetary Fund (IMF) 39
international tourism demand 2

**J**
J-Test 59
Jarque-Bera (J-B) test 55
Johansen maximum likelihood (JML) cointegration approach 31, 102, 127; empirical example 131–37; forecasting performance 192, 193; selection criteria 182
joint hypothesis 78–79, 81–83, 170, 175
joint significance 44

**K**
Kalman filter (KF) 143–45, 148

**L**
lagged dependent variables 49–50
Lagrange multiplier (LM) test 52, 53–54, 153
LAIDS model 32, 169–72; forecasting performance 194
leading indicator model 48, 49
learning curve model 32
Likelihood Ratio (LR) test 52
linear expenditure system (LES) 27, 32
linear functional form 8–9, 37
linear log model 37
LM test 52, 53–54, 153
log linear model 37
log-log model 37
longitudinal data 38
long-run cointegration coefficients 90
long-run cointegration regression 90, 92, 94
long-run cointegration vectors 137
long-run equilibrium regression 72, 91

**M**
MAE 102, 185
MAPE 184–85, 192
marginal revenue (MR) 11
marketing expenditure variable 6, 30

maximum likelihood (ML) estimation 171
mean absolute forecasting error (MAE) 102, 185
mean absolute percentage error (MAPE) 184–85, 192
mis-specification test 55–56
ML (maximum likelihood) estimation 171
model estimation 39–42
model selection criteria 182–83
model specification 37
model structure instability 138
Monte Carlo simulations 76, 79, 80, 129
multiple regression model 54, 58

**N**
naïve model 185
non-causal models 183
non-stationary time series 72–73, 74–76
normality test 55
null hypothesis 63–64, 76–80, 83–85, 87, 94, 107, 117–18, 151, 170

**O**
oil crises, effects of 7–8, 30, 139
OLS (ordinary least squares) 35, 37, 39–41, 46–47, 56–57, 62–63, 80, 85, 91–92, 94
omitted variables 62
one-off events variable 8, 30, 139
one-tailed *t* statistic 43
ordinary least squares (OLS) 35, 37, 39–41, 46–47, 56–57, 62–63, 80, 85, 91–92, 94
outbound tourism demand model 46
own-price variable 4–5, 29

**P**
panel data analysis 32, 149, 164–65; empirical study 153–64; fixed and random effects 151–53, 160–64; model specification and estimation 150–53; poolability testing 150–51, 159–60; selection criteria 183
partial adjustment model 48, 50
partial adjustment process, testing for 64
Phillips-Perron tests 78
point elasticity 9
policy evaluation 44–45
POLS model 151, 152

poolability testing 150–51, 159–60
pooled data 38
pooled ordinary least squares (POLS) model 151, 152
population variable 3
power functional form 9–10, 37
predictive failure 138
price elasticity of demand 11, 33, 155
price variables 4–5

**Q**
qualitative effects 7–8

**R**
Ramsey RESET test 55–56
random effects (RE) model 151–53
random walk 74, 143–46, 179
recursive least squares procedure 57, 139–42
recursive OLS estimates 139–42
relative tourism price 29
RESET test *see* Ramsey RESET test
RMSE 102
RMSPE 184–85, 192
root mean square forecasting error (RMSE) 102
root mean square percentage error (RMSPE) 184–85, 192

**S**
Schwarz Bayesian criterion (SBC) 42, 78, 86, 92, 100, 108
seasonal time series 79
seasonal unit roots 79–81
seemingly unrelated regression (SUR) estimation 171
Sims test 112, 113
Sims' general (unrestricted) VAR model 106
single-equation methods 167
specific-to-general modelling 47
spurious correlation 70
spurious regression 31, 70–72
standard error 43
static model 48–49; testing for 63
stationary time series 73–74, 75
Stock and Watson maximum likelihood estimator 127
structural equation model 32
structural instability 138–39; tests for 56–57, 139–42
structural time series model (STSM) 32
substitute destinations 2
substitute prices variable 5

sum of squared residuals (SSR) 40–41, 51–52
SUR estimation 171
system-of-equations approach 32, 167, 168; *see also* almost ideal demand system (AIDS)

**T**
*t* statistic 43, 78–80
tastes variable 5–6
time horizon of forecasts 183
time series 38, 73–76
time varying parameter (TVP) model 31, 34, 138–39, 147–48; forecasting performance 192, 193; and Kalman filter 143–45; selection criteria 183; worked example 145–47
total revenue (TR) 11
tourism demand analysis 1, 12; data frequency 27; demand elasticities 8–12, 33–34; dependent variable 2–3; determinants 1–8; explanatory variables 3–8, 28–30; functional form 8–12, 30; measures of demand 27–28; *see also* traditional methodology
tourism expenditure 153–54, 173
tourism prices variable 29
traditional methodology 35–45, 46; data collection 37–39; forecasting and policy evaluation 44–45; hypothesis formulation 36–37; hypothesis testing 43–44; limitations 45; model estimation 39–42; model specification 37
transfer function model 32
translog utility function 32
travel costs variable 29
TVP model 31, 34, 138–39, 147–48; forecasting performance 192, 193; and Kalman filter 143–45; selection criteria 183; worked example 145–47

TVP-EC-LAIDS model 32, 179–80, 194–95
TVP-ECM model 193
TVP-LAIDS model 32, 179, 194–95
two-tailed statistic 43

**U**
uncompensated price elasticities 171
unit roots 74–76; Dickey-Fuller (DF) tests 76–78; seasonal 79–81; testing procedure 78–79; tests, examples of 81–84
unrestricted VAR model 106

**V**
VECM 128, 129, 131, 132, 136
vector autoregressive (VAR) model 32, 105–8; and cointegration 126–37; example 114–26; forecasting error variance decomposition 110–11, 123–25; forecasting performance 125–26, 192, 193; Granger causality and exogeneity 112–14; impulse response analysis 108–10, 120–23; selection criteria 182
vector moving average (VMA) process 109

**W**
Wald test 52
Weighted least squares (WLS) 38
White test 54–55
Wickens-Breusch one-stage approach (WB) 31, 91–92, 97–100, 182, 193
Working-Leser model 168
World Tourism Organization (WTO) 38
Wu-Hausman test 67
Wu-Hausman statistic 67

**Y**
*Yearbook of Tourism Statistics* 39
Young's theorem 170

For Product Safety Concerns and Information please contact our EU
representative GPSR@taylorandfrancis.com
Taylor & Francis Verlag GmbH, Kaufingerstraße 24, 80331 München, Germany